A CIVILISED SAVAGERY

A CIVILISED SAVAGERY

Britain and the New Slaveries in Africa, 1884-1926

KEVIN GRANT

Routledge
New York • London

Published in 2005 by
Routledge
Taylor & Francis Group
270 Madison Avenue
New York, NY 10016
www.routledge-ny.com

Published in Great Britain by
Routledge
Taylor & Francis Group
2 Park Square
Milton Park, Abingdon
Oxon, OX1 4RN
www.routledge.co.uk

Routledge is an imprint of the Taylor & Francis Group, a Division of T&F Informa.
Copyright © 2005 by Taylor & Francis Books, Inc.

10 9 8 7 6 5 4 3 2 1

Library of Congress Cataloging-in-Publication Data
  Grant, Kevin, 1965-
    A civilised savagery : Britain and the new slaveries in Africa, 1884-1926 / Kevin Grant.
    p. cm.
    Includes bibliographical references and index.
    ISBN 0-415-94900-9 (alk. paper)—ISBN 0-415-94901-7 (pbk. : alk. paper)
    1. Slavery—Africa, Sub-Saharan—History—19th century. 2. Slavery—Africa, Sub-
Saharan—History—20th century. 3. Great Britain—Colonies—Africa—History—19th century.
4. Great Britain—Colonies—Africa—History—20th century. I. Title.

  DT1321.G73 2005
  306.3'62'096709034—dc22

                                                                              2004011423

I dedicate this book to my parents,
Don and Anita Grant,
because it is as much theirs as mine.

While we have been dreaming of progress and benevolence, there has grown up among us a strange product, born of the union between greed and science, suckled on cynicism and schooled in the subtleties of the law. It is nothing less than a civilised savagery, infinitely more dangerous and terrible than primitive barbarism, because free from all passion, and working in an atmosphere of cold and sinister calculation that admits neither reform nor repentance. It is fortified by a monied command of brain-power in every country, and armed in its own work with all the machinery of destruction that science has given to modern man....Here lies, let us clearly understand, the chief peril of the modern world.

Harold Spender, "The Great Congo Iniquity,"
The Contemporary Review (July 1906): 45

Contents

Acknowledgments

Thank you to Lisa Trivedi. And thank you to Don and Anita Grant, and Navin and Karen Trivedi, for their encouragement and support at every turn.

This book owes much to the good judgment and advice of other scholars. Thank you to Thomas Metcalf, who provided expert guidance to the dissertation upon which this book is based. I am one of many former students who continue to appreciate Tom's friendship and intellectual generosity. I have also benefited greatly from the advice and support of Andrew Porter, who oversaw my archival research and enabled me to recognize at an early stage that my initial thesis was entirely wrong. Many other colleagues have contributed to this project in formal and informal ways. I am particularly grateful to Antoinette Burton, J. B. Close, Deborah Cohen, Caroline Cox, Tabitha Kanogo, Tom Laqueur, Philippa Levine, David Lieberman, Sudipta Sen, Frank Trentmann, James Vernon, Clarence Walker, Andrew Walls, and Richard Webster. At the outset, I benefited from the camaraderie and insight of participants in the Empire Studies Reading Group at Berkeley. I gratefully acknowledge my fellow participants (some of whom appear above): Alice Bullard, Durba Ghosh, Carina Johnson, Anne Keary, Barbara Metcalf, Lisa Pollard, Rachel Sturman, Krystyna von Henneberg, and Darren Zook. Since 1997, Hamilton College has also provided me with a productive working environment. I thank all of my colleagues in the History Department for their high standards in both scholarship and teaching. I am especially grateful to Shoshana Keller, Al Kelly, and Tom Wilson for their readings of my works-in-progress over the past several years, and to Robert Paquette for directing me toward relevant works on slavery and abolition. And thank you to members of the interdisciplinary reading group for their critical eyes and telling questions: Chris Georges, Martine Guyot-Bender, Adam Lutzker, Onno Oerlemans, Kyoko Omori, Bonnie Urciuoli, Edward Wheatley, and Steve Yao. I further acknowledge my debts to the first-rate staff of Burke Library, and especially Kristin Strohmeyer and Joan Wolek, who always find what I cannot.

I initially drafted the most important parts of this project in an unlikely place: Ahmadabad, India. I am pleased to convey my longstanding appreciation for the gracious hospitality and assistance of our friends and neighbors, Lalit and Madhu Shah.

The research for this book was made possible by the financial support of the Fulbright Foundation, the Mellon Foundation, the American Historical Association, and the Williams Watrous Couper Fund.

Finally, and again, thank you to Lisa Trivedi, partner in all things.

Introduction

The path is strewn with dead men's bones. You see the white thigh-bones lying in front of your feet, and at one side, among the undergrowth, you find the skull. These are the skeletons of slaves who have been unable to keep up with the march, and so were murdered or left to die.[1]

Henry Nevinson, a British journalist, thus recounted his travels through the Hungry Country, an arid region of sandy terrain and forests of barren trees, along the main slave route in the Portuguese colony of Angola. He had departed in 1905 from the coastal town of Benguela, then followed the route through the district of Bié and across the Luanza River into central Africa.[2] It was a path of age-old suffering and new euphemisms. The Portuguese government had long since outlawed slavery, so the slave traders now called themselves "labor merchants." These merchants traveled deep into the interior to exchange guns and liquor for slaves, whom the merchants then marched back to the coast to be sold. Up to half of the slaves did not survive the march to the coast, leaving an intermittent trail of bones and shackles that stretched for hundreds of miles.

Those slaves who did survive were sold as "contract laborers" (*serviçaes*) to the European representatives of sugar plantations in Angola and cocoa plantations on the Portuguese islands of São Tomé and Príncipe in the Gulf of Guinea. Each laborer signed a five-year contract in the presence of a Portuguese magistrate, presumably of his own free will. Subsequently, most contract laborers did not receive their promised wages, they were subjected to flogging, their children were born into servitude, and they never regained their freedom. Nevinson observed, "The difference between the 'contract labor' of Angola, and the old-fashioned slavery of our grandfathers' time is only a difference of legal terms."[3] With this thought in mind, Nevinson entitled his exposé on Portuguese West Africa *A Modern Slavery*, contributing a powerful case study to a growing public debate in Great Britain over the so-called new slaveries of European imperialism in Africa. Writing against the backdrop of this and other contemporary controversies over brutal labor exploitation in the Congo Free State and British South Africa, Nevinson declared:

> I am aware that…the whole question of slavery is still before us. It has reappeared under the more pleasing names of "indentured labor," "contract labor," or the "compulsory labor" which Mr. Chamberlain [the former British Colonial Secretary] has advocated….The whole thing will have to be faced anew, for the solutions of our great-grandfathers no longer satisfy.[4]

* * *

This book is about the British campaigns against the new slaveries of European imperialism in Africa in the late nineteenth and early twentieth centuries. It illuminates a pivotal period in British anti-slavery protest after the legendary age of emancipation, bridging the gap in historical scholarship between the Victorian era of abolition and the rise of labor law and human rights protest under international government. It begins by outlining the development of the ideologies of British humanitarianism and empire through the Victorian era, then examines three interrelated campaigns against new slaveries in the Congo Free State and Britain's Transvaal Colony in South Africa, and on the islands of São Tomé and Príncipe. These case studies illustrate how advocates of evangelical philanthropy and human rights influenced British responses to the new slaveries, and how the ensuing debates reflected divisive class and partisan politics, as well as the calculations of big business. Finally, this book demonstrates that Britain's humanitarian responses to the new slaveries in Africa played a central role in establishing the foundations of twentieth-century international government and labor law as a "sacred trust" under the League of Nations.

The concepts of free labor and slave labor carried highly charged political connotations in Britain in the late nineteenth century. Slavery was anathema to the British nation, which took pride in its own civil liberties and in its leading role in the abolition of the Atlantic slave trade after 1807 and the emancipation of chattel slaves in much of the British Empire after 1833.[5] By contrast, free labor was regarded as a natural and potentially virtuous act, a means to cultivate discipline and self-reliance while contributing to the welfare of one's broader community. Despite Dickensian horrors of exploitation in industrial Britain, it was possible for the employers of free laborers to attain recognition as benevolent benefactors by offering fair wages, education, and moral recreation to their employees. By the end of the Victorian era, the British people had come to believe that maintaining the line between free labor and slave labor was fundamental to legitimate commerce and government both at home and abroad. This line marked the divide between civilization and savagery. Indeed, in the humanitarian politics of the British Empire, no issue was of greater importance than labor.[6]

Frederick Cooper has demonstrated that the British regarded free labor as essential to the legitimacy of imperial rule in Africa. "Free labor," Cooper explains, "became a vital concept distinguishing the progressive colonizer of the early twentieth century from the…buyers of human flesh who had for past centuries represented Europe overseas."[7] Moreover, British abolitionists regarded the emancipation of slaves as an integral part of a larger, multifaceted process of colonial reform. This had been true in the early decades of the nineteenth century, and it remained true a century later. John Harris, the Secretary of the British and Foreign Anti-Slavery and Aborigines' Protection Society, declared in 1921 that the British had to do more than free Africans from slavery. As the leading representative of British abolitionists after the First World War, Harris urged imperial officials to "encourage the indigenous producers by means of secure land tenure, education, and instruction in agricultural science, to an ever increasing volume and quality of raw material." According to Harris, this raw material should be produced for the mutual benefit of Africans and European merchants and manufacturers in the imperial economy.[8]

The historical scholarship on British anti-slavery protest has generally assumed a simple dichotomy between slavery and freedom, focusing on campaigns against chattel slavery in the plantation economies of the Caribbean and North America between the 1780s and 1870.[9] This scholarship does not generally examine the fluidity of the concept of slavery in the age of emancipation, a fluidity that was clearly acknowledged by contemporary humanitarians and imperial officials, and that has since been illuminated by historians of labor in Africa, the Americas, and Asia.[10] Throughout the colonial world, Europeans attempted to trace the blurred lines between conditions of slave labor and free labor. They struggled to understand the cultural bases of different forms of bondage, as Paul Lovejoy demonstrates in surveying "transformations in slavery" in Africa, and as Indrani Chatterjee demonstrates in colonial India.[11] More to the point, Europeans found that the lines between slavery and freedom remained blurred even after legal emancipation, which commonly gave way to what abolitionists such as Harris called "slaveries in disguise."

A small number of historical studies have addressed British anti-slavery campaigns that focused on labor systems beyond the American plantation complex. The most important of these studies are those by Howard Temperley and Suzanne Miers, who have examined aspects of British anti-slavery that the present study references and complements. Temperley has demonstrated how Victorian abolitionists attempted to build an international crusade against "slavery in all its forms" prior to 1870.[12] Miers has addressed British anti-slavery politics and Africa prior to 1890, with a distinct emphasis on British Colonial Office and Foreign Office policies.[13] More recently, Miers has surveyed campaigns and legislation against slavery after the First World War, demonstrating the influence of British officials and policies in shaping international labor laws under the League of Nations and the United Nations.[14] The present study of British anti-slavery is centered on the era of high imperialism between the 1880s and the 1920s, overlapping at either end with the subjects of Temperley's and Miers's research.[15] It takes a comparative and integrative approach to the ideologies and campaigns of a variety of private organizations and government institutions that protested against, supported, and occasionally equivocated in the face of the new slaveries in Africa.

As in the Caribbean and the United States, the abolition of the slave trade and the manumission of slaves in colonial Africa did not immediately rectify the imbalance of economic and political power between the imperialist and the imperial subject. Freedom did not come with the stroke of a pen. Imperial officials commonly overlooked the enforcement of new labor laws, or their central governments provided them with alternative, legally sanctioned systems through which to compel people to work. These systems of labor mobilization were legitimized in terms of taxation and criminal law, or by the categorization of projects as "public works," which justified the coercion of labor in the public's presumed interest. Since the "free laborers" of colonial Africa did not have the vote, they could not participate in defining or enforcing their own rights through legislation. Emancipation was consequently a long-term process in which laborers, employers, and imperial governments worked at cross-purposes.

British critics of the new slaveries in Africa conveyed a keen sense of betrayal. The British government, and the other European great powers, had built these imperial labor systems with the declared purpose of supplanting indigenous slaveries. European imperialists had, furthermore, concealed their violent exploitation of Africans behind the rule of law. Despite the various brutal, if legal, forms of labor exploitation in Africa, humanitarian critics perceived the condition of slavery in those systems that deprived laborers of their property rights and depended upon physical coercion or, in extreme cases, atrocity. As accounts and images of the new slaveries reached Britain, many people responded with outrage to this evidence that the civilizing mission had been not only betrayed, but transmogrified. "While we were dreaming of progress and benevolence," observed Harold Spender, a radical journalist, "there has grown up among us a strange product, born of the union between greed and science, suckled on cynicism and schooled in the subtleties of the law. It is nothing less than a civilised savagery."[16]

The defenders of the new slaveries acknowledged that violence played a part in making imperial subjects work, but then, they added, it should. Imperial regimes were sanctioned by their laws to use violence to maintain economic and social order. Since these same laws forbade slavery, or overlooked the presence of slavery, the defenders of imperial labor policies could effectively argue that the new slaveries did not, by legal definition, exist. Cooper has observed that coercive labor systems, sanctioned by law, were commonplace among European regimes in Africa.[17] This observation is borne out by an extensive body of scholarship, including Paul Lovejoy and Jan Hogendorn's study of British labor policies in Nigeria, Martin Klein's work on French West Africa, and Gervase Clarence-Smith's and Patrick Harries's studies of Angola and Mozambique under the Portuguese.[18] All of the European powers reformed their imperial labor policies to affect the appearance of free labor before or after the turn of the twentieth century, and all experienced some measure of public criticism because their reforms were either ineffectual or too slow.

This book might have also examined British controversies over German labor policies in the Cameroons and South West Africa, French labor policy in Senegal, or British labor policies in Nigeria and East Africa. I do not, however, aspire to address all of the new slaveries in Africa, but to explain the dominant forces in British opposition to the new slaveries. While scholars of colonial labor have paid substantial attention to the new slaveries, there is as yet no multifaceted study of those whom we might call the new abolitionists. This book highlights the British reform campaigns against the Congo Free State, Britain's Transvaal Colony in South Africa, and Portuguese West Africa because these were Britain's largest campaigns against the new slaveries in Africa, and because these campaigns were closely connected in British imperial and domestic politics. (See Figure 1 for map.)

This book focuses on Britain because it was not only the dominant European imperial power, but also the center of humanitarian political protest and debate over European imperial labor policies between the 1880s and the 1920s. Moreover, British humanitarians and imperial officials played the central role among Europeans in crafting a new international law against slavery under the League of Nations. In staging their campaigns against the new slaveries in Africa, Britain's new abolitionists found support from pressure groups in other European nations, but this foreign support did not sustain or direct the British campaigns, and the foreign pressure groups did not achieve national exposure comparable with that of their allies in Britain.[19] The British activists and officials who addressed the new slaveries in Africa were conscious of their leading role among their European counterparts. In fact, they believed that in combating "slavery in all its forms" they were upholding a national tradition—but a tradition that did not blind them to new slaveries within their own empire. While the British believed that the line between freedom and slavery marked the divide between civilization and savagery, they acknowledged that this line could shift beneath their own feet.

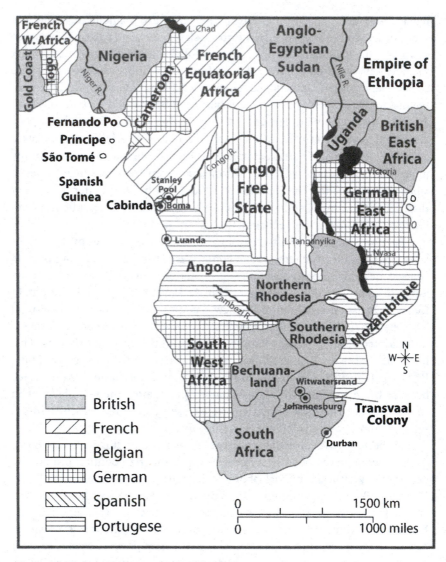

Figure 1. Colonial sub-Saharan Africa, 1904.

There were three distinct ideological branches of British humanitarianism that influenced controversies over the new slaveries in Africa. This study articulates these ideologies through the words and deeds of particular reform campaigns, grounding imperial discourses in the practices of organizations and institutions. The first of these humanitarian ideologies, trusteeship, had been a cornerstone of the moral authority of British administration overseas since the late eighteenth century. Edmund Burke, and other prominent advocates of trusteeship, asserted that the British should serve as imperial "trustees" because they occupied a higher level of civilization than the peoples of other races around the world. The British civilization was distinguished by its political organization, by its economy and technology, and by its Protestant culture. God's Providence had entailed a Christian duty to enhance the moral and material welfare of Britain's imperial subjects, but the imperial government and its chartered companies did not fulfill this duty solely through a program of spiritual conversion. Rather, the British imperial regime was to promote Christian ethics and culture by incorporating foreign peoples into the imperial economy as laborers and consumers.

Burke, as a member of the House of Commons in the late eighteenth century, famously described Britain's political rule and economic dominance over the people of India as a "sacred trust."[20] Under this trust, Britain had the right to manage, but not to claim sovereignty over, the property of its imperial subjects, just as a trustee would manage the property of a child for the child's benefit. This trusteeship had a theoretical end point: the moment at which the formerly savage wards achieved a civilization comparable to that of the trustee and learned to govern their own affairs in an accordingly civilized manner. Even the arch-imperialist Cecil Rhodes would later advocate "equal rights for all civilized men."[21] Political rights and privileges were thus premised on a civilized culture that, in principle, all people, regardless of race, could achieve.

The principle of trusteeship was useful to imperial administrators because, although it placed theoretical limits on the duration of their rule, it allowed these same administrators to decide when their rule should actually end. Consequently, imperial administrators were apt to prioritize their immediate interests in maintaining social and economic stability over their presumed, long-term interests in making themselves obsolete. This point was not lost on twentieth-century nationalists, such as the Kenyan leader Jomo Kenyatta, who criticized "those 'professional friends of the African' who are prepared to maintain their friendship for eternity as a sacred duty, provided only that the African will continue to play the part of an ignorant savage so that they can monopolize the office of interpreting his mind and speaking for him."[22]

The rise of evangelicalism in Britain in the late eighteenth century produced the second ideological branch of British humanitarianism: evangelical philanthropy. Evangelicals took leading roles in the British anti-slavery movement and in the development of British overseas missions, which grew dramatically over the course of the nineteenth century. Remarkably, historians of British anti-slavery have generally overlooked the ways in which missionary societies appropriated and advanced anti-slavery politics to rally support for their own expansion into Africa after the middle of the nineteenth century.[23] At the same time that the memberships and budgets of Britain's anti-slavery societies dwindled, Britain's major missions to Africa were growing, following the lead of Dr. David Livingstone in condemning slavery as the "open sore" of

Africa. It is no wonder that missions would take a leading role in advancing Britain's anti-slavery movement. British popular support for abolition had always been motivated by a moral calling, and specifically a calling that invoked the moral virtue of free labor.

Like the advocates of trusteeship, evangelicals believed that they could promote Christian ethics and culture by incorporating foreign peoples into the imperial economy as laborers and consumers. However, in the process of freeing people from bondage and saving souls, evangelicals also instigated social reforms, provoking unrest that imperial administrators wished to avoid. Although both imperial administrators and evangelicals invoked Protestant Christianity to legitimize their intervention in foreign societies, they subscribed to different conceptions of reform and different time frames for the transition from savagery to civilization. This tension was exacerbated after the 1870s, when British missionary societies took over the British anti-slavery movement and joined in a general movement for "the evangelization of the world in this generation."

At the turn of the twentieth century, the advocates of trusteeship and evangelical philanthropy were challenged by proponents of "the elementary rights of humanity," or human rights. Two distinct groups within the British imperial economy advanced this rights-based agenda. The trade unionist movement, which became increasingly involved in imperial issues after 1900, was primarily concerned with defending the rights of British workers. The second group was a powerful combination of British merchants, who established a strategic alliance with the Aborigines' Protection Society (APS), the oldest anti-slavery organization in Britain.[24] These merchants and the APS were initially concerned with defending the merchants' rights to trade in foreign imperial territories in West and central Africa, but their agenda grew to encompass the rights of Africans as well. This group asserted that the rights of British merchants to trade with Africans would guarantee Africans' human rights. Borrowing from the Victorian liberal tradition, this humanitarian lobby argued that human rights were based on property ownership, and that the exchange of property through commerce would ensure the fundamental human right of freedom from suffering.

The advocates of evangelical philanthropy and human rights came into conflict over issues of culture and political sovereignty in tropical Africa. Evangelicals generally endorsed cultural reform and political deference, while the advocates of rights endorsed a significant degree of cultural relativism, as well as political autonomy, for Africans. In the latter regard, the advocates of human rights also came into conflict with imperial officials. In contrast to the indeterminate time frame of trusteeship, rights did not, in principle, depend on historical development for their efficacy. Rights constituted, in themselves, an imperative to reform, and it was not clear where claims to rights might end. In these respects, rights were a potential threat to imperial rule.

As we will see in the chapters that follow, these three branches of British humanitarian ideology were mutually constitutive. The advocates of trusteeship, evangelical philanthropy, and human rights sometimes worked together and sometimes at odds, adapting and refining their particular approaches to slavery. One might reasonably argue that their differences were actually outweighed by their shared commitments to capitalist development and racial hierarchy. In fact, each group declared its principles to be universal, but these principles were similarly circumscribed in practice by capitalism and racism. In acknowledging these and other limits of humanitarianism in retrospect, one must be careful, however, to set aside the assumption that humanitarianism was either morally good and unselfish or fraudulent and hypocritical. One cannot grasp the historical significance of humanitarianism by addressing it as either a myth or a reality.[25] Humanitarianism has been historically contingent on myriad factors, including religion, class, race, gender, nationalism, and sovereignty. In order to perceive the historically contingent and dynamic nature of humanitarianism, one need only consider that the current international laws governing the human rights of labor are based on precedents in imperial labor law, as discussed in chapter 5.[26]

This history of British humanitarianism, anti-slavery politics, and European imperialism in Africa follows a general chronology. It begins by outlining the ideological origins of the main humanitarian principles with which the British legitimized and criticized imperial labor systems and the European "scramble for Africa" in the late nineteenth century. It then examines three British reform campaigns against new slaveries in Africa in the early twentieth century. The first of these controversies, and certainly the most famous, focused on reports of forced labor and atrocities in the Congo Free State, ruled by King Leopold II of Belgium. The second controversy involved the exploitation of indentured Chinese laborers in the gold mines of Britain's Transvaal Colony in South Africa, and the third controversy focused on charges that a prominent British company, *Cadbury Brothers Ltd.*, had profited from cocoa produced by slaves in Portuguese West Africa.

Historians have not previously connected these controversies to any significant extent. Nonetheless, the principal leaders, events, and outcomes of these controversies were inextricably linked. I have chosen to address them in separate chapters because I wish to strike a balance between a coherent narrative and distinct analytical emphases upon different factors that shaped humanitarian politics in Edwardian Britain. Thus, the chapter on the Congo reform campaign highlights the tension between evangelical philanthropy and human rights, stressing the predominance of evangelical philanthropy in the humanitarian politics of empire in Britain prior to the First World War. In addition, this chapter highlights the propagandistic power of new technologies of visual protest, especially lantern slides and the reproduction of photographs in the popular press. The next chapter, on "Chinese slavery," demonstrates that discourses on rights were strictly circumscribed by racial and class politics in both Britain and South Africa. By contrast, the chapter on the Cadbury scandal demonstrates how humanitarian campaigns were enlisted in the service of partisan political warfare, and how the discourses of Christian paternalism and rights could be manipulated—if not bought—by capitalists.

The last chapter of this book steps back from Britain to address the emergence of international government and international labor law in the context of European imperialism. The debates over the new slaveries in Africa before the First World War set the stage for wartime discussions about the management of Europe's imperial subjects by a proposed "league of nations." Disputes over the merits of evangelical philanthropy and human rights were promptly subsumed within debates over the definition and prerogatives of sovereignty in an international system of government. The victorious European powers ultimately employed British humanitarian discourses to legitimize their seizure and redistribution of imperial territories in Africa and elsewhere under the League of Nations' mandates system. In the end, British officials overlooked the human rights of Africans and other imperial subjects, choosing to base the mandates system on the traditional, imperial ideology of trusteeship. This ideology had changed in at least one important respect, however, since the declarations of Burke in the late eighteenth century. The new advocates of trust, including imperial officials such as Jan Smuts and Sir Frederick Lugard, characterized their trust as "sacred," but they otherwise played down the providential, Christian overtones of this principle and displayed little recognition of its theological origins. Instead, they identified Britain's trust with the maintenance of what they called "native welfare."

British evangelicals and human rights activists agreed that the test of Europe's "sacred trust" would come in the creation of specific legislation to promote the welfare of Africans under the League of Nations. Toward this end, British anti-slavery activists succeeded in 1922 in initiating the creation of an international convention against slavery. In drafting the text of the convention, however, British and European officials in the League of Nations were careful not to inhibit the existing, coercive labor systems of imperial regimes. In fact, the convention stipulated that governments should retain the privilege of mobilizing "forced labor" for their public works. British anti-slavery activists regretfully acknowledged that the Slavery Convention of 1926 outlawed the most egregious excesses of chattel slavery while sanctioning the new slaveries of European imperialism. The creation of an international government, and the codification of the human rights of labor under international law later in the twentieth century, thus rest on both the power of European imperialists and the prevailing humanitarian ideologies of Great Britain, which remained invested in the moral authority and economic order of empire.

CHAPTER 1

Humanity and Slavery in All Their Forms

Joseph Conrad's *Heart of Darkness*, published in 1899, opens on the River Thames aboard a cruising yawl, where several men wait for the tide to turn and carry them out to sea. As the dusk falls, one of the men, Charlie Marlow, begins a tale that unfolds into the novella and, more broadly, a commentary on Europe's scramble for Africa. Marlow's tale is loosely based on Conrad's own experience during a visit to the Congo Free State as a ship's captain in 1890, an experience that prompted Conrad to question the motives and morality of Europe's civilizing mission. In a series of reflections that precede his tale, Marlow observes:

> The conquest of the earth, which mostly means the taking it away from those who have a different complexion or slightly flatter noses than ourselves, is not a pretty thing when you look into it too much. What redeems it is the idea only. An idea at the back of it, not a sentimental pretence but an idea; and an unselfish belief in the idea—something you can set up, and bow down before, and offer a sacrifice to.[1]

This chapter is, in part, about the origins of the idea to which Conrad referred at the turn of the twentieth century. There was actually a range of distinct, and yet related, ideas that enabled Europeans to legitimize their conquest of Africa. While Conrad generally cast an ironic eye upon the European as an "emissary of light," he primarily leveled his criticism at traders who had lost their moral compass in their search for wealth.[2] Conrad, like most other critics of European imperialism in his era, was not opposed to European intervention in Africa, and he recognized the currency and power of the idea that had rendered this intervention a humanitarian calling. From the distance of over a century, historians are apt to approach this idea as a hegemonic ideology that was based on racism, capitalism, religion, or a coherent amalgam of these and other forces at work in British and European imperial culture. Conrad and his contemporaries, however, understood that the idea meant different things to different people, and that people were prepared to argue for the superiority of their humanitarian principles over the humanitarian principles of others.

The language of humanitarian debate in Conrad's era reflected three distinctive humanitarian ideologies that provided strong moral authority to British overseas expansion. These ideologies were distinguished by their respective emphases on the political principle of trusteeship, evangelical philanthropy, and, finally, human rights. It is important to note that these ideologies developed at different times, in response to different historical circumstances. Moreover, the currency of each ideology was not constant, but waxed and waned in different political environments. Whereas the principle of imperial trusteeship originated in the political aftermath of the Reformation, evangelical philanthropy came to the fore in British humanitarian politics on the strength of the evangelical movement of the late eighteenth century. Subsequently, the politics of human rights developed in the late nineteenth century on the basis of liberal interpretations of natural rights theory, coupled with a commitment to cultural relativism derived largely from the ethnographic studies of Mary Kingsley in West Africa. This is not to say that the idea of human rights originated in Britain in the late Victorian era, but rather that a historically particular version of human rights became a significant factor in humanitarian debates over empire in Britain at this time.[3] While a strictly materialist critique of empire might collapse these three ideologies into a single historical system of capitalist exploitation, it is nonetheless true that the historical advocates of these ideologies saw themselves in different camps. Their differences, as well as their common beliefs and strategic alliances, were clearly apparent in twentieth-century debates over the new slaveries in Africa.

The perception of new slaveries was nothing new to the British. This chapter couples its introduction of humanitarian ideologies with an overview of debates over the legal guises of slavery that followed the emancipation of chattel slaves in the British Empire in 1833 and predated the onset of Europe's scramble for Africa in the 1870s. The subjects of abolitionist protest diversified throughout the Victorian era, expanding beyond the plantation complex in the Americas to include slavery under Islamic regimes in East Africa and the Middle East, as well as the international traffic in indentured Indians and Chinese. In order to combat these perceived evils, the British abolitionist movement developed new organizations at home and attempted to forge alliances with abolitionists abroad, but missionary societies soon overtook the conventional anti-slavery organizations to become the leading public authorities of British abolition by the final third of the nineteenth century. As the last section of this chapter demonstrates, missionaries were not alone in driving abolitionist debates in the years ahead. British missionaries, merchants, labor leaders, and government officials all acknowledged, decried, and exploited the problem of new slavery in the age of imperialism.

Forms of Humanity: Trusteeship and Evangelical Philanthropy

The political principle of trusteeship was a source of moral authority and a point of contention in British humanitarian debates over empire after the late eighteenth century. Yet trusteeship remains a vague and fleeting term in most scholarship on empire in the modern era. William Roger Louis observed over thirty-five years ago that there was not an adequate history of imperial trusteeship, and this remains true today.[4] Historians of the British Empire commonly refer to Edmund Burke's declaration of 1783 that Britain's rule in India was a "sacred trust," but few have considered the earlier development of this principle, or whether this principle had changed before British imperial officials, in cooperation with President Woodrow Wilson of the United States, laid the foundations of international government as a "sacred trust" under the League of Nations after the First World War.[5] Given that historians have not previously examined the origins of British imperial trusteeship, in contrast to the voluminous scholarship devoted to the sources of evangelical philanthropy and human rights, it is useful to take a brief overview of the development of trusteeship in order to gain perspective on changes in British humanitarianism in the nineteenth century.

The political principle of trusteeship developed in England during the Reformation of the sixteenth century, under the influence of Lutheran theology and radical Calvinism.[6] It was a product of the rejection of divine-right theories of monarchy, and it reflected a momentous turn in ecclesiological and political theory toward popular sovereignty and the right of resistance to unjust rule.[7] The Lutheran origins of political trusteeship are found in the principle of justification by faith, *sola fide*, which established the equality of the faithful in the eyes of God, regardless of worldly ranks and orders. In privileging an individual's trust with God, Lutherans freed commoners of their dependence on the spiritual mediation of priests and monarchs, thus laying the groundwork for a new conception of self that would, under the influence of more radical theologians, reshape the political world.

Martin Luther's foremost advocate in England, William Tyndale, articulated the relationship of faith and trust in his interpolation of Luther's *A Prologe to the Romayns*, published in Tyndale's *New Testament* of 1534:

> Fayth is then a liuely and stedfaste truste in the fauoure of God, where-
> with we committe oure selues all to gedyr vnto God, and that truste is so
> surely grounded and steketh so fast in oure hertes, that a man wolde not
> once doute of it, though he shuld dye a thousand tymes therfore. And
> suche truste wrought by the holy goost through fayth, maketh a man
> glad, lusty, cherefull and true herted vnto God and to all creatures. By
> the meanes where of, willingly and withoute compulsion he is glad and
> redy to do good to euery man, to do seruice to euery man, to soffre all
> thinges, that God maye be loued and praysed, which hath geuen him
> suche grace.[8]

Luther and his supporters in England were not advocating a new egalitarian society ordered by a common understanding of Christian duty. Rather, Luther believed that the existing social and political hierarchies were direct reflections of God's will and Providence.[9] He asserted that political authority was derived from God, and that rulers had a duty to rule their subjects not as they themselves wanted to do, but rather as God prescribed.[10] Turning to the duty of subjects, Luther referred repeatedly to St. Paul's injunction in his Epistle to the Romans that it was the subjects' Christian duty to submit themselves to the highest powers, whose rule could never be legitimately resisted with violence.[11] Thus, the Lutherans' commitment to a divinely ordained political hierarchy circumscribed the political implications of the principle of justification by faith, rendering it compatible with the authority of monarchy.[12]

The persecutions of Protestants in the course of the Counter-Reformation prompted other Protestant theologians to reject Luther's deference to political hierarchy and to formulate doctrines of resistance to unjust rulers. As Quentin Skinner explains, radical Calvinists took Luther's idea that any individual could convenant directly with God and used this idea as the basis for popular revolution.[13] These radical Calvinists claimed that God did not ordain specific rulers, but rather the standards by which a people should select a ruler. The people therefore had a Christian duty to select a godly ruler and to enforce the ruler's sacred trust not only to God but also to themselves. The Calvinists argued that if subjects found themselves oppressed by a tyrannical ruler, this could only mean that they had made a mistake in selecting him.[14] In England, Calvinists took this point farther by drawing a distinction between a public office and the individual who occupied that office. A public official who advocated ungodly acts forfeited his public status and became a private individual, who could then be opposed lawfully by his former subjects.[15] Faith therefore constituted one's trust with God, and the equality of the faithful entailed the Christian duty to enforce the sacred trust of a ruler to govern in a godly manner.

This identification of trusteeship with popular sovereignty gained currency in England in the seventeenth century, during debates over the troubled reign of the Stuarts and in the Civil Wars that preceded the execution of Charles I in 1649.[16] The king's opponents asserted that he had broken his God-given trust with the people by indulging in arbitrary government and popish reforms. Charles, by contrast, chose to privilege his own relationship of trust with God. Subsequently, the Lord Protector and Head of State, Oliver Cromwell, used the popular idea of trust to articulate his own puritanical vision of an English republic ordained by Providence.[17] Although the republic was short-lived, the politics of trust and Providence would continue to inform British government throughout the seventeenth and eighteenth centuries, assuming a central role in conceptions of trusteeship and empire under the influence of John Locke.[18]

Locke built upon the identification of trusteeship with popular sovereignty in his *Second Treatise of Government*, published in 1690. The concept of trust is fundamental to Locke's work, constituting, in the words of Peter Laslett, "both the corollary and the safeguard of natural political virtue."[19] Locke's theory of the state, in particular, centers upon a "social contract" through which free individuals in a state of nature agree to form a political society. Yet Locke uses the word "trust" much more often than he uses the word "contract," and he did not, in either case, wish to invoke a formal, legal deed for government.[20] "Trust," Laslett emphasizes, "is a matter of conscience, which may have its final and unlikely sanctions, but which operates because of the sense of duty which Locke dogmatically, unthinkingly assumes in every man he contemplates."[21]

How, then, did trusteeship apply to the governance of imperial subjects who did not explicitly volunteer to form an imperial society? According to Locke, people can also give legitimacy to government through "tacit trust."[22] This tacit trust is displayed by the continued residence of people in a given imperial territory.[23] Moreover, the imperial ruler can perceive this tacit trust from the privileged perspective of "paternal power," which prefigures political power in Locke's analysis. Parents naturally hold authority over their children due to both their superior capacity for reason and "the Affection and Tenderness, which God hath planted in the Breasts of Parents, towards their Children."[24] Parents are not to be "a severe Arbitrary Government, but only for the Help, Instruction, and Preservation of their Off-spring."[25] Their reason enables them to comprehend the natural law of God and, in turn, evaluate the development of the child according to standards of behavior and forms of culture that presumably manifest this law. According to Locke, "neither can there be any pretense why this parental power should keep the Child, when grown to a Man, in subjection to the Will of his Parents any farther."[26] It is, nonetheless, for the paternal authority to determine when the child, like the imperial subject, has reached maturity. As Uday Mehta has argued in a related vein regarding Locke, "Behind the capacities ascribed to all human beings there exist a thicker set of social credentials that constitute the real bases of political inclusion."[27]

Locke identifies the grounds upon which imperial subjects can deny their tacit trust and legitimize rebellion against their paternal governors. "The Power of the Father," Locke explains, "doth not reach at all to the Property of the Child, which is only in his own disposing."[28] The property of the child, like the property of the imperial subject or any human, is composed fundamentally of his own person and his own labor.[29] The arbitrary coercion of the body, or the use of coercion to extract labor, constitutes a violation of tacit trust. In *A Letter Concerning Toleration* Locke further explains that imperial subjects retain these fundamental property rights even if they are not Christians.

> Not even Americans, subjected unto a Christian Prince, are to be punished either in Body or in Goods for not embracing our Faith and Worship. If they are perswaded that they please God in observing the Rites of their own Country, and that they shall obtain Happiness by that means, they are to be left unto God and themselves.[30]

To whom, then, can the imperial subject turn for relief, given that he has a tacit trust with the same imperial government that oppresses him? In the case of Englishmen, as Laslett explains, "There is no final judge of these things on earth, the ultimate appeal can only be to God."[31] Likewise, the imperial subject can appeal to God only in the last resort through the mediation of Christian representatives in the legislature of the imperial government.[32] This legislature is, after all, in Locke's words, "the Soul that gives Form, Life, and Unity to the Commonwealth."[33] In Lockean terms, then, imperial trusteeship depends fundamentally upon tacit trust, toleration of cultural differences over forms of faith and worship, and final recourse to God through an appeal that must be mediated by Christian representatives within the imperial government.

Linda Colley has demonstrated that in the eighteenth century, "Protestantism, broadly understood, provided the majority of Britons with a framework for their lives."[34] Political trusteeship was one means to connect this national Protestant identity to the emerging, modern imperial identity of the state. British officials used trusteeship, for example, to legitimize the extension of the British Empire after the conclusion of the Seven Years War in 1763.[35]

Twenty years later, following the loss of the American colonies, Burke identified trusteeship as the guiding principle of the British Empire, which would henceforth focus upon Asia. Endorsing Charles Fox's India Bill in 1783, Burke declared, "All political power which is set over men, and…all privilege claimed or exercised in exclusion of them…ought to be some way or other exercised ultimately for their benefit." In short, all forms of political dominion and commercial privilege were "in the strictest sense a *trust*."[36]

Burke's conception of trust, like that of Locke, was not based on legal contract, but on Christian duty.[37] Like many of his contemporaries, Burke regarded the British Empire as providential, and he believed that Protestantism had helped to imbue Britain with a unique capacity for just rule overseas.[38] Accordingly, Britain's imperial governors were accountable to God. "The wrongs done to humanity in the eastern world," Burke declared, "shall be avenged on those who have inflicted them.…The wrath of Heaven would sooner or later fall upon a nation, that suffers, with impunity, its rulers thus to oppress the weak and innocent."[39] Burke specifically designated Parliament as the representative of the people of India before God. Despite cultural differences, Burke stated, "Men separated by every barrier of Nature from you, by the Providence of God are blended in one common cause, and are now become suppliants at your bar."[40] Burke did not believe that these suppliants were under any obligation to assimilate the culture of their distant British representatives. On the contrary, Burke argued, "If we undertake to govern the inhabitants of such a country, we must govern them upon their own principles and maxims, and not upon ours.…We have more versatility of character and manners, and it is we who must conform."[41] British moral authority was thus based on divine Providence, the representation of imperial subjects by Christian legislators accountable to God, and, finally, the acknowledgment of cultural difference, blended by God in the common cause of just rule. It was, in Burke's words, a "sacred trust."[42]

Burke believed, furthermore, that the laws of the market were divinely ordained, and that political economy was an engine for material and moral development. C.B. Macpherson observes, "The central assumption of [Burke's] political economy is strikingly like Adam Smith's 'invisible hand,' though Burke's assumption is more obtrusively theological."[43] Burke believed that the Christian principle of trust constituted the duty of each person in a position of privilege to ensure that his actions benefited those people under his power. As Macpherson further explains, "There is nothing surprising or inconsistent in Burke's championing at the same time the traditional English hierarchical society and the capitalist market economy. He believed in both, and believed that the latter needed the former."[44] In other words, capitalist competition was to be governed by the laws of God, which rendered subordination natural and respect for one's own subordination moral.

As Britain entered the age of revolution in the late eighteenth century, trusteeship was the main principle used to define the British Empire as a Christian and paternalistic regime. Burke's trusteeship would remain the preferred ideology of the imperial state, because it entailed political and economic subordination while discouraging administrative intervention to impose social reforms. Imperial officials were, and would remain, generally averse to such reforms, because these reforms tended to produce social and economic instability. The principle of trust, moreover, gave officials the authority to determine when the so-called ward had achieved civilization and become entitled to his freedom. In the late eighteenth century, there was no indication that the wards of the Indian subcontinent would ever be more than children in the eyes of their imperial trustees.

The rise of evangelicalism increasingly challenged the political principle of trusteeship after 1780. The evangelical movement began in the Church of England, then spread through more radical, nonconformist channels to transform Britain's religious landscape by the middle of the nineteenth century. Most important, evangelicals emphasized that grace was available to those who performed good works and, in the most general sense, lived in accordance with biblical precepts. In contrast to the Calvinist concept of an Elect destined for salvation, evangelicals believed that grace was accessible to all people, regardless of culture or race. Tensions subsequently arose between these ostensibly inclusive principles and the practices of evangelicals, who commonly treated foreign peoples as culturally inferior and demanded not only social, but also political, deference from their congregations.[45] Nonetheless, after the late eighteenth century, evangelicals created a global religious movement through abolitionist organizations and overseas missionary societies that regarded the social reform of foreign peoples as a moral imperative.

Previous scholars have emphasized continuity in the humanitarian politics of the British Empire across the nineteenth century, suggesting that trusteeship remained the dominant imperial ethic even in the wake of the evangelical movement.[46] This is not to say that they have viewed the concept of trusteeship as static, but rather that they have perceived it as adaptable to the tenets of evangelicalism. While there was certainly common ground between trusteeship and evangelicalism, there were also significant distinctions that constituted an ideological break in British humanitarianism in the late eighteenth century. It is important to bear in mind both the commonalities of and the differences between these ideologies in order to appreciate how evangelicalism transformed the humanitarian politics of the British Empire, particularly through the anti-slavery movement in the nineteenth century.

Evangelicals shared with the advocates of trusteeship a strong faith in the moral and cultural superiority of Christianity, and a firm commitment to capitalist development. This common ground between evangelicalism and trusteeship is illustrated by the burgeoning abolitionist organizations of the late eighteenth and early nineteenth centuries. David Brion Davis has observed, "Much of the early British antislavery writing reveals an almost obsessive concern with idealizing hierarchical order."[47] More specifically, evangelicalism was tied to the hierarchical order and ethics of capitalist production. "British antislavery," Davis explains, "provided a bridge between preindustrial and industrial values; by combining the ideal of emancipation with an insistence on duty and subordination, it helped to smooth the way to the future."[48] This duty to which Davis refers was not a product of economic self-interest.[49] Rather, this duty was a tenet of Christianity, and it was central to the humanitarian visions of Burke and leading evangelical abolitionists such as William Wilberforce.[50] Burke was, in fact, a supporter of abolition, as well as an advocate of Britain's "sacred trust" in India.

The advocates of both trusteeship and evangelicalism acknowledged a close connection between commerce and Christianity.[51] In contrast to Burke, however, evangelicals saw the combination of commerce and Christianity as an engine for comprehensive social reform. This concept was also influential among Victorian era social reformers within Britain itself who looked to the anti-slavery movement as a model for their domestic campaigns.[52] Whether addressing the lower classes in Britain's slums or the peoples of Africa, evangelicals believed that British commerce with "uncivilised" peoples served three distinctly Christian purposes. First, this so-called legitimate commerce in British commodities would undermine illegitimate commerce in immoral commodities such as slaves. Second, commerce would spread a Christian material culture and thus facilitate cultural assimilation to a civilized model. Finally, commerce would promote consumer desire for additional British goods, a desire that would drive people to achieve the Protestant virtue of self-discipline in their labor for wages to obtain more goods. The savage was thus disciplined as both a producer and a consumer, and the abolitionist or missionary thus reconciled his or her role as a paternalistic, moral educator with that of a capitalist competitor. It was precisely through exploitation that the savage would learn, and in this manner self-preservation and improvement were conflated with virtue. It was in these terms that the abolitionists envisioned the ideal plantation, as Davis describes it: "a kindly, paternalistic master ministering to his grateful Negro 'yeomen,' both subject to the administrative agents of the King and both dedicated to the commercial prosperity of the empire!"[53]

The discourse of trusteeship figured less prominently in British imperial politics in the Victorian era, giving way to principles of evangelical philanthropy that justified British expansion on the next major imperial frontier: Africa. While evangelicals, like the advocates of trust, believed in natural progress along a hierarchy of civilization, they did not believe that progress was ultimately achieved through tutelage administered by a government authority. Rather, evangelicals emphasized the roles of individual conscience, action, and revelation. One might attribute this shift in humanitarian discourse to a combination of changes in the British political environment. Given that the advocates of trust took a reticent view toward comprehensive social reform, it seems likely that their voices were muted by the rise of "Christian economics" after the 1820s, and especially by evangelicals who asserted that commercial development and social reform must be linked both at home and abroad.[54] In a related vein, the central role of the government in managing trust was arguably difficult to reconcile with the era of "free-trade imperialism," and with Britain's aversion to establishing new imperial administrations outside of the Indian subcontinent between the 1840s and the 1890s.[55]

Although the discourse of trusteeship fell into relative disuse in imperial circles, the principle of trust remained compatible with important tenets of evangelical philanthropy, especially with evangelicals' clarion call for the dual advancement of "commerce and Christianity." A leading clergyman and economist, Thomas Chalmers, argued in the 1820s that commercial relations were not governed by contract, but by "implicit trust" derived from Christian morality, an assertion to which the evangelical reformer Samuel Smiles referred approvingly in his book Self Help in 1859.[56] Trusteeship also remained an important principle for political philosophers who addressed the British Empire, including Thomas Macaulay and John Stuart Mill, and it was a point of reference for radical critics of imperialism, such as John Hobson, and for imperial officials both at home and abroad.[57] Significantly, British officials began to revive the discourse of trusteeship in the era of the scramble for Africa at the end of the nineteenth century, when Britain started to extend its administrative control over an increasing amount of territory. British officials wanted to represent the expansion of industrial capitalism as a means to promote the moral and material improvement of savages who labored for the capitalist's profit. Toward this end, in 1896 the Colonial Secretary, Joseph Chamberlain, declared: "We, in our Colonial policy, as fast as we acquire new territory and develop it, develop it as trustees of civilisation for the commerce of the world."[58] Putting the principle of trusteeship into practice, Sir Charles Eliot set out to promote "native trusteeship" as the Commissioner and Consul-General of Britain's East Africa protectorate after 1901.[59]

The connotations of trusteeship differed in these contexts, but trusteeship would resurface as a coherent and central ideology in British policies on empire and international government after the First World War. Trusteeship did not infringe, in principle, on native sovereignty, and so it suited imperial officials who wanted to seize territory and yet honor Britain's wartime pledge to support "the self-determination of small nations." Britain's seizure of territory in Africa, the Middle East, and Asia was therefore, in principle, a temporary measure that fell within the word, if not the spirit, of Britain's wartime commitments. At the same time that imperial officials revived trusteeship as their preferred ethical discourse, they added a new emphasis on the maintenance of "native welfare." Despite this change in emphasis, however, trusteeship in the 1920s still bore comparison with the speeches of Burke in the late eighteenth century. While government officials no longer characterized imperial governance as providential or in any respect theological in the 1920s, they nonetheless defined it as a "sacred duty." Like Burke, the latter-day advocates of trusteeship accepted cultural differences between peoples and preferred to avoid social reform projects. Instead, imperial officials asserted that Africans would benefit from capitalist development, with a view toward promoting liberal democracy and loyalty, and, eventually, attaining self-government within the British Commonwealth. As in the Burkean concept of trusteeship, however, imperial officials did not seriously question the social reforms entailed by capitalism itself, nor did they establish a fixed schedule or a clear set of criteria for independence from British rule.

We will return to the politics of trusteeship, in the context of international government, in the last chapter of this book. In the meantime, we turn to the new slaveries of the nineteenth century and the prevailing humanitarian politics of evangelical philanthropy and human rights.

Forms of Slavery

The original British campaigns against slavery focused on the Atlantic slave trade and the chattel slavery of Africans and their descendants on plantations in the Caribbean and North America in the late eighteenth and early nineteenth centuries. These campaigns contributed to the British government's Abolition Acts of 1806–1807, the Emancipation Act of 1833, and the subsequent reforms of labor laws under other European imperial regimes and in the United States. Although the Atlantic slave trade had been largely suppressed by 1870, British abolitionists still saw themselves surrounded by unfinished work. In the years following the Emancipation Act, abolitionists had perceived that imperial regimes could outlaw chattel slavery, only to impose new slaveries under legal fictions of freedom. Moreover, British abolitionists, missionaries, merchants, and colonial officials recognized that chattel slavery still existed beyond the reach of European sovereignty, and that abolition provided a moral imperative for expansion in conjunction with commerce and Christianity. Thus, as slavery took many forms in the age of emancipation, abolition assumed a new role in the politics of imperial expansion.

Plantation owners sought new locations and new sources of labor in their attempts to adapt to the laws against slavery and to evade the efforts of Britain's Royal Navy to enforce the abolition of the Atlantic slave trade. Europeans and

Africans developed plantations in the mid-nineteenth century on islands in the Gulf of Guinea and in the Indian Ocean, as well as on the coasts of Africa. The plantation owners exploited labor costs that were cheaper than those of their American competitors, and they built new colonial economies upon exports such as cloves, palm oil, sugar, and, later, cocoa and rubber. African rulers and traders participated in these growing trades by providing slaves for work as plantation hands and porters, receiving in exchange European imports such as firearms, ammunition, and liquor.

Slave traders and plantation owners in Africa found refuge under the laws of cooperative imperial regimes. Imperial labor laws commonly outlawed slavery at the same time that they bound the former slaves to similar, if not identical, conditions of servitude under euphemistic legal terms backed by the coercive power of the state. In the British Caribbean, the manumission of slaves had been limited by their mandatory "apprenticeship" for ten years as plantation laborers under the authority of their former masters. This transitional step between slavery and freedom had been supported by many in the abolitionist movement, reflecting evangelicals' common belief that freedom must be contingent upon social reform. Seymour Drescher explains, "Abolitionist leaders [had] declared that 'insanity alone could dictate' immediate emancipation. The abolitionists' rationale for delay [had been] straightforward: too high a proportion of Caribbean slaves were African 'savages,' debased by both superstition and enslavement. Slaves as a group required a long transition to absorb proper work habits, religion, and civilization."[60] The period of apprenticeship had therefore been established to enable the plantation owners to educate their workers in self-discipline, thrift, and other skills and habits that would ensure their welfare as free men and women. According to abolitionists and government inspectors alike, however, apprenticeship had proven to be a thin veil for slavery, and the system had been abandoned in 1838.[61]

The British employed another legal stratagem in their attempts to retain the labor of present and former slaves and, perhaps more important, to avoid social and economic instability, if not rebellion, in the Empire. The Emancipation Act had not addressed the systems of slavery in most British possessions in Asia, particularly in British India and in the numerous Indian princely states with which the British had established alliances.[62] British abolitionists soon turned their attention to India, using the World Anti-Slavery Convention of 1840 to condemn the enslavement of millions of Indians under British rule.[63] The East India Company (EIC) never considered attempting to emancipate all of the slaves in India, and it was reluctant to institute legal reforms that required administrative action toward this end. So, as Suzanne Miers explains, "[The EIC] did not outlaw slavery, but simply declared that it had no legal standing in British India."[64] After Crown rule was established in India following the Mutiny of 1857, the government of India declared slavery illegal in 1860. Yet the precedent of turning a blind, legal eye to slavery, established by the EIC, proved influential in subsequent British imperial policies in Africa. By declaring that slavery had no legal standing, imperial regimes passed the responsibility for enslavement to the slaves themselves, who were, in principle, not bound by law to their conditions of servitude. Under this calculated, legal oversight, slavery became "voluntary."[65]

Whether legal systems outlawed slavery or overlooked it, all European imperial regimes in Africa bound people to servitude under new legal categories. In Portuguese West Africa, slaves were recategorized first as *libertos* in 1869 and then as *serviçaes* after 1878, though their actual labor conditions had not changed. Subsequently, the British, the French, the Germans, and the Belgians "recruited" Africans for their militaries or mobilized "corvée labour" or "forced labor" for "public works."[66] Many European regimes also laid legal claim to Africans' labor through taxation. The taxes might be payable in currency, in kind, or in labor, but they all provided the imperial regimes with a legal basis for compelling people to work. In a fundamental sense, all systems of imperial taxation were built on the arrogation of land by European regimes, generally under the classic colonialist principle of *terra nullius*, or vacant land. Since the fifteenth century, European explorers had claimed land that was, to their eyes, uncultivated, undeveloped, and, thus, unoccupied.[67] In this tradition, the imperialists of the late nineteenth century claimed ostensibly vacant African lands, then imposed taxes on the indigenous communities as just compensation for the privilege of living on the land.[68] Failure to pay the tax constituted a violation of contract, rendering one a criminal subject to the legitimate violence of the state.

In conjunction with the mobilization of indigenous labor through a combination of coercion and taxes, British plantations in the Caribbean and Africa relied increasingly upon migrant workers, and particularly indentured Indians, to meet their labor needs.[69] Indenture was a legal, contractual relationship, unlike the illegal condition of slavery, in which one person owned another as property. Nonetheless, in the years following the first private shipment of Indians to British Guiana in 1837, British abolitionists insisted that the conditions of these indentured laborers were little different from the oppressive experiences of the slaves whom they replaced. In 1840, Lord John Russell, the Colonial Secretary, opposed a proposal that the government should administer the transfer of Indian indentured laborers to Guiana. He declared, with a famous turn of phrase, "I am not prepared to encounter the responsibility of a measure which may lead to a dreadful loss of life on the one hand, or, on the other, a new system of slavery."[70] Following a change in political leadership, the British government took charge of the indentured migration from India in 1842 and oversaw its operation until its end in 1917.

These invidious distinctions between slavery and free labor demonstrate that although the British and other European governments could nominally outlaw slavery, they could not as easily change the imperial economies that had depended upon slave labor. Local imperial officials readily compromised emancipation in the interest of profit and social stability, creating troubling discrepancies between imperial policy and practice. In the era of the European scramble for Africa and its aftermath, British imperial officials, like their European counterparts, were more likely to accommodate slavery than oppose it. The former Governor-General of Nigeria, Lord Frederick Lugard, observed in 1922, "The temporary continuance of domestic [i.e., indigenous] slavery has certain advantages as a form of labour-contract between a more advanced and a very primitive people, where the conception of labour as a saleable commodity... has not yet arisen, and currency with which to pay wages is unknown, or exists only in a very primitive form."[71]

Apart from the slave trade, which depended on overt acts of abduction and coercion, imperial officials were even more likely to overlook other forms of enslavement in Africa, such as lineage slavery. This form of slavery was not primarily directed toward labor exploitation, but toward political and social purposes. Slaves might be used as military recruits, or to bear children, or to fulfill symbolic roles in public ceremonies, such as human sacrifices at funerals. With the rise of the European plantation economies in Africa, two distinctive slave systems thus developed: one based on labor exploitation for the imperial export economy and the other on a lineage system of social reproduction. While this study focuses on the former system of slavery, it is noteworthy that Europeans were well aware of, and largely indifferent to, other systems of slavery in their midst.

Surveying European imperial labor systems at the turn of the century, British humanitarians were quick to observe that abolition had proven to be a cynical pretense for, rather than an object of, Europe's economic expansion. Reflecting upon the horrors of the Congo Free State, H.R. Fox Bourne, the Secretary of the Aborigines' Protection Society, observed in 1903:

> If the over-seas slave traffic has been suppressed and the enslavement of one native by another forbidden, the old forms of slavery have been succeeded or supplemented by new, more grinding and hateful to the victims, and for the satisfaction of white instead of black oppressors. Savage customs and institutions have been condemned and interfered with in so far as they proved inconvenient to the usurpers of land and its produce, but, for the most part with nothing but increase of savagery.[72]

The Problem of New Slavery in the Age of Imperialism

Having perceived that emancipation by law did not constitute freedom, Victorian abolitionists reconceived slavery as a protean concept and condition.

In turn, freedom became an elusive goal. In the troubled aftermath of the Emancipation Act of 1833, the APS was founded in 1837, and two years later the British and Foreign Anti-Slavery Society (Anti-Slavery Society) was established to combat "slavery in all its forms." While popular anti-slavery politics continued to focus on the Atlantic slave trade and the plantation system in the Americas, leaders of these new organizations began to address other causes, such as international indentured labor and the appropriation of land and labor from the indigenous peoples of South Africa, Australia, and Canada.[73]

Public support for these anti-slavery organizations remained strong through the 1840s, but then began to wane after the next decade. Looking back, one might attribute this decline in support to triumphant success, particularly after the emancipation of slaves in the United States. Yet leading abolitionists believed that the effects of their propaganda had been attenuated by an abundance of worthy causes, rather than their absence. In the previous generation, the definitive representation of slavery was the African in chains, kneeling in supplication and asking, "Am I not a man and a brother?" As slavery took many forms in the age of emancipation, and as abolitionists acknowledged slaves of diverse races, it became harder to define a clear subject of compassion. In addition to this lack of focus in their own propaganda, abolitionists confronted the rise of working-class politics and industrial reform in Britain, which prompted many would-be humanitarians to turn to the welfare of so-called white slaves at home. It appears that, simultaneously, a significant middle-class constituency of British anti-slavery was drawn away by another mass movement, the "free trade" campaign led by Richard Cobden and John Bright, founders of the Anti-Corn Law League.[74] While Cobden and Bright were both active supporters of the British anti-slavery movement, their own campaign at the very least offered the anti-slavery societies stiff competition for popular support.

The critics of industrial capitalism in Britain used "slavery" and "abolition" as idioms to address a variety of forms of labor exploitation and political subjugation. As Drescher demonstrates, "antislavery propaganda triggered images of deprivation which were contagious,"[75] enabling reformers to enhance the rhetorical power of their calls for the regulation of child labor or the expansion of the franchise. Subsequently, advocates of women's rights took up the idioms of slavery and abolition to articulate their grievances and claims, and these idioms similarly surfaced in controversies over sexual exploitation, particularly white slave prostitution. By the late nineteenth century, the concepts of slavery and abolition constituted complex intersections between British domestic and imperial politics, connecting issues of race, class, gender, and sexuality.[76]

The Victorian anti-slavery organizations failed to adjust to this increasingly complicated political environment. Accordingly, historians have observed that British anti-slavery drifted into irrelevance after 1870. As European expansion into tropical Africa accelerated in the next decade, Britain's traditional anti-slavery lobby was reduced to a handful of small pressure groups, the most prominent of which were the APS and the Anti-Slavery Society. These organizations were guided by committees of elderly members who were increasingly out of touch with popular sentiment. Their secretaries nonetheless maintained a prolific, if largely ineffectual, correspondence with government officials.

As the original Victorian anti-slavery organizations receded to the political margins, the leadership of the British anti-slavery movement passed to Protestant missionary societies, which embraced abolition as a central cause in their civilizing mission, especially in Africa. It was a missionary, Dr. David Livingstone, who did more than anyone else to increase the British public's awareness of slavery in Africa in the Victorian era. His *Missionary Travels and Researches in South Africa*, published in 1857, went through nine editions. The original version, priced at 1 guinea, sold more than 30,000 copies, while the cheaper, abridged edition, published in 1861 at 6 shillings, sold 10,000 copies.[77] Slavery was a prominent feature of Livingstone's portrayal of African savagery, and he and many others would subsequently invoke abolition as a justification for colonial intervention.[78] As Suzanne Miers explains, anti-slavery rhetoric became "an integral part of an ideological package which justified the subjugation of colonial peoples and the reorganization of their social, economic, and religious structures."[79]

The amalgam of "commerce and Christianity" was at the heart of Livingstone's ideology of intervention in Africa, reflecting his evangelical faith in the natural relationship between individual morality and the ethics of progress in a free market. The material and moral aspects of one's existence were thus linked in a comprehensive reform project known popularly as the civilizing mission. Fanny Guinness, a leading figure in the Congo Balolo Mission, stated in 1880: "We must seek to introduce an entirely new order of things, and in place of ignorant cruel degrading heathenism to establish social order and justice, intelligent industry, and mutual goodwill." "It is not sufficient merely to preach the gospel," Guinness declared. "We must endeavour to show them a better way *in everything*."[80] In theory, according to Guinness and other missionaries, slavery was the greatest obstacle to the civilizing mission in Africa, because it undermined property ownership, inhibited legitimate commerce, and thus enervated the African's will to work toward self-improvement.

Andrew Porter has demonstrated that the slogan "commerce and Christianity" fell out of use in missionary circles in the later decades of the nineteenth century. Rejecting the idea that there is a natural connection between commerce and Christianity, Porter traces the material interests that prompted missionaries to integrate commerce into their strategies of expansion.

As discussed previously, missionaries found that they could combat the slave trade and other obstacles by promoting what they called legitimate commerce. Porter argues that when the obstacles were removed, and when there were no new commodities to attract missionaries' attention, they chose to regard commerce as less significant in the process of evangelical expansion. Porter's definition of commerce does not account, however, for an important commodity with which missionaries remained preoccupied: labor. Missionaries, of necessity, did not lose interest in mobilizing the labor of their congregations, and this mobilization entailed social reforms that were inextricably linked to the process of conversion. For example, as Pamela Scully demonstrates, missionaries reorganized African families on a Christian model so that men and women would fill appropriate gender roles as laborers outside and inside the home.[81] Indeed, "commerce and Christianity" remained a dynamic force in missionary and imperial ideologies until at least the early twentieth century. While the slogan fell out of use, as Porter correctly argues, its tenets continued to surface under other guises, such as the idiom of "moral and material improvement."[82]

Despite their declarations against slavery, missionaries found that the exigencies of life in Africa commonly required them to tolerate, if not participate in, slavery to further their work of Christian conversion. Paul Lovejoy explains:

> On the one hand, they pledged to fight slavery as part of the general reform of African society associated with the spread of Christianity; on the other, they generally concluded that conversion to Christianity should precede the abolition of slavery. Slave holders, for example, were allowed to become Christians. Slavery was to be tolerated temporarily, so that the Christian church could be established. Only when Christians were the majority of the population would it be safe to abolish slavery.[83]

Like missionaries, merchants and imperial officials were apt to tolerate slavery. Most merchants were not particularly concerned about the welfare of Africans *per se*, and many recognized that slavery was by no means incompatible with commercial development, particularly in a plantation economy. European governments, on the other hand, made much of their abolitionist principles at home, but they seldom, if ever, put these principles into practice abroad. As statesmen in London condemned slavery, imperial officials in Africa took a reticent approach to initiating abolition. Britain's famous anti-slavery naval squadron patrolled the African coasts and intercepted foreign slave traffic, but this was as far as the British government wished to go.[84]

The leading participants in British abolitionist politics entered into intense lobbying and negotiations during the Berlin Conference of 1884–1885, which the German Chancellor, Otto von Bismarck, convened with no pretensions to

philanthropy. This conference had been conceived instead as a means to negotiate the general rules and boundaries of European expansion into West
and central Africa. It was Bismarck's intention to manipulate Anglo–French
competition on this imperial front to support a favorable balance of power in
Europe, while blocking the spread of British "paper protectorates" in Africa
for the benefit of German merchants.[85] Generally, the dominant powers at this
conference, Germany, Britain, and France, shared a desire to secure commercial access to Africa with minimal administrative responsibilities and costs.

The British government did not believe that it had crucial interests at stake
in central Africa, but it readily used the Berlin Conference as a forum for pan-
dering to humanitarian sentiment at home. The Permanent Undersecretary at
the Foreign Office, Sir Julian Pauncefote, suggested to the Foreign Secretary,
Lord Granville:

> Great Britain might carry off all the honors of the meeting by being the
> first to propose…an international Declaration in relation to the *traffic in
> slaves*…as distinguished from the institution of Slavery, making it a
> crime against the Law of Nations.[86]

When the British delegation proposed a declaration against the slave trade
in Africa, the other delegates balked at the administrative requirements of
enforcing such a policy. Ultimately, the conference made only a moral declaration against slavery and the slave trade in Africa, with no specific commitment to enforcement. Although the significance of this declaration would be
subsequently debated by humanitarians and imperial administrators, the
Berlin Act proved to be a foundational document in establishing international laws governing the rights of labor in the twentieth century, as the last
chapter of this book demonstrates. In the shorter term, British humanitarians
and, on occasion, the British government used the moral sentiment of the
Berlin Act's declaration against slavery as a rhetorical weapon with which to
criticize the labor policies and, implicitly, the legitimacy of other European
imperial powers in Africa, especially Belgium and Portugal.

While the delegates at the Berlin Conference declined to commit themselves to the administration of abolition, they endorsed commerce and Christianity as means to combat the slave trade in central Africa. The Berlin Act
established free trade for all European merchants on the Congo River, and
it guaranteed unrestricted access to the region by missionaries of all Christian denominations. Furthermore, signatories pledged under Article VI to
watch over the indigenous tribes and "to care for the improvement of the
conditions of their moral and material well-being, and to help in suppress-
ing slavery, and especially the slave trade."[87] In a series of bilateral agree-
ments, the delegates recognized the authority of King Leopold II of Belgium

over the Congo, because he had promised to manage the region as an international free-trade zone and to promote the expansion of both Catholic and Protestant missions. The participants in the Berlin Conference thus made moral capital of Leopold's support for free-market commerce and Christianity, declaring that these policies would bring slavery in central Africa to an end. On these same grounds, Leopold enjoyed the avid support of British missionaries and merchants.

The legendary atrocities of King Leopold's regime in the Congo are commonly treated as the measure of the humanitarian principles of the Berlin Conference. This is misleading, because it renders the Congo Free State exceptional, rather than representative of a general rule in European imperial administration. Although the Congo Free State used more overt methods of violence than other European regimes in Africa, all of the European governments sanctioned coercive systems of labor mobilization to control the transition from slavery to wage labor in their territories.[88] Sudden emancipation was a sure road to instability, and even reputedly progressive imperial officials, such as the future Governor-General of Nigeria, Frederick Lugard, believed that slavery should suffer a slow death. By the end of the century, each of the European regimes had seized African lands and imposed a variety of taxes designed to force Africans to work in the "public interest"—that is, for the benefit of European firms and the state.[89] Acknowledging that Africans continued to work under conditions analogous to slavery, imperial officials explained that discipline and administrative control would facilitate the adaptation of savages to civilized economies and cultures. "The new labor systems were intended as a related transition toward the establishment of wage labor," Lovejoy explains, "with the abolition of slavery as an inevitable by-product."[90] British humanitarians would condemn several of these new labor systems as new slaveries at the turn of the century. From this perspective, it becomes clear that the Congo Free State was responsible for one new slavery among many.

In the years following the Berlin Conference, Britain's traditional antislavery lobby continued to dissipate. The governing committees of the APS and the Anti-Slavery Society attempted to compensate for their weaknesses by coordinating their activities, but there was tension and quarreling among their leaders. The groups resolved their conflicts to some extent by dividing up their geographical areas of interest; for example, the Anti-Slavery Society held humanitarian jurisdiction over East Africa, while the APS oversaw South Africa. There was a flurry of activity surrounding the Brussels Conference on slavery, arms, and liquor traffic in Africa in 1889–1890, but neither the APS nor the Anti-Slavery Society played a central role in the organization of this event, which was a vehicle for the agendas of King Leopold II and Cardinal Lavigerie, the leader of the Catholic anti-slavery movement.[91]

Missionaries remained well-positioned in British imperial culture and politics to take a leading role in British protests against indigenous African slavery and the new slaveries of European imperialism. This fact was not fully appreciated by contemporary leaders of Britain's political left, and consequently many historians have missed this point in focusing on radical Liberals and labor leaders as critics of empire in the late Victorian and Edwardian eras.[92] James Ramsay MacDonald, a member of the London County Council and the Secretary of the Labour Representation Committee, observed naively in 1902: "We have surely learned the lesson that the missionary may be an excellent teacher but a most misguided politician."[93] In fact, missionary societies had already become formidable organizers and fund-raisers among all classes of British society.[94] British charitable giving to overseas missions in the early twentieth century was surpassed only by donations to education and church-building,[95] and missionaries enjoyed the support of prominent nonconformist ministers, who reached the apogee of their political power in the 1906 general election after more than fifteen years of participation in anti-imperialist campaigns.[96] Finally, missionaries were able to use their connections to leading nonconformist ministers to reach out to the growing British labor movement in the run-up to the election, especially on the issue of "Chinese slavery" in South Africa, as discussed in chapter 3. In 1906, as a leader of the newly formed Independent Labour Party, MacDonald would become the leading parliamentary representative of the Congo reform campaign, a campaign inspired and organized by missionaries.

In articulating their evangelical goals and gathering support, missionaries made expert use of photography. The beginning of the scramble for Africa in the 1870s had coincided with the development of dry-plate photography, replacing the wet-plate collodion process that had necessitated immediate processing. As a result, Europeans could now take photographs in Africa and develop these photographs later—a luxury further enhanced and simplified in 1888 by an American, George Eastman, who introduced the box camera, called a Kodak. This camera captured images on a roll of paper (transparent nitrocellulose coated with a gelatin emulsion) instead of glass plates, and its faster shutter speed eliminated the need for a tripod. Not only was the creation of photographs made easier, but their distribution was accelerated in the late 1890s, when a new method for printing photos in halftones on high-speed presses made mass production in the press possible for the first time.[97]

Victorian missionaries had been quick to bring the new, if cumbersome, technology of photography into the field. When, for example, Livingstone made his expedition from the mouth of the Zambesi to Victoria Falls between 1858 and 1863, he was accompanied by the photographic team of his brother, Charles, and Dr. John Kirk. Although this pioneering photography was regarded as scientific, missionaries soon constructed overtly propagandistic images through studio sets and, with technological advancements, photographs taken "on the spot" in Africa and around the world. In the late nineteenth century, missionaries conducted popular speaking tours in Britain in which they featured their photographs in lantern-slide lectures in church halls and theaters.[98] The missionaries of the Congo reform campaign, in particular, would rely upon their previous lantern lectures as models for their subsequent "Congo atrocity meetings," but they also departed from standard procedure by using photography and lantern lectures to mobilize international protest against an imperialist regime.

The New Abolitionists and the Politics of Human Rights

Among the hundreds of British missionaries who set sail for Africa in the late nineteenth century, a particular couple, the Reverend John and Alice Harris, would assume predominant roles in the extraordinary public controversies over the new slaveries of European imperialism. Alice Seeley had been in her early twenties, living in London and working for the civil service, when she met John Harris, a Congregationalist minister. Seeley was four years older than Harris, and better educated, having attended King's College, London. Harris had previously worked for a few years in business before devoting himself to social work and the ministry. By all accounts, Seeley was a quietly charismatic and willful personality, with a keen intelligence and a facility for writing and public speaking. By contrast, Harris was aloof in manner, but he had a talent for meticulous organization and displayed an intense desire to rise above his anonymous station and distinguish himself as an evangelical leader. Both Seeley and Harris were deeply influenced by the Reverend F.B. Meyer, a prominent Baptist minister who ultimately inspired them to pursue missionary work in Africa.

Following their engagement, the Harrises were accepted by the Regions Beyond Missionary Union (RBMU) for service in the Congo Balolo Mission. They received rudimentary training in the RBMU mission in East London and were scheduled to travel to the Congo in the spring of 1896 in the company of a group of unmarried missionaries, under the care of an elderly couple. When the elderly couple fell ill and could not make the trip, the director of the mission, Dr. Harry Grattan Guinness, suggested that Seeley and Harris move forward their marriage date and take charge. They were married on May 6, 1896, and departed four days later for the Congo. Over the course of the next decade, the Harrises would devote themselves to work on mission stations deep in the African interior, before returning to Britain to become the most influential leaders of British anti-slavery in the first half of the twentieth century. Their activities and their perspectives as evangelical philanthropists are integral to the chapters that follow.

As the Harrises left Britain for the Congo in 1896, a new British humanitarian lobby, known as the Liverpool Sect, began to assert itself in African affairs. This group originated from the Liverpool, London, and Manchester chambers of commerce, and it initially focused on defending British trading privileges in the French Congo. Over time, the group would shift its attention to the Congo Free State and advocate British trade as the guarantor of Africans' human rights. The articulation of commerce and human rights marked a shift away from the "commerce and Christianity" of evangelical philanthropy. Distinguishing this humanitarian agenda, John Holt, an influential Liverpool merchant, made blunt and dismissive reference to missionaries such as the Harrises:

> We have plenty of people trying to get to heaven by looking after the men's souls in Africa, but very few who take a living interest in their bodily or material welfare—their political and other rights are least thought of by any.[99]

This new humanitarian lobby also broke decisively from missionaries over the issue of culture. In contrast to missionaries, as discussed below, this new humanitarian lobby advocated cultural relativism as a principle that should inform imperial economic and administrative policies.

It appears that the Liverpool Sect drew the connection between commerce and rights from the Victorian, liberal interpretation of natural rights, based on property ownership and free trade. The leading spokesman of this lobby, E.D. Morel, is commonly given credit for popularizing the idea in the British humanitarian discourse of empire that rights are inextricably linked to property ownership in land, produce, labor, and, ultimately, one's own body. Morel obviously had a way with words, but he was not an original thinker. His ideas on rights appear to have been gleaned primarily from H.R. Fox Bourne, the Secretary of the APS.

At sixty-four years of age, Fox Bourne was in poor health and in the twilight of his humanitarian career when he met the young Morel in 1901. A priggish teetotaler, Fox Bourne represented an earlier generation of antislavery politics in Britain. He had been born in Jamaica in 1837, one of eight sons of Stephen Bourne, who had been sent by Lord Melbourne's government to Jamaica in 1833 to supervise the emancipation of slaves and the management of the new apprenticeship system. In his early twenties, Fox Bourne took a job as a clerk in the War Office and, at the same time, began a journalistic career writing articles for radical papers. He was a "free trader" and an avid admirer of Richard Cobden, whom he regarded "as representative of the principles by means of which English commerce [had] reached...vast proportions" in the mid-nineteenth century.[100] Fox Bourne believed that free trade with the Empire was essential to Britain's prosperity, but he was simultaneously critical of capitalists who exploited unfree labor as the basis of trade, whether at home or abroad. He published several books, for the most part on the history of British overseas trade, and, upon retiring from the War Office in 1870, he worked for most of the next twenty years as an editor of the radical *Weekly Dispatch*.[101] He became the Secretary of the APS on January 4, 1889, and committed himself wholeheartedly to lobbying on behalf of aboriginal causes, even as the stature and influence of his organization dwindled.

The APS had distinguished itself upon its foundation in 1837 as a group devoted to ensuring the land rights of aboriginal peoples in order to advance the progress of emancipation begun under the Emancipation Act. In the face of the new slaveries of the 1890s, this group argued that the overriding concern of humanitarians should be to assist Africans in keeping the customary property rights that would give them the practical means to exist in a manner commensurate with their human rights. Fox Bourne was steeped in the liberal tradition of rights derived from Locke. While he left no account of his intellectual and political education, it is certain that Fox Bourne was a careful student of Locke, given that he published a two-volume biography of Locke in 1876. As a Victorian liberal, Fox Bourne took the connection that Locke drew between rights and property ownership and then extrapolated this connection into a principle of contemporary liberation and reform, with applications far beyond Locke's historical perspective and intentions. Although Locke articulated the principle of trusteeship in conjunction with rights, Fox Bourne did not invoke trusteeship in his humanitarian campaigns, and his political disciple, Morel, would convey deep skepticism of trusteeship in later decades.

In addition to the important connection between property and rights, studies in the ethnography of African societies constituted the second major influence on the distinctive, rights-based humanitarian ideology of the Liverpool Sect. Fox Bourne, Morel, and others did not regard African cultures as equal to European cultures, but they saw these cultures as worthy of respect. Mary Kingsley, who first set out for West Africa in 1893 in search of "beetles, fishes, and fetish," was the central figure in this movement for cultural relativism.[102] As Paul Rich observes, Kingsley's writings "were...of importance in rejuvenating the cultural relativist ideal at the high point of imperial enthusiasm and went on to have a significant impact on political and anthropological thought in the years after the Anglo–Boer War [1899–1902]."[103] Kingsley argued through publications and lectures that Europe's perception of African savagery displayed Europe's inability to understand Africans on their own terms.[104] Africans, Kingsley asserted, were different from Europeans and should not be compelled to conform to European social customs, moral standards, and modes of production.

Kingsley took a dim view of missionaries and their practices of acculturation, a view that was commonly shared by traders and imperial officials.[105]

She advocated tolerance of polygamy and other aspects of African culture that missionaries abhorred.[106] In a typically derisive tone, Kingsley explained that missionaries in Africa "wrote their reports not to tell you how the country they resided in was, but how it was getting on towards being what it ought to be."[107] Time and again, Kingsley asserted that missionary "civilisation" caused African "degeneration" by undermining the traditional order of African society.[108] In contrast to missionaries, Kingsley asserted, merchants and traders promoted the constructive development of African societies. More broadly, she was a strong proponent of the importance of commercial relations and free trade between Africans and Europeans.

Kingsley preferred commerce to "commerce and Christianity," but she did not advocate commerce between equals. She asserted that the difference between Africans and Europeans was not "a difference of degree but of kind," and she believed that this difference in kind was reflected in "a large number of anatomical facts" and "a far larger number" of "mental attributes." "I feel certain," Kingsley stated, "that…the mental difference between the two races is very similar to that between men and women among ourselves. A great woman, either mentally or physically, will excel an indifferent man, but no woman ever equals a really great man."[109] Kingsley believed that the African mind was acute but lacked discipline, that Africans were prone to sloth, and that they were deficient in the mechanical arts. "They have never made, unless under white direction and instruction," Kingsley pronounced, "a single fourteenth-rate piece of cloth, pottery, a tool or machine, house, road, bridge, picture or statue."[110] She believed that through commercial relations with Europeans, Africans would develop discipline of mind and mechanical skills that would enhance their welfare in their native societies. In Kingsley's opinion, commerce between unequal peoples could be mutually beneficial, provided that each party respected the other's differences.

Kingsley was not alone in articulating a hierarchical concept of cultural relativism that was informed by racial essentialism. Advocates of cultural relativism among British missionaries and ministers had stirred debates in British missionary societies and chapels, where their views—as The Spectator once put it—"must have sounded to many…as a lecture on the sacredness of dynamite would sound to an audience of kings."[111] The influence of cultural relativism could also be heard in the labor movement, as labor leaders expanded their political platform to address imperial affairs. MacDonald declared upon his return from a visit to South Africa in 1902: "If we seriously mean to face the problem of native civilisation we must take him in his own way of doing things, and modify him without fundamentally altering him."[112]

Kingsley was not solely responsible for propagating cultural relativism in late Victorian Britain, but she did exert considerable personal influence over a number of future humanitarian leaders, especially Morel. In eulogizing Kingsley after she died in 1900 as a volunteer nurse to Afrikaner prisoners during the South African War, Morel characterized her in the pages of the *British Empire Review* as "a visionary."[113] In the several years after Kingsley's death, when Fox Bourne began to slow considerably with age, Morel assumed leadership over the new humanitarian lobby in African affairs, and soon rose to national prominence as the Secretary of the Congo Reform Association.

Morel had been born George Edmond Pierre Achille Morel-de-Ville in Paris in 1873.[114] His father, who was French, had worked in the French Home Office. His mother was English and a member of the Society of Friends. Educated in England between the ages of eight and fifteen, Morel became involved in African affairs in 1891, when he took a position as a shipping clerk with the Liverpool shipping firm *Elder Dempster*. Morel's fluency in French helped him to secure a position in charge of *Elder Dempster's* shipping to the Congo Free State. Soon thereafter, he aspired to become a journalist, and he used his work with *Elder Dempster* to develop a journalistic specialty in West and central African trade.

Morel became a naturalized British citizen in 1896 upon marrying Mary Florence Richardson, the daughter of a Liverpool printer. He continued to develop his journalistic expertise, walking a fine line between his increasingly critical views of the Congo Free State and his employment with *Elder Dempster*. In 1901 he published a series of anonymous articles in *The Speaker* that were highly critical of the Congo Free State, articles that caught the eye of Fox Bourne. Morel subsequently resigned from *Elder Dempster* on good terms and became assistant editor of a trade journal, the *African Mail*. He founded his own publication, the *West African Mail*, in 1903 with the financial support of British merchants including Alfred Jones, the owner of *Elder Dempster* and the Consul of the Congo Free State in Liverpool. By this time, Morel was well connected in the leading circles of African affairs, as both a member of the West African Trade Section of the Liverpool Chamber of Commerce and as a correspondent with influential figures in Britain's African empire.[115]

Morel and his allies were committed to property rights, free-market commerce, and cultural relativism as the bases of freedom and development for Africans. Yet, as Frederick Cooper observes regarding this humanitarian lobby, "The deeper questions of the peculiar nature of capitalistic economic rationality and the difficulties of transporting it to Africa lay unexamined."[116] The same humanitarians who advocated cultural relativism did not evaluate how European capitalist expansion in Africa might entail cultural crises of its own. In fact, Morel asserted that African culture was impervious to such change. He declared in the first issue of the *West African Mail*: "Equatorial Africa…is virgin ground of enormous natural wealth; and the African, unlike the Asiatic, will never become a manufacturing and commercial rival of the White-man on a scale sufficiently great to constitute a danger. The vast bulk of the African race is essentially agricultural and arboricultural; it is the ingrained character-istic of the race."[117]

The humanitarian politics of the British Empire had thus reached a cross-road at the turn of the twentieth century. The predominance of evangelical philanthropy, and its program of global reform, were increasingly challenged by the advocates of human rights, who prioritized commercial development and endorsed cultural relativism. Moreover, humanitarian protest could now be conveyed through the new, popular media of the lantern-slide lecture and photographic reproductions in the press. Humanitarian activists would fur-ther benefit from the proliferation of newspapers, illustrated magazines, and, especially, the "sensationalist press" in Britain after the 1890s. And just as the principles and media of humanitarian protest were changing, so also were its leading political participants. British trade unionists were on the move in the late nineteenth century, building upon the expansion of the franchise under the second and third Reform Acts of 1867 and 1884. They consolidated their political platforms and organized behind representatives whom they placed in Parliament to assert their concerns and demands. At the turn of the century, British labor decisively linked its domestic agenda to imperial policy in debates over the South African War and, subsequently, tariff reform. In the interest of the welfare and rights of the British working class, MacDonald and other labor leaders would contribute their growing political power to protests against the new slaveries in Africa.

Aside from these significant developments in British humanitarianism, sev-eral points of continuity are striking. First, all major factions within British humanitarianism supported the Empire, and none advocated direct political representation for Britain's nonwhite imperial subjects. Second, evangelical philanthropy remained the dominant ideology and motive force in British anti-slavery politics. Fox Bourne, Kingsley, and Morel were members of a rad-ical lobby with no popular base of support at the turn of the century, and they would subsequently gain this support only through their association with missionaries, nonconformist ministers, and the Labour Party. Their relatively progressive views on African culture had no currency in Britain at large prior to the First World War, and Morel, like Kingsley before him, remained invested in a concept of racial essentialism that was common in his era.

Previous studies have treated this humanitarian era in teleological terms, as a turning point toward contemporary human rights politics and protest.[118] Indeed, this book represents this era as a political bridge between the Victorian age of emancipation and the twentieth-century age of human rights activism. Yet, one must bear in mind that the leading participants in the anti-slavery protests of the early twentieth century in Britain saw themselves work-ing within a long-standing tradition. Specifically, these latter-day abolitionists saw themselves as inheritors of the mantle of the legendary abolitionists

Thomas Clarkson and William Wilberforce, and as defenders of the Victorian principle of free trade, often in a Cobdenite mold. While one might dispute the accuracy of this self-representation by a disparate group of missionaries, merchants, radicals, trade unionists, and politicians, their conception of their own place in history poses a significant question to which this book will return in its final chapter and its epilogue: To what extent did British humanitarianism in the twentieth century remain indebted to the ethics of the British Empire in the nineteenth century? As we will see, this question has still larger implications, given the influence of British humanitarian activists and imperial officials in laying the foundations of the institutions and ideologies of international government under the League of Nations.

CHAPTER **2**^{*}

Bodies and Souls: Evangelicalism and Human Rights in the Congo Reform Campaign, 1884–1913

Alice Harris was at the Congo Balolo Mission station at Baringa, 1,200 miles inland from the west coast of Africa, in the territory of the Congo Free State. She and her husband, the Reverend John Harris, had established the station as a mission outpost on the Upper Congo in September 1900, and they had been recently joined by a medical missionary, the Reverend Edgar Stannard. John Harris was attending a missionary meeting downriver on this particular day, May 14, 1904, when two African boys arrived suddenly at the station and attempted to convey some pressing news. Alice Harris and Stannard surmised that a detail of African "sentries" of the Anglo–Belgian India Rubber Company (ABIR) had attacked a village in the vicinity for failing to provide the company with rubber in accordance with its assigned tax. Shortly thereafter, Harris and Stannard encountered two men from the village who were proceeding to the local ABIR agent to protest against the attack, bearing the proof of their claims in a small bundle of leaves. At the missionaries' request, one of the men, who identified himself as Nsala, opened the bundle and displayed the freshly cut hand and foot of a small child. Harris gathered from Nsala's explanation that the sentries had killed his wife and daughter, then devoured them, leaving behind only the daughter's hand and foot. Appalled by this revelation, Harris persuaded the man to pose with the child's remains for a photograph.[1]

Harris framed the photograph on the veranda of her home, with the child's hand and foot upon the floor and Nsala gazing at them in profile.

---

^{*} This chapter is significantly expanded from an earlier essay: Kevin Grant, "Christian Critics of Empire: Missionaries, Lantern Lectures and the Congo Reform Campaign in Britain," *Journal of Imperial and Commonwealth History* 29:2 (May 2001): 27–58.

Fig. 2.1 Nsala with child's remains. (Reprinted from E.D. Morel, *King Leopold's Rule in Africa*, London: Heinemann, 1904.)

When John Harris returned to Baringa on the following day, Alice told him about the massacre and showed him the photograph, which she had developed. John wrote to the Director of the Congo Balolo Mission (CBM), Dr. Harry Guinness: "The photograph is most telling, and as a slide will rouse any audience to an outburst of rage, the expression on the father's face, the horror of the by-standers, the mute appeal of the hand and foot will speak to the most skeptical."[2]

The "slide" to which John Harris referred was a lantern slide, a popular feature of missionary lectures in Britain since the early 1890s. The prospective audience for this slide would be composed of local missionary auxiliaries, chapel congregations, workingmen's meetings, and, in the broadest sense, the British public. The Harrises had already participated in the missionary lecture circuits in Britain, the private and public forums of missionary publicity known among missionaries as "deputation meetings." Photographs, projected as lantern slides, had become powerful instruments of missionary propaganda, and the Harrises now proposed to use photography to serve their mission and, in turn, the peoples of the Upper Congo by exposing the atrocities of the Congo Free State.

Missionaries played a central role in mobilizing popular support for the Congo reform campaign in Britain, the largest humanitarian movement in British imperial politics during the late Victorian and Edwardian eras. The Congo reform campaign was, moreover, the largest of several interrelated British protests against the new slaveries of European imperialism in Africa. Recalling the legendary activism of abolitionists in the mid-nineteenth century,

E.D. Morel declared in the preface of his book, *The Congo Slave State: A Protest against the New African Slavery*:

> In the days of the over-sea slave trade, Europeans went down the West Coast of Africa to capture the inhabitants and carry them away to labour on European and American plantations. That wickedness was put an end to by a few men, who, after incredible difficulty, heart-breaking set-backs and soul-tearing toil, with pen and voice succeeded in rousing the conscience of the world. An evil perhaps as great—possibly greater—and accompanied by concomitant dangers which the over-sea slave trade was innocent of, faces us to-day.[3]

Historians have identified the Edwardian critics of empire as advocates of a secular, liberal ideology based on natural rights and a radical critique of capital, distancing them from the Victorian tradition of evangelical philanthropy.[4] For more than fifty years, historians have argued that one such radical, Morel, drove the Congo reform campaign to defend the rights and cultures of African societies, while promoting free trade on the Congo on behalf of British merchants. This story has been most recently retold by Adam Hochschild, who offers a hagiographic treatment of Morel in *King Leopold's Ghost*.[5] This chapter demonstrates, contrary to the claims of Hochschild and his predecessors, that the Congo reform campaign achieved popular support in Britain only after missionaries, and especially John and Alice Harris, popularized the lantern lecture as a mode of protest and transformed the campaign into an evangelical crusade.[6] The success of missionaries in the Congo reform campaign suggests that evangelical Christianity, rather than radicalism and the nascent politics of human rights, remained the predominant force in the humanitarian politics of the British Empire in the early twentieth century.

British missionaries supported the creation of the Congo Free State to further their own expansion into central Africa, and they withdrew their support only after the state's policies on property rights and commerce stifled their work of proselytization. In this respect, it is significant that British missionaries did not attempt to end European expansion on the Congo, but rather to correct the evils of "imperialism" as a particular, malignant form of overseas rule. Missionaries shared to a significant extent in the economic critique of European expansion espoused by radicals such as John Hobson, who published the best-known statement of this critique, *Imperialism: A Study*, in 1902. This radical critique defined "imperialism" as a product of industrial capitalism, driven by international financiers who manipulated European governments to establish coercive monopolies for their own profit, rather than for the benefit of the general populace at home or abroad.[7] Like Hobson, Morel, and other radicals, missionaries condemned "imperialism" as a betrayal of the liberal principle of free trade, which had been a tenet of the Victorian civilizing mission of empire. In contrast to radicals, missionaries supported free trade in the service of a distinctly evangelical project of expansion.[8]

In joining the Congo reform campaign, missionaries utilized their auxiliary organizations, political contacts, and formidable fund-raising skills. They especially capitalized on decades of experience as photographers and, more recently, as presenters of lantern lectures in church halls and theaters.[9] As James Ryan explains, "To many Victorians, photography seemed to be a perfect marriage between science and art: a mechanical means of allowing nature to copy herself with total accuracy and intricate exactitude."[10] From numerous town halls to the Royal Albert Hall, missionaries of the Congo reform campaign exploited this "evidential force" of photography to render the suffering of Africans real to British audiences.[11] In Samuel Clemens's satire, *King Leopold's Soliloquy*, the vilified ruler of the Congo Free State declares, "The Kodak has been a sore calamity to us....I was looked up to as the benefactor of a down-trodden and friendless people. Then all of a sudden came the crash! That is to say, the incorruptible *Kodak*."[12] While it is reasonable to see the Congo atrocity photographs as precursors of the broader genre of atrocity photography and humanitarian protest in the later twentieth century, one must also bear in mind that these photographs were framed in historically particular ways to achieve historically specific, religious objectives. Aside from the mechanics of visualization and realization, the Congo atrocity photographs were incorruptible in the eyes of the British public because missionaries produced them and narrated their significance to promote evangelical reform.[13] On the strength of their lantern lectures, missionaries transformed the Congo reform campaign into a national movement, manifesting the central role of Christianity in defining popular views toward the moral authority of empire in Edwardian Britain.

The State of British Missions on the Congo

King Leopold II of Belgium employed an expansive imagination and limited resources to establish his empire in central Africa. Since the 1850s, he had become increasingly committed to the acquisition of colonial territory as a means to bolster Belgium's economy and enhance its national prestige. He had evaluated regions ranging from Southeast Asia to South America, but his imperial schemes had been frustrated by a lack of interest among the Belgian populace and Parliament, and by competition from larger European powers. In the 1870s, Leopold's attention was drawn to central Africa by a series of exploratory expeditions, and particularly the transcontinental journey of Lieutenant Verney Lovett Cameron between 1873 and 1875.[14] Cameron's letters extolled the richness of the African interior, recounting mineral deposits and crops of rubber, sugar, and other potential commodities.[15] Cameron also claimed that the Lualaba River was connected to the Livingstone River (as the Congo River was then called), affording a possible trade route into central Africa.

Less than two years later, in August 1877, Henry Stanley tracked the Livingstone River and its major tributaries for over 2,000 miles to the coast of West Africa. King Leopold subsequently hired Stanley to go back up the river in 1879 as an employee of the *Comité d'Études du Haut-Congo*, created by the King to conduct scientific investigations and, more discreetly, to negotiate territorial treaties with African leaders and conduct reconnaissance for the King's imperial expansion.[16] As Leopold's employees subsequently negotiated and otherwise fought their way through local African communities and African slave traders on the Congo River, the King busied himself winning support in Europe for his would-be empire. The French and the Portuguese governments were also attempting to gain control over the Congo at this time, and the King was in no position to oppose them without allies. Ultimately, Leopold secured his objectives in Africa by playing upon the larger imperial interests of Great Britain, France, and Germany. Toward this end, he formed the *Association Internationale du Congo* (AIC) and cultivated relationships with British missionaries, merchants, and abolitionists, who would serve as both avid proponents and, eventually, the most formidable critics of his African administration.

British missionaries participated in the earliest stages of the European occupation of the Congo River basin. As Stanley was tracking the Livingstone River in 1877, the Baptist Missionary Society (BMS) and the Livingstone Inland Mission (LIM) had been preparing to expand inland from the lower river at Boma. The British missions had allied themselves in this venture with Leopold, who successfully concealed his interests in acquiring the Congo as an imperial territory. Under the guise of philanthropy, Leopold had supported the initial explorations of the BMS and LIM in 1878, even before he had hired Stanley to go back up the river in the following year.[17]

King Leopold cultivated relations with British missionaries, merchants, and abolitionists in the hope that they would lobby the British government to support his interests in the Congo against those of his European rivals, France and Portugal. Leopold's British allies were convinced that a French or Portuguese regime would be hostile to their proselytization, trade, and campaigns against slavery. They were therefore receptive to Leopold's promises to promote free trade, sponsor the expansion of all Christian missions—whether Catholic or Protestant—and to fight against the slave trade on the Congo. The King was so vociferous in his condemnation of the slave trade in Africa that the Anti-Slavery Society enlisted him as an honorary member, a decision that it would soon regret. When the European powers gathered to discuss their expansion into West and central Africa at the Berlin Conference during 1884 and 1885, Leopold used these same promises to secure the backing of the British government, which was pleased to avoid a new administrative role in central Africa, even as it exploited the conference's humanitarian rhetoric.[18]

British missionaries celebrated their good fortune when, in February 1885, the Berlin Act placed the Congo under the authority of the AIC. Six months later, Leopold unilaterally dissolved the AIC and met no opposition when he declared his personal sovereignty over a vast African territory, which he named *L'État Indépendant du Congo*, known commonly in Britain as the Congo Free State. Although Leopold's claim was bold, he had calculated correctly that the European powers would defer to his initiative for the same reasons that they had recognized the AIC. They had always known that they were negotiating with Leopold, so it was no surprise to them when the King dropped the political facade of the AIC and announced, in effect, "*L'état, c'est moi.*"

In the early years of the Congo Free State, imperial officials often found themselves fighting for their lives, and the outcome of their struggles was far from certain. Leopold sank part of his personal fortune into the state's deficits, while a small number of European officers and their African troops attempted to mold the indigenous populace into a labor force with which to gather ivory, rubber, and other commodities for the state's profit. Officials readily negotiated with slave traders and employed forced labor, utilizing punitive expeditions to coerce the African villages that resisted their demands for work or supplies. One of the basic problems confronting the state was the continuing strength of the slave traders who opposed the state's commercial intrusions upon their territories. This problem was perpetuated by the state's lack of financial resources. Under the terms of the Berlin Act, the state was prohibited from imposing import duties and other forms of taxation with which it might have funded its administrative and military expansion. Seeking additional money for his regime, King Leopold agreed to host the Brussels Conference in 1889. At this conference, Leopold and his philanthropic allies persuaded the European powers to sanction a new system of taxation in the Congo for the purpose of combating the slave trade and developing a viable infrastructure.[19]

The philanthropic declarations of the Brussels Conference were subsequently ignored by state officials, who launched military campaigns to compel Africans to provide them with labor or supplies under the pretense of taxation (*prestation*). In 1891, the state issued a decree that arrogated to itself all "vacant lands" in the Congo, as well as the produce of those lands which now fell under its ownership. Leopold then gave tens of thousands of acres of land to concessionaire companies in which he held major investments, thus expanding his exploitation of the Congo without incurring the cost of a large imperial administration. Captain Guy Burrows, a former Commissioner of the Aruwimi District, estimated that by the mid-1890s there were only 670 Europeans in the region of the Upper Congo, of whom about half were state officials. "These white officials," Burrows remarked, "are stationed in some fifty Government posts, each...the administrative centre, so to speak, of 14,000 square miles more or less. To properly administer such a country under existing conditions is clearly a physical impossibility."[20]

The Political Economy of Conversion and Protest

Protestant missionaries viewed the Congo Free State's subjugation of Africans with ambivalence. The Reverend George Grenfell reported the brutality of the state's expeditions to the BMS Secretary, Alfred Baynes, in January 1886. Grenfell derided the image of "peace and plenty" in the Congo which state propagandists projected to Europe, and he claimed that he was tempted to "throw light" upon these "very erroneous ideas." Grenfell chose not to publicize his views, however, because he suspected that any such criticism might turn the state against his mission. Grenfell prioritized his long-term evangelical work and reflected that "with a strong and just government and a fair system of commerce, which we hope are not far distant, facilities for our work will greatly increase."[21]

Members of the two British missions on the Upper Congo, the BMS and the CBM, had witnessed state-sanctioned slavery and seen or heard about atrocities by the mid-1890s.[22] The missions tolerated these practices due to their dependence upon the state for security, transportation services, and African labor, which they received in exchange for taxes. Although the British missions made occasional protests to the state, they generally declined to protest publicly in Europe for fear that the state would expel them from the river. In June 1890, Grenfell reported to Baynes that he had seen slaves chained neck to neck at the Congo State station at Npoto, and he further observed that officials regularly abducted women as hostages to be held until their men performed assigned tasks or paid ransom in kind or in the local currency of brass rods. Grenfell cautioned Baynes that this information was "strictly private and confidential. For altho' I think it right that you should know our circumstances yet I do not feel called upon to publicly question the action of the State—our difficulties are serious enough without having the whole weight of officialdom against us."[23] Thirteen years later, Grenfell would comment to Baynes that he still regretted "the wrong doings of officials and the sufferings of the people," but that he believed the conditions of Africans would eventually be improved by "the opening up of the country and the letting in of the light."[24]

It was, in fact, not slavery or atrocities *per se* that pushed missionaries to convey their protests to the British government and public, but other state practices that threatened their work of conversion. The missions' problems intensified at the turn of the century on two fronts. First, the rubber industry on the Upper Congo grew rapidly after the mid-1890s, and the increasing labor demands of the state and the concessionaire companies interfered with the missionaries' access to African communities. In 1897, the Reverend John Weeks of the BMS complained regarding the state's punitive expeditions: "We consider this to be altogether opposed to the philanthropic objects of the State, and also a great hinderance to our work here as missionaries, as such actions keep the people in constant turmoil and fear."[25]

A more important factor in turning the missionaries to public protest was the state's refusal to grant new stations to British Protestant missions, at the same time that it encouraged the growth of Belgian and French Catholic missions, which took a more circumspect view toward its brutal practices.[26] Since the 1870s, the British missionary societies had been contemplating the creation of a chain of mission stations across equatorial Africa. This idea had caught the imagination of Robert Arthington, a great benefactor of missionary work, who persuaded the BMS to attempt to expand eastward from the Congo to link up with the London Missionary Society at Lake Albert. When Arthington died in 1900, he left the BMS the funds to realize this vision.[27] Grenfell accordingly proposed a plan to reach out from the eastern BMS station at Yakusu toward Lake Albert and connect with the westernmost station of the Church Missionary Society at Mboga, a distance of about 370 miles.[28]

In 1898 Grenfell had called for an exploratory trip to find potential sites for new stations, but the Congo Free State had rejected this request on the grounds that the region had not yet been pacified.[29] The BMS leadership interpreted this as a sign of favoritism toward Catholic missions, and by 1901 Grenfell had become concerned that Catholics were expanding rapidly to the east.[30] The correspondence between Grenfell and Baynes between 1898 and 1903 reflects their increasing certainty that Protestants were literally losing ground to Catholics in central Africa. In a revealing letter in August 1903, Grenfell urged Baynes to call home the Reverend Lawson Forfeitt for a consultation on the current "crisis" on the Congo. This crisis did not concern the conditions of African labor. Rather, Grenfell said of Forfeitt:

> He regards the contravention of the General Act of the Conference of Berlin, and especially in the matter of blocking the way of Protestant missions while favouring the enterprises of Roman Catholics, as the principal charge at the present juncture for us to maintain against the Congo State.[31]

In July 1895 the BMS Secretary had observed to the Secretary of State for the Congo, Edmund Van Eetvelde, that the state was clearly opposed to an increase in the number of British missionaries in the region. Van Eetvelde denied this, remarking upon the BMS stations: "They constitute invaluable auxiliaries for the State."[32] Three months later, Baynes had reported to Van Eetvelde that state troops, under the command of a European officer, had attacked a village near the BMS station at Monsembe. According to the Reverend W.H. Stapleton, these troops had threatened to make prisoners of the missionaries and to shoot the mission's schoolchildren. Stapleton subsequently asserted, "The B.M.S. had established all too intimate connexions with the Congo State, and, through seeking favours from the State, had sacrificed its independence; if this had not been the case, State officials would never have dared commit such an outrage as that which had now taken place."[33] Yet even as these sectarian concerns mounted within the rank and file of the BMS, the mission's leadership maintained a cordial public rapport with the Congo Free State. In January 1903, a deputation from the BMS went to Brussels and thanked King Leopold for his philanthropic support. In return, the King made Baynes an *Officier de l'Ordre de la Couronne*.[34]

At no time did the Protestant missions on the Congo establish a closely united front in opposition to the state's policies, nor did the majority of the brethren in any mission participate actively in public protests against the regime. It was only after years of failed attempts to expand inland that the executive of the Congo Balolo Mission condemned the Congo Free State in the British press in April 1903, with the Baptist Missionary Society following suit in October 1905.[35]

The British Foreign Office had been hearing critical reports about the Congo Free State since 1891, when consular officials in West Africa began to report the mistreatment of British subjects employed by the state.[36] In the course of investigating these charges, W.C. Pickersgill, the British Consul at Luanda, Angola, traveled to interview the Reverends Charles Banks and E.V. Sjoblöm of the American Baptist Missionary Union (ABMU) at Bolenge in 1896. Unlike the two British missions on the Congo, members of the ABMU had already begun to voice strong public criticisms of the Congo Free State, successfully inducing the U.S. State Department to make a representation to the state in 1895.[37] Banks, an Englishman, and Sjoblöm, a Swede, gave Pickersgill secondhand reports of massacres and stated that they had seen evidence of atrocities of mutilation. Pickersgill was persuaded by their testimony, as the Foreign Office was persuaded by his subsequent "atrocity report." Although the British government occasionally complained to the Congo Free State about its treatment of British subjects during the 1890s, it declined to make these complaints public.[38]

Reports and rumors of atrocities on the Congo reached Britain throughout the 1890s, arriving from consular officials, British employees of the Congo Free State, merchants, and brethren of the ABMU.[39] Members of the ABMU were the first Congo missionaries to criticize the Congo Free State in the British media. The Reverend John Murphy of the ABMU station at Bolenge published the initial firsthand account by a known author regarding systematic atrocities on the Congo. His story, printed in *The Times* on November 18, 1895, was subsequently treated by most humanitarians as the first reliable indictment of the Congo regime.[40] Murphy, an Irishman with nine years of experience on the Congo, reported that state officers regularly forced Africans into labor, through either punitive expeditions or hostage-taking. Perhaps the most shocking of Murphy's revelations was his claim that state sentries severed the hands of their victims to present to their European officers. All the more shocking was Murphy's explanation of this practice: "These hands, the hands of men, women, and children, are placed in rows before the commissaire, who counts them to see that the soldiers have not wasted the cartridges." In light of the Congo Free State's declarations against slavery, he concluded: "These wretched slaves soon find they have only changed masters."

The Reverend Sjoblöm, one of Murphy's brethren in the ABMU, traveled to Britain on furlough in 1897 and publicized his criticisms of the Congo Free State at a meeting hosted by the Aborigines' Protection Society in London. Sjöblom recounted an experience on January 30, 1895, in the town of Ebira, where he witnessed a state sentry become angry with an old man because this man had chosen to go fishing instead of collecting rubber. To Sjoblöm's horror, the sentry shot the man and then told a boy to cut off the man's right hand:

> The man was not quite dead, and when he felt the knife he tried to drag his hand away. The boy after some labour, cut the hand off and laid it by a fallen tree. A little later this hand was put on a fire to smoke before being sent to the commissary.[41]

Murphy's article and Sjoblöm's testimony only added to the Congo Free State's problems in Britain after 1895. Earlier that year, the British press had expressed outrage over a report that an Irish trader, Charles Stokes, had been summarily executed by a state officer, Captain Lothaire, for selling arms to Africans.[42] The "Stokes affair," coupled with Murphy and Sjoblöm's testimonies, provoked anxiety among officials of the Congo Free State in Brussels and on the Congo River. These concerns were compounded by the private remonstrances of mission officials and the prospect of further public revelations. Two years later, in 1897, Charles Dilke, a Liberal MP and a longtime ally of the APS, raised the Congo for the first time in the House of Commons.

"From 1896 to 1900," Jean Stengers explains, "[King Leopold] passed through several periods of agony. 'We are condemned by civilized opinion,' he wrote in September 1896 to his Secretary of State for the Congo, Van Eetvelde. 'If there are abuses in the Congo, we must make them stop. If they are perpetuated, this will be the end of the State.'"[43] Van Eetvelde appreciated the King's concerns, having written to Leopold, "Many of our officers are brutal men and I believe that it is necessary to make examples."[44] Significantly, neither the authorities on the Congo nor those in Brussels were prepared to make an example of Lothaire, the official who was most infamous in Europe. Instead, the Congo Free State prosecuted a small number of isolated cases, never building the Congo's tiny judiciary into an effective instrument of justice.

The state's public responses to missionaries' criticism consisted of conciliatory gestures and direct challenges to the missionaries' information. In September 1896, the state established the Commission for the Protection of the Natives, composed of several prominent Catholic and Protestant missionaries, including Grenfell as the Secretary. These missionaries were all based on the Lower Congo, far from the atrocities occurring in the rubber districts on the Upper Congo. The commission convened only twice, and never took action. By contrast, Baron Wahis published a letter in *The Times* of May 31, 1897, in which he attacked the claims of Murphy and Sjoblöm, rejecting any assertion that the Congo Free State sanctioned the severing of hands and further claiming that Sjoblöm was well known for his attempts to incite rebellion against the Belgian regime. In similar fashion, the state commonly attacked its missionary critics by asserting that they themselves were complicit in the crimes that they condemned, especially the coercion of Africans and the redemption of slaves as servants.[45] Although there is no comprehensive, documentary proof of these claims, there is significant evidence that supports the state's charges. With respect to the redemption of African slaves as servants, it is significant that the BMS deemed it necessary to bar its missionaries from this practice in 1897.[46] With respect to coercion, both Grenfell and John Harris faced criticism from their missionary brethren for sanctioning the flogging of Africans on their stations.[47] These particular incidents did not subsequently surface during the Congo controversy in Britain.

The Congo Free State also invoked missionaries' testimonies and silences in its own defense. In early 1897, there were 223 missionaries on the Congo: 115 Catholics and 108 Protestants.[48] The state observed that only a small fraction of the missionaries had made complaints against the regime, and it represented the silent majority as its supporters. The state also highlighted missionary statements in its defense. In his letter to *The Times* noted above, Wahis quoted Grenfell as follows: "I am convinced that in each of the districts where our society is represented by a station the rule of the State is infinitely more beneficent than any native regime I have known, and that life and property are more and increasingly secure."

Public discussion of the "Congo question" in Britain was soon eclipsed by two other imperial events, the Fashoda Crisis of 1898 and the South African War of 1899–1902. Despite these larger controversies, however, important developments continued in the British lobby committed to Congo reform.

Toward the end of the decade, a new pressure group assembled against the Congo Free State under the leadership of Fox Bourne, the Secretary of the APS, and members of the Liverpool, Manchester, and London chambers of commerce. This group protested initially against the state's violation of British rights to trade on the Congo under the terms of the Berlin Act. Fox Bourne and his merchant allies advocated, by contrast, free trade as an ethical means of imperial development that was mutually beneficial to Europeans and Africans. The issue of the state's exploitation of Africans was a secondary concern, one which presumably would be alleviated by eliminating the monopolies of the Congo Free State and the concessionaire companies.

Morel entered the Congo controversy in these years as an aspiring journalist and an employee of the shipping firm, *Elder Dempster*. He would soon become the primary spokesman for the merchant lobby, arguing, like Fox Bourne, that Africans should have property rights and be permitted to trade freely with British merchants. He asserted, moreover, that these rights, coupled with the self-interest of merchants, would ensure Africans' freedom. As Morel explained in the *Liverpool Daily Post*:

> The right of the native to his land and to the fruits of his land; his right to sell those fruits to whomsoever he will; his right as a free man to his freedom—those are the real principles at stake. The British merchant, in fighting primarily for himself, is indirectly fighting the new form of slavery which has been introduced into Africa with such fatal results by the Sovereign of the Congo State, and in taking the stand he has done the British merchant is rendering a great service to humanity.[49]

Morel had strong ties to British merchants. In April 1903 he began publication of a trade journal, the *West African Mail*, specializing in reports and statistics on West African shipping and commerce. Morel's journal quickly became the leading organ of protest against the Congo Free State, featuring articles critical of state policies, alongside shipping schedules. This juxtaposition of criticism and schedules represents Morel's own dual roles as a humanitarian advocate of African welfare and a member of the West African Trade Section of the Liverpool Chamber of Commerce. His commercial connections initially played a major part in dissuading missionaries from cooperating with him. As Grenfell would observe to the BMS Secretary in early June 1904: "Tho' Mr. Morel has a wonderful grip on Congo affairs, he is too manifestly the agent of the Liverpool and Manchester Chambers of Commerce, and the Belgians believe he is cleverly trying to exploit 'Exeter Hall' in the interests of British Trade."[50] This criticism was not unjustified.

Morel and Fox Bourne shared an aversion to missionary "enthusiasm," and they regarded missionaries as unreliable allies in the reform of the Congo Free

State. They were wary of missionaries primarily because they believed that missionaries would compromise the work of merchants and the welfare of Africans in the interest of conversion. Morel had received this critical view of missionaries from his first two mentors in African affairs, the explorer and ethnographer Mary Kingsley and the Liverpool merchant John Holt.[51] Incensed by the reluctance of the British missions to join British merchants in criticizing the Congo regime, Morel declared in the *Manchester Guardian*: "Missionaries who shut their eyes to the nameless atrocities and excesses which the system...daily entails may, if they wish, continue to endeavour to influence public opinion; but, if so, they must be prepared for the protests of others who interpret differently the teachings of the religion of which such missionaries are the professed followers and expounders."[52]

Morel and Fox Bourne realized that they nonetheless needed British missionaries to testify against the Congo Free State in order to persuade the British public and, in turn, the government to take up their cause. Morel approached the BMS in 1901 and was rebuffed in light of its efforts to win approval from the Congo Free State for further expansion into the Congo interior. In 1902, he approached Guinness of the Congo Balolo Mission, who confirmed that slavery and atrocities were occurring on the Congo. Guinness explained that the British government was not likely to intervene, so any public protest by his missionaries would only undermine their long-term evangelical goals. Within a year, however, the CBM had given up hope that the Congo Free State would permit its expansion, and Guinness allied himself with Morel despite their ideological differences.[53]

On May 20, 1903, Herbert Samuel, a young Liberal MP, initiated the first parliamentary debate on the Congo, supported by a small group of MPs who had been drawn to the issue by British merchants and the APS. Speaking before "a very thin house," Samuel requested the Conservative government of Prime Minister Arthur Balfour to intervene in the affairs of the Congo Free State by conferring with the other signatories of the Berlin Act "in order that measures may be adopted to abate the evils prevalent in that State." Samuel's motion joined African welfare to European commercial interests, noting that the Congo Free State had "guaranteed to the Powers that its native subjects should be governed with humanity, and that no trading monopoly or privilege should be permitted within its dominions." Morel and Fox Bourne had provided Samuel with statistics, testimonies, and other evidence for his speech, just as they had provided the general arguments employed by all five of the speakers supporting the motion. Samuel and his supporters highlighted missionary testimonies as the most significant evidence regarding exploitation and atrocities on the Congo, but the speakers did not discuss evangelical work or the sectarian disputes between the Protestant missions and the state.

The speakers instead justified the British government's intervention on two grounds: the Congo Free State's violation of international privileges to free trade under the Berlin Act, and its violation of the rights of Africans as human beings. In defining these rights, Samuel was quick to point out that "he was not one of those short-sighted philanthropists who thought that the natives must be treated in all respects on equal terms with white men." Rather, Samuel asserted vaguely, "There were certain rights which must be common to humanity. The rights of liberty and of just treatment should be common to all humanity."[54]

Commerce was the key to the defense of these rights. According to Alfred Emmott, a Liberal MP and an advocate of British business in West Africa, "the best method of civilising natives was by trade, by the gradual permeation of honest and upright trade methods." Making no mystery of the commercial interests which he represented, Emmott announced that "he believed the right policy in regard to this question was to stand at the back of our John Holts, and men of that kind, and to help them to develop their trade."[55] Again and again, speakers returned to the basic thesis that "a system" of government-sanctioned monopoly had led to the abuse of Africans and merchants. This malevolent system was based primarily on the state's appropriation of land and the products of the soil, as well as its coercion of Africans to labor on its behalf. This system left Africans with inadequate means to survive, and placed their labor and their bodies at the disposal of the state for its figurative and literal consumption. Dilke declared:

> The military system in the Congo State consisted of bringing in cannibal tribes, marching them without any commissariat through the country to be attacked, and rationing them on the bodies of the killed, carrying dried bodies with them for the purpose.[56]

Responding to these statements, the Undersecretary of State, Lord Cranborne, observed that the British government had no clear recourse to intervention in the Congo under the Berlin Act. Moreover, Cranborne insisted that "the real truth" about conditions on the Congo was still disputed. Balfour refused to condemn "a friendly Government" without a thorough inquiry. Balfour and Cranborne promised to take action on the issue, and in return Samuel agreed to decrease the intensity of the accusations in his motion, which passed in modified form.

The Congo Free State's Defense

In the summer of 1903, following the British Parliament's first debate on the Congo in May, the Congo Free State began to mobilize an international propaganda campaign in its own defense. The state organized the *Fédération pour la*

Défense des Intérêts Belges a l'Étranger (Federation for the Defense of Belgian Interests Abroad), which published the first issue of its monthly organ, *La Vérité sur le Congo* (The Truth about the Congo), in July. The *Vérité* presented its accounts and commentaries in three columns of English, French, and German. It was distributed in Belgium, Britain, France, Germany, and Switzerland through news vendors and on the seats of trains. To a lesser extent, the *Vérité* was also distributed in major cities on the east coast of the United States, primarily in Washington, Baltimore, Boston, and New York. In Britain, the Congo Free State also relied on three principal representatives: Alfred Jones, the head of *Elder Dempster* and the state's Consul in Liverpool; Charles Sarolea, the newly appointed state Consul in Edinburgh; and Sir Hugh Gilzean Reid of the Baptist Missionary Society.

The Congo Free State presented a comprehensive outline of its position in the June issue of the *Bulletin Officiel de l'État Indépendant du Congo* (Official Bulletin of the Congo Free State). Responding directly to Samuel's assertions in the House of Commons, the state declared boldly, "The freedom of commerce is complete in the Congo and there is no restriction by any monopoly or privilege."[57] The state observed that its decrees and penal code reflected its full compliance with the Berlin Act, having opened the Congo to merchants of all nationalities and to Africans as well. Responding to criticism about its policy on "vacant lands," the state argued that its policy was no different from that of the other colonial powers, citing German East Africa, the Cameroons, the French Congo, Angola, and British East Africa. Indeed, the state could accurately declare, "This principle has been written into the codes of all the civilised countries; it has been sanctioned by all of the colonial legislations."[58] Similarly, the state demonstrated that its decrees for the protection of African cultures and land rights were comparable to those of other powers.[59] The state pointedly responded to Samuel by drawing a clear connection between African rights and the legitimacy of its broader economic policy: "Just as it is an inexactitude to say that the natives have been deprived of their customary rights, it is another to assert that the policies of the State have aimed at the exclusion of private commerce for the greatest advantage of its own commercial enterprises."[60] The state conceded that unfortunate acts of violence had been committed against Africans on the Congo, but emphasized that this violence was similar in degree to that under other colonial administrations in central Africa. Moreover, criminal statistics indicated that crime was no greater on the Congo than elsewhere. The state stressed, in both respects, that it had established a judicial system that consistently punished offenders and maintained law and order. Africans in the *Force Publique*, the state's army, had occasionally overstepped their orders, but this body was, on the whole, well-regulated, and discipline would certainly improve with a greater number of white officers.[61]

The Congo Free State recounted its benevolent work of development, high-lighting its efforts to suppress the slave trade and the illegal traffic in arms and liquor. Moreover, the state had improved transportation and communication, and it had established a judicial system, hospitals, schools, and the administration of labor contracts. According to the *Bulletin Officiel*, "The measures are taken for safeguarding the individual freedom of blacks and avoiding particularly that the contracts of service between blacks and non-natives degenerate into disguised slavery."[62] Finally, the state justified its African labor policies on three grounds: the moral value of labor, the state's right to compensation for its benevolent work of protection and education, and treaties with chiefs. The *Bulletin Officiel* characterized criticism of the Congo as an affront to Belgian national honor, and particularly to those Belgians "who, for years, gave their lives to develop civilisation and commerce in the Congo."[63]

The state's defense made virtually no mention of the work of missionaries, except in passing reference to their roles as educators. There were, however, two aspects of the statement that Protestant missionaries would have found foreboding. First, the state challenged its critics by observing that Catholic missionaries had not complained publicly about its conduct.[64] Second, the state asserted that the Berlin Act had placed no restrictions on its property rights. The state could dispose of property as it saw fit, so long as it did not clearly violate the Berlin Act as a commercial monopoly.[65] It was on this legal basis that the state later confronted the misinformed demands of the BMS for new stations "in pursuance of the terms and stipulations of the Berlin Treaty, which guarantee such concessions of land to Missionary Societies without distinction of Church or creed."[66]

Bodies of Evidence

Following the British parliamentary debate in May 1903, the Foreign Office instructed a consular official in West Africa, Roger Casement, to gather "authentic information" regarding the conditions of Africans on the Upper Congo. Casement had not traveled in the region for about fifteen years, but he had heard enough from missionaries and traders on the Lower Congo to be predisposed against the regime. He urged his friend at the Foreign Office, Harry Farnall, to assist Morel in his humanitarian protests. "I don't know the man," wrote Casement, "but I'm told he is honest and his articles on Congo misrule have appealed to me."[67]

Casement's investigation covered approximately 1,600 miles between early June and mid-September 1903. He traveled up the Congo to the Lulonga River, which he then followed to its tributary, the Lopori. Having ascended the Lopori approximately 130 miles to Bongandanga, he then traveled around Lake Mantumba and descended again to Leopoldville. His investigation and subsequent report focused on the testimonies of Africans and were hailed by

British humanitarians as irrefutable proof of the Congo Free State's brutal labor practices. Between Casement and the Africans, however, stood missionaries who had their own interests to advance. While Casement suspected that state officials would readily manipulate his investigation to serve their own ends, he was not critical of missionaries' prejudices and biases. Casement believed that missions were the only European agencies on the Congo that exerted influence upon Africans with no immediate interest in their exploitation.[68] He rented a steamer, the *Henry Reed*, from the ABMU, and informed the Foreign Office, "[My]… journeys can now be undertaken independent of anyone else."[69]

On the contrary, Casement was entirely dependent on missionaries. He had long-standing friendships with missionaries such as Grenfell and Forfeitt of the BMS. He had managed the BMS station at Wathen from December 1888 until April 1889, parting on excellent terms with his employer, the Reverend William Holman Bentley. In June 1901 Casement had asked Grenfell to join him on a tour of the Upper Congo in the BMS steamer, *Goodwill*, but Grenfell had already returned home to England on furlough, so Casement had postponed his plans.[70] When Casement finally did tour the Upper Congo in 1903, he instructed the Foreign Office to send his correspondence through the CBM station at Leopoldville.[71] His steamer was captained by a Danish missionary and engineer, H.J. Danielson, who had, until recently, managed a steamer for the CBM.[72]

Missionaries acknowledged that they had to handle Casement with care to ensure that he saw their side of the story. John Harris at Baringa informed the local Standing Committee of the CBM that he wanted Casement to visit his station to see how punitive expeditions had depopulated the region and pushed Africans beyond the mission's reach.[73] Members of the BMS also cooperated with Casement, although it appears that the BMS leadership had not been notified of his trip. It is, in fact, arguable that Protestant missionaries exercised so much influence over Casement's investigation that his report might be read as a work of missionary propaganda. Missionaries provided Casement with transportation, shelter, guidance, translation services, and even publicity in neighboring African villages. On at least one occasion, Casement was even mistaken for a missionary by an African sentry of the state.[74]

Casement generally stayed with Protestant missionaries during the course of his journey, traveling from one station to the next. He visited stations of the BMS, the CBM, and the ABMU, conferring extensively with missionaries regarding their views on the Congo regime. Among the BMS ministers, Casement encountered criticism of both the state *and* the BMS leadership in London. Some missionaries on the Congo were especially critical of the BMS deputation that had gone to Brussels in January to thank King Leopold for his philanthropic work. As Casement observed in his diary entry of July 18 at

Bolobo: "Howell and Clarks read over to me the draft of the letter of protest they sent to Baynes on the Deputation—It was a very emphatic protest indeed and does them credit. I wish they would publish it. They ought to."[75]

Casement was struck by the apparent decrease in the population of the Upper Congo since his initial travels there as a member of the Sanford expedition in 1887–1888. Missionaries were preoccupied with the effect of this depopulation on their evangelical work, and they frequently highlighted this issue for him. On July 25, Casement noted in his diary: "Arr. Lukolela. Whitehead and Mrs. W met us and I walked into village....Population dreadfully decreased—only 93 people left out of many hundreds." On August 5, the Reverend W.H. Stapleton told Casement that he was convinced that the state had swept away the population wholesale.[76] Casement subsequently emphasized the depopulation of the Upper Congo in his report, publishing two letters from Reverend Whitehead to the Governor-General on this subject.

In addition to providing Casement with their views in their own words, missionaries arranged for him to interview Africans. Missionaries acted as Casement's interpreters, and they enlisted the services of bilingual Africans associated with their stations. In rare instances, the transcripts of Casement's interviews with Africans reveal preconceptions about European imperial politics which suggest that missionaries had previously advised Africans on these issues. The first enclosure of Casement's report contains an English transcript of his interview with a group of African refugees. One of these refugees stated:

> We heard that letters came to the white men to say that the people were to be well treated. We heard that these letters had been sent by the big white men in "Mputu" [Europe]; but our white men tore up these letters, laughing, saying: "We are the 'basango' and 'banyanga' [fathers and mothers, i.e., elders]. Those who write to us are only 'bana' [children]." Since we left our homes the white men have asked us to go home again. We have heard that they want us to go back, but we will not go.[77]

Casement was wary of African informants. "That everything asserted by such a people…is strictly true I should in no wise assert," he reflected. "That discrepancies must be found in much alleged by such rude savages, to one whose sympathies they sought to awaken, must equally be admitted."[78] Aside from the doubtful veracity of his informants, Casement furthermore regarded the spoken word as a slippery form of evidence. While his cultural and racial biases made him wary of Africans' testimony, he also acknowledged that the meanings of words shifted through translation. During Casement's inquiry into the mutilation of a boy named Epondo at the village of Bosunguma, his own servant, Vinda Bidiloa, translated Casement's statements into Bobangi for another African in the service of the CBM, named Bateko, who then conveyed Casement's words to Epondo and the villagers in their local language and to the accused, Kelengo, in Mongo.[79]

Casement's understanding of events was largely determined by missionaries' choices in translating and contextualizing Africans' testimonies. He also, however, sought an objective confirmation of Africans' accounts by measuring the words which he heard against his reading of the bodies that he saw. This process is apparent in Casement's record of an interview with African refugees in July: "Three of the men sat down in front of me, and told a tale which I cannot think can be true…I repeatedly asked certain parts to be gone over again while I wrote in my note-book." The people recounted forced labor, punitive expeditions, and terrible acts of mutilation sanctioned by white officers. Despite the consistency of their narratives, it was the Africans' body language that persuaded Casement. "There was no doubt that these people were not inventing," he observed. "Their vehemence, their flashing eyes, their excitement, was not simulated. Doubtless they exaggerated the numbers [of the murders by state troops], but they were clearly telling what they knew and loathed."[80]

Beyond mere body language, Casement found the sight of a mutilated body to be so powerful that it could confirm not only the act of violence but also the cause. Suffering effectively sanctified the claims of the victim, lending significance even to the victim's past silence. For example, Casement asked a man why he had not complained to senior officials about a local official who had taken his canoe from him without compensation. According to Casement, "He pulled up his loin cloth and, pointing to where he had been flogged with a chicotte [a whip], said: 'If I complained I should only get more of these.'"[81] Remarking upon the mutilation of Epondo and others whom he had seen, Casement wrote in his report: "The fact that no effort had been made by these people to secure relief from their unhappy situation impelled me to believe that a very real fear of reporting such occurrences actually existed among them." Casement concluded, "Their previous silence said more than their present speech."

While Casement attempted to describe mutilations in his notebook, one of the missionaries who accompanied him, the Reverend W.D. Armstrong of the CBM, took photographs of mutilated Africans whom they had interviewed. Armstrong had his subjects wrap white cloth around their bodies to create a backdrop against which the stumps of their limbs could stand in stark relief. In a subsequent interview by a state official, the boy named Epondo said that the white men instructed him to hold the stump of his arm in clear view for the camera.[82] All of the photos in this series picture African men and boys gazing forward with their mutilated limbs held across their stomachs, against white cloth. Casement brought these photos back to Britain, where they would circulate in books and lantern-slide lectures to become powerful symbols of misgovernment on the Congo.

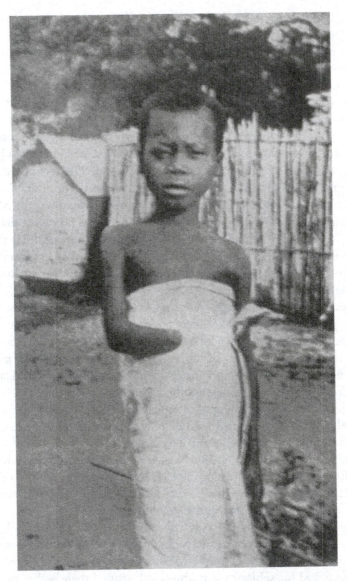

Fig. 2.2 Epondo. (Reprinted from Samuel Clemens, *King Leopold's Soliloquy*, London: T. Fisher Unwin, 1907.)

Although there is no documentary evidence that explains Armstrong's objectives in taking these photos, it is at least certain that he wanted to publicize them in Britain. Missionary organizations had long since promoted their work in Britain through lantern lectures, so it would have been reasonable for a missionary to convey criticism of an imperial regime through photographs as well. But, one might ask, why did not Armstrong or other missionaries distribute "atrocity photos" earlier? It is possible that this was a new idea proposed by Casement, but it is also likely that Armstrong came upon this idea while watching Casement interpret the mutilated bodies of Africans as decisive proof of the state's brutality. Ultimately, Casement was himself responding to a symbolic vocabulary that Africans showed to him.

In the second week of September, Casement decided to end his investigation, reporting to the Foreign Secretary, Lord Lansdowne: "I do not think I shall go again up river unless your Lordship desires it. I have seen enough."[83] Casement was convinced that atrocities had occurred on the Upper Congo with government sanction. "Of the fact of this mutilation and the causes inducing it there can be no shadow of doubt," he declared. "It was not a native custom prior to the coming of the white man; it was not the outcome of the primitive instincts of savages in their fights between village and village; it was the deliberate act of the soldiers of a European Administration."[84]

As Casement traveled to London to write his report on the Congo Free State, British missionaries were left to struggle in his wake. Among these missionaries were John and Alice Harris, stationed at Baringa, in the infamous ABIR concession, which Robert Harms aptly describes as "a plundering and tribute-collecting empire of the crudest sort."[85] Even before Casement's tour, the Harrises' relations with local traders and officials had become strained as the company's demands for African labor undermined the evangelical work of the mission. The company then turned decisively against the missionaries in the months after the CBM Home Council condemned the Congo Free State in April 1903 and after Casement completed his investigation. Although Casement had not traveled as far as Baringa, the Harrises were made to suffer for the support offered to Casement by their brethren. Following Casement's investigation, John Harris explained in a letter to Harry Guinness, the CBM Director, "We have been repeatedly given to understand that the continuance of missionary work, even to a limited extent, depends upon our silence regarding the outcome of the methods of administration."[86] When the Harrises subsequently complained to local officials about the brutality of the "native policy" at Baringa, the ABIR Director, Albert Longtain, forbade the neighboring villages to sell food or labor to the mission station. By June 1904, the Harrises were subsisting on tinned foods and goats' milk. John Harris observed to a state official in July, "I must say …that the treatment permitted to us for trying to help the State carry out its laws is such as tends to close our mouths here and drive us to the public in Europe."[87] A month later, the local company agent, Raoul Van Calcken, ordered his sentries to torment the Harrises by "firing…guns across and in the vicinity of the mission at all hours."[88] It was under these circumstances that Alice Harris sent her first atrocity photographs to Britain.

The Reverend W.D. Armstrong had established a precedent for Alice Harris's photographic representation of atrocity, but it is not clear that Harris knew about Armstrong's atrocity photographs before she took her own. Nonetheless, several months later, Harris also privileged African bodies as evidence of atrocity. After taking the photograph of Nsala and the child's remains, featured at the beginning of this chapter, Harris wrote to the company agent, Van Calcken, protesting against the alleged massacre of the previous day. In proving her accusations, Harris stated, "We have seen the hand and foot of the child, Boali, who with her mother was eaten by the sentries or their servants."[89]

The Harrises experienced some relief from their hardship later in the year, following an investigation by a state-sponsored commission of inquiry.[90] In a subsequent letter to the CBM Home Council, John Harris articulated the direct connection between his decision to protest and his goal of conversion. Reflecting upon the damning evidence that he and his wife had presented to the commission, he concluded, "When this is made public it will without doubt create the profoundest sensation. One effect will be a greater confidence in missionaries and in missionary enterprise. Do you not think it highly probable that the near future will demand a considerable advance in missionary effort on the Congo?"[91]

Commerce, Rights, and E.D. Morel's Failed Strategies of Protest

Morel believed that the nascent Congo reform campaign in Britain would "grow into a movement as big as the Anti Slave Trade movement," but neither he nor Fox Bourne had experience in grassroots political mobilization.[92] They advocated free trade and rights for Africans, but their rallying cry moved only a small, if influential, clique of merchants, journalists, and politicians. Missionaries, by contrast, believed that they could rally the British public to the cause of Congo reform in evangelical terms. Guinness wrote to Morel, "I am anxious that you may not mistake where your real supporters will be. Believe me that they will largely be found amongst those who are pronounced Christian men and women."[93] Morel responded, "We want to convert not only the religious people, but hard-headed men of the world. Now nothing, rightly or wrongly, acts upon such men as a greater deterrent than the feeling that 'religious fervor' or missionary enthusiasm is the controlling motive."[94]

Guinness, the son of a prominent evangelical family, was a dynamic and well-known Baptist minister. In the early 1890s he had begun giving lantern lectures to promote the work of his mission, having previously operated a photography studio while serving as a missionary in South America.[95] On the basis of this experience, Guinness developed a lecture titled "A Reign of Terror on the Congo," which he began to deliver in a series of "Congo atrocity meetings" in Scotland in November 1903, drawing thousands of people with the promise of lantern slides.

The strong evangelical tone of the lecture was established at the outset, as Guinness opened with organ music and a hymn, "Thou whose mighty word—chaos and darkness heard," followed by a simple prayer. He then delivered an hour-long presentation, weaving a story of promise, betrayal, and redemption. In setting the stage for his story, Guinness provided an overview of the geography, environment, and peoples of the Congo. He then presented a heroic account of the era of European exploration and King Leopold's philanthropic pronouncements. In a standard lecture, Guinness would then have focused upon the savagery of the Congo people, highlighting practices of slavery, polygamy, and cannibalism, which would be ended by Christian conversion. However, in the pivotal stage of "A Reign of Terror on the Congo," Guinness focused instead upon the savagery of the Congo Free State, realizing its betrayal of humanity through the display of atrocity photographs.[96] These photographs were contextualized with what missionaries later called "horror narratives": descriptions of the events that preceded and caused the alleged atrocity, the process through which the atrocity was committed, and the aftermath of the event. As Guinness commented to Morel, "Some of the slides are immensely effective."[97] With images of atrocity still clear in the minds of his audience, Guinness concluded his lecture in standard fashion with a glowing account of the CBM. He promised a bright future for Africans with the assistance of missionaries whose good works depended upon generous donations, which he duly received.

Looking toward the publication of Casement's damning consular report on the Congo Free State in early 1904, Guinness conducted a series of mass meetings in eleven town halls in Scotland, beginning at Aberdeen on January 17 and concluding at Greenock on February 19. Meanwhile, a Deputation Secretary of the CBM, the Reverend Peter Whytock, spoke on the Congo question in smaller towns around Glasgow and Edinburgh. Whytock had been a missionary on the Congo from 1889 to 1892, and he was the first of more than a dozen former Congo missionaries to play an instrumental role in condemning the Congo Free State before the British public. Employing a standard mode of advertising for missionary deputation meetings, Guinness and Whytock arranged for local ministers to announce their lectures during Sunday services, an approach that proved to be remarkably effective. Guinness spoke to an audience of 3,000 in Aberdeen, another 3,000 in Dundee, 2,000 in Edinburgh, and 4,000 at St. Andrew's Hall in Glasgow, the largest hall in Scotland. "I am having a grand time," Guinness wrote to Morel, "everywhere crammed to the door—and greatest enthusiasm!"[98]

Guinness's evangelical representation of the Congo crisis, replete with hymns and prayers, troubled Morel and his allies. Lady J.A. Chalmers, a friend of Morel, attended Guinness's meeting in Edinburgh and reported, "The lecture was admirable and most convincing but, between ourselves, I must say

I was personally repelled rather by the sensational and emotional character attempted to be given to it by the singing, etc." Morel concurred with Chalmers's impression and confided, "For my part, I am so constituted that the very talk of religion in a matter of this kind sets my teeth on edge."[99] Morel and Fox Bourne were particularly worried that Guinness would promote divisive sectarian politics on the international level and alienate support for their campaign among Catholics in Britain.[100] Morel's apprehensions were later realized by the strident criticism that the Congo Reform Association (CRA) would receive from Irish Catholics in the House of Commons and the Catholic press in England. Most important, King Leopold was initially able to exploit the Protestant character of the Congo reform campaign to rally support in Catholic Belgium.[101]

The success of Guinness's lectures brought tensions to a head within the Congo reform lobby. Fox Bourne withdrew the endorsement of the APS from Guinness's meetings, asserting that Guinness was using these meetings to advertise and finance the religious work of his mission rather than to advocate the rights of Africans.[102] Casement, however, believed that Guinness's evangelical approach could serve the Congo reform campaign immensely.[103] He negotiated a settlement between Guinness, Fox Bourne, and Morel, extracting an empty promise from Guinness that he would henceforth present his lectures on "non-sectarian" lines.[104] Casement had recognized that Guinness could reach a broader spectrum of British society than Morel and Fox Bourne in their efforts to gather support for Congo reform. Acknowledging the limitations of his personal contacts, Morel conceded to Lady Chalmers that "the advantages of co-operating with Guinness are that he can tap a lot of religious philanthropic people for the Association, which I cannot tap."[105]

Casement proposed the creation of a Congo Reform Association in January 1904, and he persuaded Morel to serve as the Honorary Secretary. From the start, the two men conceived of the CRA as a vehicle for advocating human rights. Just days after consulting Morel, Casement explained to Charles Dilke:

> It is this aspect of the Congo question—its abnormal injustice and extraordinary invasion, at this stage of civilised life, of fundamental human rights, which to my mind calls for the formation of a special body and the formulation of a very special appeal to the humanity of England.[106]

As advocates of human rights—also commonly identified as "the elementary rights of humanity"—Morel and Casement asserted that Africans had fundamental rights to property in their bodies, in the land, and, through the mixing of their labor and the land, to the produce of the soil. Moreover, Africans had their own distinctive cultures that should be respected. Following the standard agenda of the APS, Morel and Casement argued that the overriding concerns of humanitarians should be to assist Africans in keeping their property rights, so that on the basis of commerce they could improve their lives. As Morel declared on numerous occasions, "*The root is in the land.*"

It was on the issue of cultural difference that Morel and Fox Bourne broke with missionaries, whose goals of conversion required social reform. Their criticism of Guinness involved a range of issues, but it basically marked a clash between universalistic ideologies. Morel and Fox Bourne advocated rights that were possessed by all humans in the present; rights that were ensured by property ownership and that transcended cultural and religious differences. By contrast, Guinness and other evangelicals advocated the conversion of souls as a moral imperative based upon articles of faith with universal superiority over alternative cultures and creeds. It is important to note that Morel and his allies never critiqued the reforms entailed by their own preferred catalyst for moral and material improvement: commerce. Neither did they believe that Africans required or merited political representation to defend their rights. Nonetheless, this rights-based, imperial ideology was regarded in its own time as a radical departure from Guinness's evangelical goals.

Despite the presumed universal appeal of this human rights agenda, the creation of a human rights campaign soon exposed dissension in Britain's humanitarian ranks. Although Fox Bourne approved of the CRA in principle, he also perceived it as a threat to his own organization. Fox Bourne argued that the CRA should be an affiliate of the APS, and he initially refused to join a group that would compete with the APS for funding and prestige. The APS was chronically running short of money, having received only £694.17.6 in fiscal 1903, and its prestige now rested firmly upon its reputation rather than on its relevance to current policy makers. The conflict between Fox Bourne and Morel was further complicated by a clash in personal styles. Whereas Fox Bourne was an elderly, unobtrusive, tradition-bound character who preferred to pull his strings of influence from behind the scenes, Morel was a young man with expansive ambition who desired fame. Morel was also a far more imaginative and compelling writer than Fox Bourne, being capable of conveying moral outrage and urgency, rather than mere cold facts, through his publications. As the head of a moribund organization, Fox Bourne was in no position to stifle Morel's drive and the advance of the CRA, so he resigned himself to an alliance for the sake of their common cause.[107]

After the publication of Casement's parliamentary white paper on the Congo in February 1904, the Congo reform lobby began to make arrangements for the inaugural meeting of the CRA in Liverpool. The organization of this meeting was handled by the Reverend W.G. Pope, a Deputation Secretary of the Regions Beyond Missionary Union, of which the CBM was a subsidiary. The RBMU put up a portion of the funding for the meeting, and Pope enlisted numerous local ministers to publicize the event from their pulpits.[108] Approximately 2,000 people attended this first meeting of the CRA, which was held on March 23, 1904, at Liverpool's Philharmonic Hall. The CRA came into existence before a boisterous house, though its leadership did not have a definite plan for future action. As the Secretary, Morel dictated that the "Programme of the Congo Reform Association" should be "to secure for the natives inhabiting the Congo State territories the just and humane treatment which was guaranteed to them under the Berlin and Brussels Acts."[109] This just and humane treatment would be ensured "by the restoration of their rights in land, and in the produce of the soil, of which preexisting rights they have been deprived by the legislation and procedure of the Congo State."[110]

The Preliminary Committee of the CRA determined that its central task was to disseminate information about the Congo Free State through meetings and publications. The committee also proposed to form auxiliaries in Britain and to establish alliances with humanitarian groups overseas. These were heady days for the CRA, as it coasted on its initial momentum. Guinness and Morel spoke to an audience of over 2,000 at Exeter Hall, and Guinness continued to give lantern lectures in Scotland and London. Morel, a prolific writer, published a number of exposés, including the book *King Leopold's Rule in Africa*, featuring several of Alice Harris's photographs.[111] In September, Morel went to the United States, met with President Theodore Roosevelt, and convinced Samuel Clemens (more commonly known by his pseudonym, Mark Twain) to lend his pen to Congo reform by writing a satire, *King Leopold's Soliloquy*, which featured atrocity photographs by the Reverend W.D. Armstrong, Alice Harris, and the Reverend Henry Whiteside, all of the Congo Balolo Mission.

The lists of the CRA's subscribers and public supporters in its first year of operation provide a general perspective upon the group's strengths and limitations. It is noteworthy that the CRA did not keep a systematic account of funds received until 1907, so the following figures are merely suggestive.[112] These figures, which cover the period from March 1904 to January 1905, are drawn from 128 subscriptions and donations gathered from a partial list of donors and from acknowledgments of gifts in Morel's correspondence files.

British merchants who traded with West Africa provided a significant portion of the CRA's initial funding. This group provided more than a third of the CRA's budget of approximately £895 between March 1904 and January 1905. Moreover, most of the CRA budget in this period was composed of large donations: only five people donated a total of £400.0.0, and less than a third of CRA subscribers gave under £1.0.0, although the basic subscription rate was 10 shillings. These relatively large donations suggest that the CRA gathered much of its funding from a wealthy and middle-class constituency. Smaller donations from the working class were so rare that, two years later, Morel would remark in a letter to his patron, William Cadbury, that the CRA had received "five shillings from a working man with a very touching letter."[113] At least half of the CRA's early financial supporters resided in Liverpool or London, and it appears that most CRA funding was initially drawn from these cities. Finally, only twenty-one—or about 17 percent—of the 128 gifts were attributed to women by name, a percentage that would increase in later years under the influence of missionaries.

Turning to the published list of CRA supporters, one sees that as a parliamentary lobby the organization could cross party lines, winning endorsements from equal numbers of Liberal and Conservative MPs.[114] Guinness exerted his influence by recruiting several prominent nonconformist ministers, including four past presidents of the National Council of Evangelical Free Churches.[115] There were also some conspicuous absences from the CRA's list of supporters. For instance, the CRA did not have public endorsements from labor leaders.[116] It is also remarkable that the CRA supporters included only a few members of the Society of Friends, given that several prominent Friends had already joined the Congo reform campaign under the auspices of the APS. Finally, the CRA supporters included only one Catholic, Lord ffrench, and they did not include representatives of the BMS, the largest British mission on the Congo.

Despite a promising start, the Congo reform campaign began to falter in Britain in the autumn of 1904. By July 6, the CRA had gathered a respectable £653.17.11, but subscriptions had then diminished alarmingly. The CRA received just over £6 in October 1904, and Morel discovered, to his dismay, that his wealthy merchant sponsors would not relieve the CRA's financial distress. In assessing the attitude of the general public in December, Casement declared, "Interest in the Congo question is practically dead. No one cares a d—n about it."[117] Morel did not know how to raise funds outside of his personal circle of commercial contacts, and he did not know how to overcome the public's apathy. Surveying the remnants of the Congo reform campaign at the end of the year, Morel remarked to his friend Alice Stopford Green, "Things look very black."[118]

Although the Foreign Office acknowledged the moral basis of Casement's proposals, it proved reluctant to weigh the welfare of the Congolese peoples into the balance of Britain's international relations. Moreover, the Foreign Office was wary of bringing scrutiny to bear upon its own empire. As Lansdowne later wrote in a minute concerning the Congo regime: "Ghastly, but I am afraid the Belgians will get hold of the stories as to the way the natives have apparently been treated by men of our race in Australia."[119]

Casement regarded the Foreign Office as a fiefdom of conniving bureaucrats, but it must be said that the Foreign Office's attitude toward the Congo Free State reflected its standard priorities. Ultimately, the Foreign Office viewed Europe as the central stage upon which its policies performed, and even the staff of the African Department saw the Congo as an extension of European diplomacy. The Foreign Office hesitated to interfere with the Congo Free State because it judged that Britain had far more to lose in Europe than it might gain in Africa by challenging the sovereignty of King Leopold II. The British government did not have designs on the Congo River basin and British business did not have major economic interests in the region, certainly not in comparison with Britain's territories in southern and eastern Africa. Furthermore, the Foreign Office feared that its criticism of the Congo Free State might alienate Belgium's elected government and undermine the long-standing Anglo–Belgian alliance, which had become a cornerstone in Britain's defense against German expansion, particularly in view of the Anglo–French entente of 1904.[120] Even the fiercest British critics of the Congo regime chose to avoid indicting the Belgian nation for the imperial policies of its monarch. Meanwhile, Leopold successfully equated his interests with those of the Belgian nation in order to isolate his critics at home.

Lantern Lectures and the Revival of the Congo Reform Campaign

The CRA had drifted in a state of limbo between the autumn of 1904 and the spring of 1905. Its funding had dried up and its public lectures had been suspended. Its "plan of campaign" had not been instigated to any effect and, most significantly, the CRA had not expanded its base of support in Britain. Toward the end of this period, however, Morel began to forge links with the Society of Friends that would bolster the CRA in the years ahead. William Cadbury, of the cocoa company *Cadbury Brothers Ltd.*, and William Albright were among the most influential Friends who assisted Morel. Albright, a member of the Friends' Anti-Slavery Committee and the Committee of the Anti-Slavery Society, raised the Congo scandal for the first time at the annual meeting of the Society of Friends in May 1905.

Subsequently, the Honorary Secretary of the Friends' Anti-Slavery Committee, E.W. Brooks, began to correspond with Morel.[121] Although Morel appreciated this political support from the Friends, he was primarily interested in tapping their wealth to finance his own agenda. In this respect, Cadbury surpassed Morel's wildest expectations by donating £1,000 to the CRA in June 1905.[122] Ironically, *Cadbury Brothers* was at this time facing accusations that it had sanctioned slave labor on cocoa plantations in Portuguese West Africa. Morel would soon become Cadbury's confidant and advise him on how to refute these charges of slavery, as Cadbury continued to fund the Congo reform campaign. Cadbury's strategic use of the Congo controversy to divert attention from his company's own scandal is discussed in chapter 4.

In August 1905, John and Alice Harris arrived home on furlough from the Congo and proposed to conduct a speaking tour of Britain to rally support for the creation of CRA auxiliaries. Morel hesitated to support this initiative, perhaps due to his difficulties with Guinness, but he quickly bowed to pressure from Cadbury and Casement, who recognized that the Harrises' brand of evangelical philanthropy might reinvigorate the Congo reform campaign.[123] While the Harrises subsequently embraced Morel's radical views on property rights and free trade, they incorporated Christian ethics and the rhetoric of duty into their call for reform. John Harris explained to Morel, "You appeal to the more educated classes and politicians, what I want to do is to appeal to the popular mind." Harris was prepared to advocate property rights and free trade for Africans, but, he added, "the ordinary Englishman is quite in ignorance of this subject and therefore we want to be careful to hit his intellect on the right spot."[124] The "right spot" was Britain's Christian conscience, and the tool for hitting that spot, as John and Alice Harris understood, was the lantern slide image of atrocity.

The lantern lectures of the Congo reform campaign were initially financed by a missionary society, they were generally staged in religious institutions, and, most important, they were narrated by missionaries. As employees and representatives of the RBMU, the Harrises took advantage of the mission's relations with numerous nonconformist ministers to arrange local meetings throughout England. At the same time, Cadbury gave them access to the Society of Friends, enabling John Harris to address the Society of Friends' Meeting for Sufferings in October 1905.[125] On the bases of these contacts, the Harrises and other missionaries would hold the largest number of their "atrocity meetings" in Baptist and Congregationalist chapels and at Friends' meetings. Moreover, John Harris spoke regularly to Pleasant Sunday Afternoon Society (PSA) brotherhoods, as on October 1, 1905, when he addressed a PSA meeting of over 1,000 workingmen at Christ Church in London.[126]

Like Guinness, the Harrises framed the image of atrocity within a narrative of promise, betrayal, and redemption. The civilizing mission had been betrayed by the Congo Free State and, by extension, the British government, which had naively supported Leopold some twenty years earlier at the Berlin Conference. Invoking their faith in the essential morality of Britain and their shame over Britain's complicity in the creation of the Congo regime, the Harrises rallied their audiences to protest as an act of Christian duty.

The display of lantern slides was timed to realize Leopold's act of betrayal and to drive home the missionaries' call for redemption. In the middle of a standard, hour-long presentation of some sixty images, there were twelve "atrocity photographs."[127] The images were often complemented by "Congo hymns," from which the following stanza is drawn:

Britons, awake!
Let righteous ire
kindle within your soul a fire,

let indignation's sacred flame
burn for the Congo's wrongs and shame.[128]

The prospect of the redemption of "civilization" on the Congo was closely identified with missionaries. In the course of a standard lecture, the accounts of atrocities were followed by an image of John Harris and a chief of Baringa. "Ladies and Gentlemen," the speaker would declare, "amid all these tales of darkness there is just one ray of light"—the missionary. The next slide displayed "natives at a Missionary's house," accompanied by the statement "The villagers know that the missionary is their friend."[129] Contrary to the claims of the Congo Free State that the "native" was lazy and incapable of improvement, the speaker displayed images of Africans making bricks and palm oil. "He is willing to learn," the speaker asserted. "He listens to the white missionary and yields to the influence of love."[130] The problem, the speaker asserted, was that the missionary's work was undermined by the state, which treated the natives as slaves and drove them from the mission stations.[131] "Are the Churches of Christ to remain silent?" asked the speaker. "Will the heart of civilisation remain unmoved? Surely not." The speaker then concluded his or her call for reform by declaring, "Let us demand that suitable sites shall be granted for the erection of mission stations. And if our legal and reasonable requests are refused, then let us send a man-of-war to the mouth of the Lower Congo, with orders to prohibit the entry or departure of steamers or craft of any kind until they are granted."[132]

It is important to note that the photographic evidence of the Congo reform campaign did not go unchallenged. In the case of Epondo, discussed above, the advocates of the Congo Free State asserted that his hand had not been cut off by a state sentry, but had been bitten off by a wild boar. This assertion produced various conflicting testimonies that threatened to undermine the veracity of the missionary narrative. Moreover, the state attempted to provoke doubt about the authenticity of the photograph of Epondo by publishing a satirical, doctored photograph that featured Morel. Figure 2.3, which appeared in *La Vérité sur Congo* on November 15, 1905, was captioned "A photographic proof.—Mr. MOREL has just killed Epondo's wild boar."[133] While this photograph demonstrates that the "reality" of Congo atrocity photographs was subject to dispute, there is no indication that the Congo Free State's propaganda campaign could compete in Britain with missionaries' authority.

Yet photography and, particularly, lantern slides were only means to an end. Three larger political factors changed the course of the Congo reform campaign in the last half of 1905. First, trade unionists culminated their protests against "Chinese slavery" in Britain's Transvaal Colony in South Africa, giving broad exposure to ethical debates over imperialism in the run-up to the general election of 1906 and setting the stage for the entry of British labor

Fig. 2.3 Doctored photograph of Morel with wild boar. (Reprinted from *La Vérité sur le Congo,* November 15, 1905. This photograph was originally published in *Petit Bleu,* October 17, 1905.)

leaders into the Congo controversy. Second, the report of Leopold's commission of inquiry was published in October. Finally, missionaries assumed leading roles in mobilizing grassroots support for Congo reform in Britain.

It is impossible to evaluate precisely the impact of "Chinese slavery" on the Congo reform campaign. It is clear, however, that this controversy made antislavery discourse a central feature of partisan political debate in Britain during 1905, as demonstrated in chapter 3. Furthermore, British labor led this protest against the Conservative government's imperial policy in cooperation with influential nonconformist ministers, who, having been drawn into the Congo reform campaign by missionaries, enabled Morel to make contact with British labor for the first time. In the aftermath of the election, James Ramsay MacDonald would chair a new parliamentary Congo Committee and then remain a political ally of Morel until the 1920s. Remarkably, however, Morel and other leaders of the Congo reform campaign initially saw the "Chinese slavery" controversy as a threat to their own interests. Alfred Emmott cautioned Morel, "Do not let us forget, Chinese labour, West Australian irregularities, and Nigerian expeditions are the deadly foes of our Congo movement. We can't help that."[134]

As the CRA watched the growing "Chinese slavery" controversy with apprehension in 1905, it also awaited the publication of the report by King Leopold's commission of inquiry. This report caused a sensation in Belgium upon its release in October, because it condemned the Congo Free State and vindicated the claims of British humanitarians. The commission's report also served as a pretense for the BMS to enter the Congo campaign in Britain, much to the surprise of Morel and others. In August 1905, Morel had complained to John Harris that the BMS was still refusing to cooperate with him. "Probably when they get that report," Morel had speculated bitterly, "they will send another grovelling mission over to King Leopold to lick his boots again."[135] By July, however, the BMS General Committee had already decided to publicize its criticism of the Congo regime. The BMS executive had been driven to this desperate act by its realization that the Congo Free State would not allow it to purchase land for new stations. Moreover, the BMS anticipated that the report of the state commission would be damning, and, discretion being the better part of valor, it opted to condemn the state in light of the state's self-indictment. As Grenfell wrote to Baynes in August, "I quite see the wisdom of your decision to await the publication of the Commission's Report before you make a further move."[136] Under increasing public pressure, however, the BMS General Committee deemed it advantageous to pre-empt the commission's report and break with the Congo regime in a resolution of October 17, 1905.

The Congo atrocity meetings, arranged and led by missionaries, raised the profile of Congo reform in Britain, riding the wave of evangelical politics that brought an unprecedented number of nonconformists into Parliament in the general election of 1906. The election finally persuaded Morel of the power of religion in British politics. In February he wrote to the prominent minister and mentor of John and Alice Harris, the Reverend F.B. Meyer, regarding the Congo campaign: "You will have been busy with election fury up to now. Is there any chance of pushing a bit now, through Nonconformist Bodies throughout the country?...If Nonconformity is in earnest in this matter, it can MAKE the Government take action."[137] Morel continued to develop his strategic alliance with nonconformists through John and Alice Harris's mediation, and by January 1907 he was personally distributing CRA subscription forms to ministers to place upon the seats in their chapels.[138]

Following the general election, the Congo reform campaign experienced a dramatic increase in requests from chapel congregations for missionary lantern lectures. In an effort to manage this emerging reform movement, John and Alice Harris became the Joint Organizing Secretaries of the newly formed London auxiliary of the CRA in May 1906. The RBMU continued to pay their salaries, and it characterized their service to the CRA as a "loan."[139] The RBMU would finance the Harrises' work until the CRA began to pay their salaries in September 1908.[140]

John and Alice Harris gave over 300 lectures and arranged many others in the auxiliary's first year of operation. The auxiliary sponsored almost 300 more meetings in its second year. Despite the Harrises' best efforts, however, they were overwhelmed by requests from chapel congregations for lantern lectures, so they recruited other Congo missionaries to join them as speakers, including members of the BMS.[141] When requests for speakers continued to exceed their means, the Harrises distributed standard lectures, accompanied by slides, for ministers to use in their sermons.[142] Recognizing the importance of lantern lectures in its propaganda campaign, the CRA formed its first Finance Committee in March 1907 to acquire and manage the funds necessary for the increasing number of "atrocity meetings."

Morel had initially recorded the missionary lectures in the *CRA Official Organ*, but by the middle of 1906 he could not provide enough space to list the many meetings that were taking place. Morel's correspondence indicates, furthermore, that missionaries and ministers regularly neglected to notify him of meetings, which suggests that the lists of hundreds of meetings in the *Official Organ* are far from complete. There is, nevertheless, a particular group of meetings, known as Town Meetings, which offer some perspective on the scope of the revival of the Congo reform campaign under the Harrises' management. Town Meetings specifically functioned as forums for the establishment of CRA auxiliaries. The Harrises laid the foundation for these meetings by mobilizing support among chapels, Friends' meetings, and, to a lesser extent, trade unions. These groups, in turn, submitted memorials to their mayors, who then convened and chaired the fifty-three Town Meetings mapped below. After the Harrises and other lecturers had set the stage for a Town Meeting, Morel would often attend as the official representative of the CRA.[143] The Town Meetings represent areas of particularly strong support within a reform campaign that extended from Devon to lowland Scotland. The first Town Meeting occurred in Liverpool on January 4, 1906, followed by a meeting at Sheffield on May 29. It was in December 1906, however, that the meetings began to increase rapidly, proliferating throughout 1907 on the basis of hundreds of local lantern lectures by missionaries and ministers (see Figures 2.4 through 2.6).

Missionaries used their lantern lectures to transform the Congo reform campaign in important ways. After 1906 these "atrocity meetings" served as catalysts for the creation of CRA auxiliaries, which then lobbied local government officials, raised funds, and disseminated information. The first auxiliary was established in Liverpool in March 1906, but it was the London auxiliary, established in May 1906 under the management of John and Alice Harris, that was designated as the main fund-raising and propaganda agency of the CRA. In addition to producing lantern lectures, the London auxiliary managed the distribution of CRA literature, including tens of thousands of free pamphlets and leaflets. There were approximately two dozen CRA auxiliaries established after 1906, most on the occasion of a Town Meeting. Several of these auxiliaries disappeared after brief flurries of activity, but nineteen survived to stir up local interest in Congo reform in the next several years. Few records remain for these

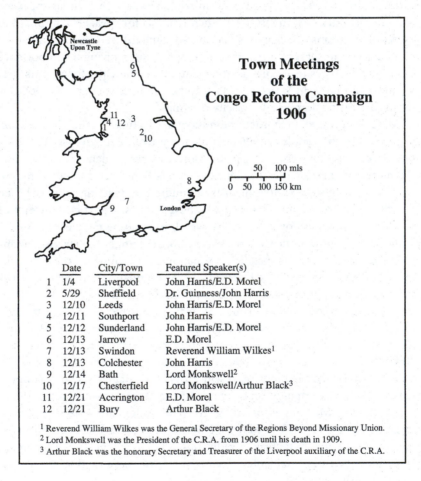

**Town Meetings
of the
Congo Reform Campaign
1906**

	Date	City/Town	Featured Speaker(s)
1	1/4	Liverpool	John Harris/E.D. Morel
2	5/29	Sheffield	Dr. Guinness/John Harris
3	12/10	Leeds	John Harris/E.D. Morel
4	12/11	Southport	John Harris
5	12/12	Sunderland	John Harris/E.D. Morel
6	12/13	Jarrow	E.D. Morel
7	12/13	Swindon	Reverend William Wilkes[1]
8	12/13	Colchester	John Harris
9	12/14	Bath	Lord Monkswell[2]
10	12/17	Chesterfield	Lord Monkswell/Arthur Black[3]
11	12/21	Accrington	E.D. Morel
12	12/21	Bury	Arthur Black

[1] Reverend William Wilkes was the General Secretary of the Regions Beyond Missionary Union.
[2] Lord Monkswell was the President of the C.R.A. from 1906 until his death in 1909.
[3] Arthur Black was the honorary Secretary and Treasurer of the Liverpool auxiliary of the C.R.A.

Fig. 2.4 Town meetings of the Congo Reform Campaign, 1906.

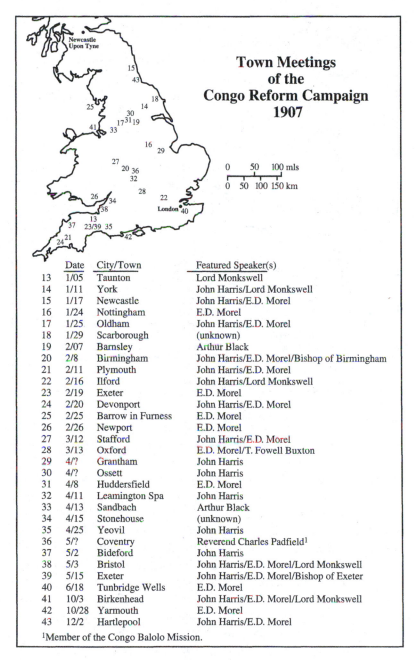

Fig. 2.5 Town meetings of the Congo Reform Campaign, 1907.

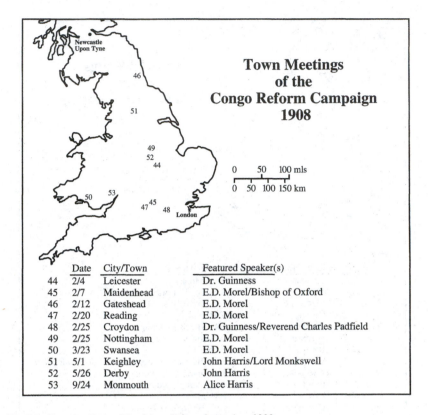

**Town Meetings
of the
Congo Reform Campaign
1908**

	Date	City/Town	Featured Speaker(s)
44	2/4	Leicester	Dr. Guinness
45	2/7	Maidenhead	E.D. Morel/Bishop of Oxford
46	2/12	Gateshead	E.D. Morel
47	2/20	Reading	E.D. Morel
48	2/25	Croydon	Dr. Guinness/Reverend Charles Padfield
49	2/25	Nottingham	E.D. Morel
50	3/23	Swansea	E.D. Morel
51	5/1	Keighley	John Harris/Lord Monkswell
52	5/26	Derby	John Harris
53	9/24	Monmouth	Alice Harris

Fig. 2.6 Town meetings of the Congo Reform Campaign, 1908.

groups, but it is possible to give a chronological and geographical overview of their development (see Figure 2.7).

Nonconformist ministers were the backbone of the new CRA auxiliary network. The importance of ministers is apparent in a published list of auxiliary committees in October 1907. Of 210 committee members, more than a quarter (58) were ministers. This strong religious influence had been manifested earlier in 1907, when the National Council of Evangelical Free Churches declared April 14 to be "Congo Sunday," instructing its affiliated ministers to preach on what it characterized as "the Congo crime."

The growth of CRA auxiliaries produced a significant increase in CRA funding. The group's income leaped from £815.0.3 in fiscal 1906–1907 to £1,720.7.0 in fiscal 1907–1908. This increase reflects the input of at least nine auxiliaries established after February 1907 and a rise in funds generated by "passing the hat" at lantern lectures.[144] The 1907–1908 fiscal year proved to be the first in which the CRA operated in the black, and it would stay in the black until it wound up in 1913. This is remarkable in view of the finances of two comparable philanthropic organizations, the APS and the Anti-Slavery

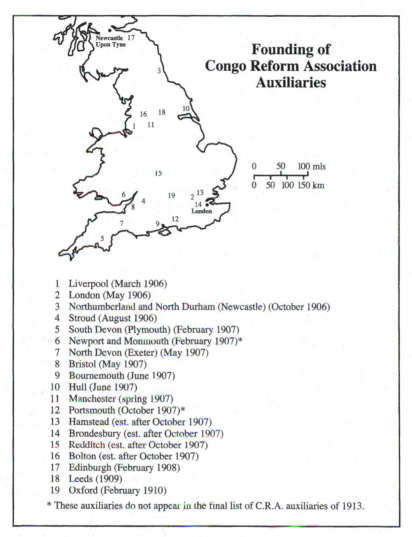

Founding of Congo Reform Association Auxiliaries

1 Liverpool (March 1906)
2 London (May 1906)
3 Northumberland and North Durham (Newcastle) (October 1906)
4 Stroud (August 1906)
5 South Devon (Plymouth) (February 1907)
6 Newport and Monmouth (February 1907)*
7 North Devon (Exeter) (May 1907)
8 Bristol (May 1907)
9 Bournemouth (June 1907)
10 Hull (June 1907)
11 Manchester (spring 1907)
12 Portsmouth (October 1907)*
13 Hamstead (est. after October 1907)
14 Brondesbury (est. after October 1907)
15 Redditch (est. after October 1907)
16 Bolton (est. after October 1907)
17 Edinburgh (February 1908)
18 Leeds (1909)
19 Oxford (February 1910)

* These auxiliaries do not appear in the final list of C.R.A. auxiliaries of 1913.

Fig. 2.7 Founding of Congo Reform Association Auxiliaries.

Society, which labored under perpetual deficits, with meager budgets of several hundred pounds.

The growth of auxiliaries shifted the main sources of CRA funding away from businessmen in the African trade. In 1907–1908, the CRA recorded 474 gifts, aside from small donations at "atrocity meetings," for a total of £1,057.7.5. There were twenty gifts of £10 or more for a total of £575.0.0, and among these larger donations only two came from businessmen with prominent commercial interests in Africa.[145] Morel observed in this period that approximately half of the CRA's funding had come from the Society of Friends.[146] Also, of these 474 gifts, 136 were attributed to women by name, indicating a more open approach to women that missionaries brought to the Congo reform campaign.[147]

Despite the success of the missionaries' reorganization of the CRA, Morel was by no means reconciled to permitting the campaign to assume a religious character. In April 1906 both the BMS and the RBMU suggested that they might break away from the CRA and conduct independent campaigns. Morel responded aggressively: "The idea that the Baptist Society or Guinness are going to dictate to me, shows if they entertain it, that they don't know who they have to deal with....It would be a fatal mistake for the CRA to allow itself to be swamped by any denomination; this would never do."[148]

By February 1907 the CBM attempted to prevent its missionaries from sending information directly to Morel, creating a rift in allegiances between Morel and John and Alice Harris.[149] Morel perceived that the missions had allied themselves with the CRA in order to win administrative reforms that would permit them to expand their evangelical work, rather than to secure Africans' property rights and trade with British merchants. In fact, the BMS and the RBMU had never ceased to appeal to the Congo Free State, through the British Foreign Office, for new station sites.

As dissension split the ranks of the Congo reformers, their campaign gathered momentum throughout 1908. In November of that year, Leopold bowed to international and domestic pressure and sold the Congo Free State to Belgium, marking a turning point in the life of the CRA. The organization's goal had been partially achieved, but, by consensus among its officers, the CRA opted to continue its work until practical reforms on the Congo had been completed. "Atrocity meetings" continued in Britain and money poured into the CRA treasury.[150]

Morel's skepticism of missionaries was substantiated in 1909. The Congo Free State, now under Belgian national authority, offered new stations to the CBM, and the mission's brethren in the field began to report a decrease in state violence. As a result, the CBM Home Council expressed public support for the new regime and instructed its missionaries to stop publicizing their evidence of continuing abuses. Morel criticized the mission for caving in to the Congo Free State, which had not yet given guarantees that it would abolish its oppressive system. Morel wrote to the Secretary of the CBM in August 1909: "The Belgian Government is doing its utmost to undermine the British movement for a radical alteration of this fundamental iniquity by throwing sops to the British Missionary Societies, and by other traditional maneuvers."[151] Morel's remonstrations and appeals had no effect. In May 1911 he commented: "The Baptist Missionary Society are still kept out of their stations, and are getting cross. The Congo Balolo Mission people are dumb."[152]

In 1910, John and Alice Harris left the CRA due to personal conflicts with Morel and became the Joint Organizing Secretaries of the recently amalgamated

British and Foreign Anti-Slavery and Aborigines' Protection Society.[153] Lantern lectures and donations decreased precipitously in the Harrises' absence, and Morel turned his attention toward administrative policy in Nigeria and "secret diplomacy" over Morocco. By 1913 it was apparent that British popular interest in the Congo had dissipated, and that the Foreign Office would soon recognize the Belgian regime. The CRA thus chose by default to declare victory, although it continued to receive reports of misgovernment on the Congo. Its leadership believed that they had waged a battle of historical significance, and they voted to use their surplus funds to enable Morel to write a history of the Congo reform movement.[154]

The perspective of this history was presaged in the final, celebratory meeting of the CRA, held in Liverpool in June 1913. Morel was lionized by his allies, but John and Alice Harris and the other missionaries who had mobilized popular support for the Congo reform campaign in Britain were absent from the stage. "In point of fact," John Harris remarked two years later, "none of those who had borne the heat and burden of the day were even invited on to the platform when the meeting was held for closing up the work of Congo Reform!"[155] Morel had exploited missionaries' organizational skills and the appeal of their evangelical message, but he had never reconciled himself to the role of religion in humanitarian politics. Subsequently, he wrote religion out of the history of the Congo reform campaign, representing his own human rights ideology as the mainspring of popular support for the CRA.[156] Historians have been quick to praise Morel, finding in his commitments to property ownership, free trade, and cultural relativism the framework of a contemporary secular, liberal model of human rights politics.[157] Although Morel's ideas certainly resonate today, these ideas were not the ones that proved most powerful in building the campaign for Congo reform in Britain in the early twentieth century.

Missionary lantern lectures and grassroots organization made the Congo reform campaign into the largest sustained protest against imperialism in the decades before the First World War. In 1908, the Foreign Secretary, Sir Edward Grey, had observed: "No external question for at least thirty years has moved the country so strongly and so vehemently as this in regard to the Congo." Although historians have commonly identified the campaign with the radical politics of Morel, Grey's statement belies this impression. Grey alludes to the controversy over the Bulgarian atrocities, which William Gladstone mobilized as an evangelical crusade, laying the groundwork for his famous Midlothian campaign. This was an apt precedent for the Congo reform movement, which was characterized by evangelical politics as articulated by British missionaries who returned from the Congo to carry their protests through Britain's chapels. In joining the public protest in Britain, missionaries set aside Morel's demands for human rights and the preservation of African customs. Although missionaries employed Morel's discourses on property rights and free trade, they refigured these discourses in their "atrocity meetings" in terms of their own evangelical goals of expansion and conversion. John Harris had told Morel in 1905 that he and his wife would transform the Congo reform campaign by hitting the intellect of the "ordinary Englishman" on "the right spot." As Grey recognized in 1908, this spot marked the British public's understanding of imperialism as a civilizing mission based upon both commerce and Christianity.

CHAPTER 3

"Chinese Slavery" in South Africa and Great Britain, 1902–1910

On May 13, 1904, an Anglo–Chinese convention cleared the way for indentured Chinese laborers to work in the gold mines of Britain's Transvaal Colony in South Africa.[1] Twelve days later, a shipment of 1,052 indentured Chinese men departed from Hong Kong aboard the S.S. *Tweeddale,* which berthed across the bay from the city of Durban in Natal, on the east coast of South Africa, on June 18. Officers of the Transvaal Foreign Labour Department registered the Chinese passengers and conducted physical examinations on the *Tweeddale's* deck. The officials found that three of the Chinese had died of beriberi in transit, and that another forty-three now had the disease. Of these men, forty would be sent home and three would die on board the ship. The remaining 1,006 men gave their fingerprints to the authorities and received "passports": tin tickets stamped with their registration numbers and the name of their employer, the *New Comet Gold Mining Company.* Accompanied by British officials, interpreters, and police, the men then traveled northwest by train, leaving behind the tropical coast of Natal for the arid expanse of South Africa's high veldt. They passed through Johannesburg, a boomtown built upon gold, and finally reached their destination, the New Comet Mine, located on an outcrop of the main gold reef in an area called the Witwatersrand or, more commonly, the Rand. The Chinese entered the premises of the mine and surveyed the above-ground plant, as well as the European, American, and African employees who paused to survey them in turn. They then passed a sentry at the gate of their compound, a fenced enclosure trimmed with barbed wire, and filed into several long, one-story buildings of brick and corrugated iron where they set their bags upon the wood-plank beds that stood against the walls.[2]

The arrival of these indentured Chinese on the Rand had been preceded by vociferous debates in South Africa and Great Britain. Both the supporters and the critics of this indenture scheme framed their arguments against the backdrop of the South African War of 1899–1902. This war had produced an acute labor crisis in the Transvaal's gold mines, a crisis that British officials now hoped to resolve by importing the Chinese. The employment of Chinese laborers was not easily reconciled, however, with the declared goals of Britain's Conservative government in fighting and winning the recent war against the Afrikaners, or Boers, of South Africa. Previous scholarship on this subject has dwelled upon colonial policy-making and the partisan claim that "Chinese slavery" exposed the collusion of the Conservative government and international capitalists.[3] This chapter, by contrast, examines the anti-slavery politics of this controversy and demonstrates how the rights of labor were circumscribed by class and race.

Prime Minister Arthur Balfour and his Colonial Secretary, Joseph Chamberlain, had justified the South African War on three grounds: as a defense of the political rights of British subjects living under the Afrikaner governments of the Orange Free State and the South African Republic; as a war for valuable territories that would provide economic benefits and, especially, jobs for British working-class families; and, finally, as a war to liberate black Africans from their alleged enslavement by the Afrikaners. Trade unionists and Liberals cast the importation of indentured Chinese to the Transvaal as a betrayal of wartime promises of employment to the British working class. Furthermore, these critics portrayed the working conditions of the Chinese as damning evidence of the Conservatives' support for new slaveries to serve the same "capitalists" who had allegedly orchestrated the South African War at the expense of the British soldier and taxpayer alike.

Trade unionists and Liberals asserted that the Conservative government would sooner enslave Chinese under the legal pretense of indenture than order the mine owners on the Rand to pay fair wages to British working-class immigrants. Approximately 85 percent of whites employed on the Rand in 1904 had been born in Britain, and the opponents of Chinese labor claimed, with little evidence, that there could be a great wave of British immigration in the near future.[4] Regardless of the viability of this immigration scheme, the popular resentment provoked by indentured labor in the Transvaal made a clear impression on British politics. At a mass demonstration against Chinese labor in Hyde Park on March 26, 1904, a common buttonhole badge pictured a cadaverous Chinese man above the caption, "The New British Miner."[5]

As in Britain, the controversy over "Chinese slavery" in the Transvaal reflected class conflicts. Since early 1903, the proposed importation of indentured

Chinese had provoked intense controversy in the colony, focusing on the disputed merits of a Chinese labor force and the perceived threat of a Chinese community to the socio-economic stability and health of whites and blacks. The main advocates of Chinese labor were an influential group of mine magnates and the British High Commissioner in South Africa, Lord Alfred Milner. The majority of the active opponents of Chinese labor came from the Transvaal's white artisanal class of mine workers, represented by a former mine manager, F.H.P. Creswell. These whites regarded Chinese labor as a threat to their wage scale and employment as skilled laborers, economic issues that were inextricably linked to strong racial biases. The Afrikaners were also strongly opposed to the importation of indentured Chinese, but they chose to avoid public debates on the issue. The Afrikaner leader, Louis Botha, asserted that because Afrikaners had no representatives in the imperial government, they should not dignify the regime by participating in its policy decisions. Only after the importation of Chinese laborers, when the imperial government bore the full responsibility for its policy, did Afrikaner leaders begin to protest openly.

Despite other differences of opinion, all of the white political parties in South Africa agreed that the Transvaal should be a "white man's country," free from the settlement of so-called Asiatics. South Africa's white community at large was keenly aware of controversies over the growing Indian community in Natal. This community was composed of "passenger Indians," who had freely immigrated to set up businesses in South Africa, and indentured Indians, who had been imported to work on Natal's plantations after 1860. Many Indians who had indentured themselves to work in Natal had chosen to remain after their contracts ended, moving into trade and other commercial fields where they competed, often successfully, with whites.[6] Whites' hostility to this growing Indian community contributed to anti-Chinese sentiment, and South Asians and East Asians were commonly maligned with little distinction.

The critics of Chinese labor in the Transvaal and in Britain were certainly aware of each other's activities, but they did not coordinate closely. The political protests in the Transvaal and Britain shared emphases on race and class politics, but there were also important distinctions. Most significantly, it appears that trade unionists in Britain were the first to use anti-slavery rhetoric to condemn Chinese labor, calling upon their nation's abolitionist tradition to win popular support. In April 1904, for example, a labor demonstration in Brighton, England, passed the following resolution:

> That this Mass Meeting of Inhabitants of Brighton in open air assembled denounces the South African "Labour Importation Ordinance, 1904," and demands the withdrawal of that measure, as imposing slavery on the Chinese to be imported thereunder, as inflicting an injury

and an indignity on British labour and as violating the best traditions of the Empire.[7]

Throughout this controversy, the Conservative government tried desperately to discredit portrayals of the Chinese as slaves.[8] The taint of slavery was more than a political liability in Britain. The Victorian tradition of abolitionist politics had become a basic component of both British national identity and the moral authority of the British Empire. The Conservatives wanted to discredit "Chinese slavery" in large part because slavery carried an absolute moral imperative to enact reform, which would have derailed the government's postwar efforts to revive the Transvaal mine industry. The Conservatives argued that because the Chinese had entered freely into their indentures, the word "slavery" did not accurately describe their employment. Such attempts to fix the definition of slavery proved futile, however. The scandal over Chinese labor in the Transvaal revealed slavery as a protean concept which could serve different political agendas. This chapter demonstrates that the controversy over "Chinese slavery" reflected, above all, the alienation of British labor from the Conservative government, rather than a concern for the Chinese. Only in these domestic political terms did the Transvaal become a major issue in the 1906 general election.

Abolitionist discourse played a central role in British protests against labor policies in the Transvaal, as it did in the contemporary protests against the Congo Free State. Both of these reform campaigns identified abolition and free trade as traditions of the Empire, and both condemned self-serving capitalists and monopoly as being incompatible with ethical imperial governance. Yet the connotations of the abolitionist discourses regarding Chinese and African laborers were dramatically different in important respects. Whereas popular support for the Congo reform campaign was mobilized through an evangelical rhetoric of Christian duty and principles of redemption and salvation, the protests against "Chinese slavery" generally emphasized rights—not the rights of the Chinese, but the rights of British and South African white workers to economic welfare and employment. As Jonathan Hyslop observes, "[The] critique of 'slavery' directed venom against the Rand-lords' exploitation of the Chinese, apparently demanding the liberation of those who would in fact be deprived of work. The effect was to protect white skilled workers against 'cheap' labour competition while wrapping this cause in a cloak of morality."[9]

Although the Chinese were identified as slaves, they did not receive sympathy from any political quarter among whites in Great Britain or South Africa. Instead, they were regarded as a threat to British working-class employment and to the white mine workers and rural Afrikaner communities in the Transvaal. British politicians conjured all the power of their nation's anti-slavery tradition in condemning the use of Chinese labor in the Witwatersrand mines, but there was no latter-day equivalent of the classic abolitionist image of the African in chains, imploring, "Am I not a man and a brother?" By contrast, the Chinese were caricatured as conniving, depraved, ridiculous, and, occasionally, pathetic.

British representations of "Chinese slaves" bore no resemblance to the representations of African slaves in the Congo Free State which were discussed in the previous chapter. This juxtaposition of anti-slavery discourses in the Edwardian era suggests, more specifically, that overseas slavery had been racialized by the turn of the century in Britain as a quintessentially African experience. Indentured Chinese laborers could be portrayed as slaves, but in the midst of Africans in the Transvaal they were also interlopers. Moreover, the British regarded the Chinese as racially superior to Africans, and thus less pitiable by comparison. The Chinese were typecast at worst as immoral and cunning; the Africans, as lazy, slow-witted, and impressionable. The British public condemned the use of Chinese labor, but only insofar as the Chinese usurped white employment and threatened the authentic slaves: Africans. This privileging of the African slave was further reflected in the British Labour Party's support for the revived Congo reform campaign after the 1906 election, at the same time that it lost interest in the Chinese on the Rand.

The Aborigines' Protection Society (APS) shared this critical view of the Chinese, warning that the Chinese would "contaminate" Africans with their supposed vices and unhygienic practices. Meanwhile, leaders of the Congo reform campaign viewed the Chinese slavery controversy as a distraction from, rather than a complement to, their own cause. When the *Morning Leader* likened the conditions of labor in South Africa to those on the Congo, E.D. Morel, the Secretary of the Congo Reform Association (CRA), asked Herbert Samuel, the Liberal MP: "Don't you think it is a great pity…that the suggestion of a parallel should be drawn between the Congo business *and anything else in the world?*"[10]

As political parties in South Africa and Britain continued to argue over the importation of indentured Chinese to the Transvaal after 1904, the Chinese on the Rand found their own sources of discontentment and took matters into their own hands. Some men staged strikes over wages, and others rebelled violently against abusive managers or dishonest merchants. The mine owners had hoped that the Chinese would provide a stable workforce, but the Chinese commonly left the mines for days or weeks at a time without authorization, seeking temporary relief from the hardships of mine labor or seeking a way home. Tensions escalated in 1905, when the British press reported the flogging of Chinese mine workers, as well as stories of "outrages" committed by marauding Chinese gangs on Afrikaner farms. This news was greeted with chagrin by both the mine owners and the Conservative government in Britain, which would be shadowed by the "Chinese slavery" scandal during the impending general election.

The cynicism of the Liberals' partisan declarations against Chinese slavery was exposed after their landslide electoral victory in January 1906. The new government of Henry Campbell-Bannerman promptly disavowed "slavery" in defining the condition of the Chinese in the Witwatersrand gold mines. Winston Churchill, the new Parliamentary Undersecretary of State for the Colonies, explained disingenuously that one could not classify the Chinese as slaves "without some risk of terminological inexactitude."[11] After abolitionist rhetoric had served its purpose in demolishing the Conservative Party, the Liberals sanctioned the continuance of Chinese indentured labor in the Transvaal until it could be conveniently discarded without harming the mine industry and the economy of the colony's white community.

The Turn to Chinese Labor in the Transvaal

Since the middle of the nineteenth century, Chinese laborers, or "coolies," had traveled in increasing numbers to the gold mines of New South Wales, the salmon-canning industry of British Columbia, the sugar estates of British Guiana, and other destinations within the British Empire. British imperial authorities viewed these Chinese laborers with ambivalence, but the white settler communities for whom the Chinese worked became decidedly hostile to the Chinese over time. By the end of the century, British Columbia, Australia, and New Zealand had passed legislation to deter the immigration of Chinese laborers and make it difficult, if not impossible, for them to remain in these territories as anything but transient employees. White South Africans, whether British or Afrikaner, shared in this growing, discriminatory movement against "Asiatics."

Only a small number of "free Chinese" businessmen and their families had immigrated to South Africa by the late nineteenth century.[12] Whites nonetheless interpreted their presence as the first wave of a potential "Asiatic" invasion. The white governments in all parts of South Africa passed discriminatory laws in the 1880s and 1890s that were primarily aimed at the growing Indian population, but which covered the Chinese as well. These laws established educational criteria for settlement in particular regions, or they proscribed property ownership in the urban centers where most of the Chinese lived. In 1885, for example, the South African Republic passed a law that prohibited "Asiatics" from owning fixed property. This law was amended in 1886 to permit Asiatics to own property, but "only in the streets, wards, and locations which the Government shall for sanitary purposes point out to them for habitation."[13]

The decision of the Witwatersrand gold mines to import Chinese laborers in 1904 was driven by chronic shortages of African labor, and by the need for relatively inexpensive labor to bring the mines back up to their pre-war levels of production. In the decade following the discovery of the massive gold reef on the Rand in 1886, the South African Republic had become the world's leading source of gold. Yet, as Alan Jeeves observes, "from the earliest days of the industry... mine labor recruiting remained an unstable, expensive, conflict-ridden enterprise."[14] The process of recruitment was further complicated by the outbreak of the South African War in 1899, which had a devastating effect on the productivity of the mines. In contrast to the 3,637,713 fine ounces of gold that had been produced in the nine months preceding the war, the mines produced only 606,793 fine ounces during 1900 and 1901. Both investments and dividends fell precipitously, and by the end of 1901 the Rand's gold production stood at its lowest figure since 1888.[15]

After the war, the mines found it harder than ever to recruit Africans, due to a combination of factors, including poor working conditions, decreased wages, and postwar opportunities for employment elsewhere. Whereas 107,482 Africans had worked in the mines in 1899, only 70,608 were employed in May 1904, while the number of whites had remained steady at approximately 12,400.[16] The mine owners did not want to import additional white laborers, due primarily to their higher wage scale and other economic factors. There was some concern about the prospect of trade union unrest, but, as Peter Richardson explains, "The union aspect of the dispute tended to obscure the greater economic significance of the industry's objection to this type of labour. Its high unit cost, unreliability, and its association with greater mechanisation and higher capital overheads were all inconsistent with the developing low-grade [ore] policy of the industry."[17] Furthermore, neither the mine owners nor the British High Commissioner, Alfred Milner, wished to foster the growth of a large proletariat of unskilled white laborers in the Transvaal. Sir George Farrar, the President of the Transvaal Chamber of Mines and the Chairman of the powerful Anglo–French Group, observed in 1903: "We do not want to use white men for subordinate labour, because if you do you will have a white man who walks arm in arm with the native."[18] Both the mine magnates and Milner wanted to make the Transvaal into "a white man's country," but only for men of the proper class.

In view of the shortfall in African labor, the Transvaal Chamber of Mines began seriously to discuss the importation of Chinese men soon after the South African War ended with the signing of the Vereeniging Treaty in May 1902. The Chamber was initially divided between those who perceived the immediate necessity of importing Chinese laborers to salvage the industry and those who believed that the Chinese might deepen the industry's crisis by destabilizing the Transvaal's social order. Harold Strange, chairman of the mines' recruitment agency, the Witwatersrand Native Labour Association, feared that the Chinese might totally displace the African workforce, which would then become discontented and rebellious.[19] Within a year, however, the industry's continuing crisis induced most of the Chamber to agree to the importation of

Chinese laborers on an "experimental" basis.[20] In December the Chamber commissioned an investigation into the prospect of importing Chinese laborers, and it dispatched two representatives, H. Ross Skinner and Herbert Noyes, to China in February 1903. In anticipation of a favorable report, the Chamber drafted a labor importation ordinance in the same month and sought the support of the High Commissioner for its new proposal.[21]

Milner perceived the mine industry as the engine of the Transvaal's postwar economic development, and he recognized that the industry had been hurt by labor shortages. Ultimately, Milner saw the recovery of the mines as a practical prerequisite for the realization of his own imperial vision for the Transvaal. In the aftermath of the war, he intended to transform the colony into a white settlement dominated by British immigrant farmers, merchants, and artisans, all carried on the backs of an African labor force. Milner's vision of the Transvaal did not, however, include a white proletariat, and so he shared the mine owners' aversion to the immigration of the British working class. In Milner's opinion, indentured Chinese laborers were an acceptable solution to the mines' present labor problems because, after fulfilling their contracts, the Chinese could be forced to leave. In the short term, Milner informed his superiors that "Asiatic labour" would relieve the Transvaal's economic crisis, which, in his opinion, now threatened the political stability of the colony.

Milner's arguments failed to impress the Colonial Secretary, Joseph Chamberlain, who advocated a more cautious approach to the Rand's labor shortage, observing that the British public would condemn the importation of Chinese laborers in light of the government's wartime promises. Chamberlain anticipated correctly that the use of indentured Chinese would be construed as proof of the government's indifference to British working-class interests. Moreover, during a visit to Johannesburg in January 1903, Chamberlain had talked with representatives of the white political community and encountered general opposition to Chinese labor. At the very least, Chamberlain believed that importation was an untenable policy without the endorsement of the Transvaal's white population by referendum.[22]

As the mine owners maneuvered for support within the imperial government and attempted to circumvent Chamberlain, Farrar initiated a public campaign in the Transvaal for the importation of Chinese labor. On March 31, 1903, he addressed a meeting of hundreds of employees of the East Rand Proprietary Mines at Driefontein. He asserted that the well-being of the mines was the basis of the well-being of all whites in the Transvaal. It was standard procedure for the mine owners to equate their interests with those of the white community at large, and in this case Farrar asserted that Chinese labor was the key to their mutual prosperity. With the long-term employment interests of his audience in view, Farrar advocated only the use of unskilled Chinese laborers, who would be repatriated at the end of their indentures.[23]

Not all of the Witwatersrand's white working class saw their common interest in Farrar's proposal, and many viewed low-paid Chinese laborers as a threat to their livelihoods. On April 1 an estimated 5,000 people assembled in Wanderers' Hall in Johannesburg to protest against Chinese labor under the auspices of the White League. The *Transvaal Leader* reported, "The meeting was essentially a working-men's one." The White League, which had previously promoted boycotts against Indian and Chinese storekeepers, condemned indentured Chinese laborers as a threat to white, and especially British, employment on the Rand. The main speaker provoked outcries when he asked whether Britons had fought their recent war for the benefit of mine magnates and Chinese laborers.

The campaign against Chinese labor never achieved significant influence because it could not compensate for the weakness of trade unions in the Transvaal. Artisans on the Rand had unionized in 1892, but their unions exerted little influence and would not be recognized by the mine owners until 1915.[24] Mining capital dominated labor in the colony, and by July 1903 the mine owners had mobilized employees into a pro-Chinese pressure group, the Labour Importation Association, which staged meetings at mines and in several towns during August and September. The mine owners were also not averse to using strong-arm tactics to gather support, as when Farrar presented a petition in favor of Chinese labor to his employees on payday. On August 5 the Witwatersrand Trades and Labour Council, representing the majority of artisans on the Rand, complained to the Colonial Office that mine owners were forcing employees to sign pro-Chinese petitions.[25] When opponents of Chinese labor tried to hold a second mass meeting at Wanderers' Hall on December 14, the mine owners transported employees to pack the hall and disrupt the meeting. There was an audience of more than 5,000 people in the hall and an overflow meeting of several thousand more at the local sporting arena. The audience in the main venue was rowdy, erupting into songs and chants including "Who are, who are, who are we? We are the people who want the Chinee!" The first speaker against Chinese labor, a bakery owner named J.W. Quinn, was assaulted by a man from the crowd, prompting his colleagues on the platform to throw a table at the audience. Quinn was never able to speak over the noise in the hall, though he waited at the podium from eight o'clock in the evening until midnight.

The British mine workers opposed to Chinese labor never found their voice in the Transvaal. The Afrikaners, meanwhile, chose to remain silent until the policy was in place. Botha believed that most Afrikaners opposed the importation of Chinese labor, but he urged them not to sign petitions on the issue, since they did not have a representative government to which they could appeal. According to Botha, "The responsibility must rest entirely upon the shoulders of those who wish to bring 'the yellow danger' into the country."[26]

By April 1904, opposition to Chinese labor in the Transvaal had collapsed. In an effort to lobby the British government, the labor leader F.H.P. Creswell had traveled to London, where he confided to Major John Seely, a Liberal MP, "Local opposition for the moment is dead as mutton."[27]

As the mine magnates busied themselves in crushing dissent, they cooperated with Milner in constructing a semblance of popular support for their labor policies. In July 1903, Milner appointed a Labour Commission "to enquire what amount of labour is necessary for the requirements of the Agricultural, Mining and other industries of the Transvaal, and to ascertain how far it is possible to obtain an adequate supply of labour to meet such requirements from central and southern Africa."[28] The findings of the majority report, published in November, were a foregone conclusion. The majority of the commission declared that Africans could not meet even half of the Transvaal's labor requirements. At about the same time, the Chamber of Mines' envoys to China, Skinner and Noyes, returned to present their favorable report on the potential for importing indentured Chinese workers.[29]

On the basis of the Labour Commission's majority report, the Chamber of Mines pushed an importation ordinance through the Transvaal's Legislative Council. The draft of this ordinance, submitted on December 28, made a strategic concession to skilled white laborers on the Rand. It stipulated not only that "indentured unskilled coloured laborers" would be repatriated, but also that they would be employed in the mines "as unskilled workmen only."[30] In its final version, the ordinance formalized in law a racial division of skilled and unskilled labor that established a precedent for the "colour bar" among laborers on the Rand in decades to come. Since 1893, certain skilled jobs in the mines had been reserved for whites with appropriate certification. According to Robert Davies, the 1904 Labour Importation Ordinance took this practice farther. "For the first time," Davies explains, "an extensive list of jobs, covering skilled, supervisory and less skilled positions, were reserved by law for whites."[31]

The Transvaal Legislative Council was an appointed body, weighted heavily with mine interests, and it was not representative of the Transvaal's white community at large. In fact, Botha and another prominent Afrikaner leader, Jan Smuts, had refused to serve on the Council. When the draft ordinance proceeded to London for the sanction of the imperial government, both the Cabinet and the permanent staff at the Colonial Office called for assurances that the ordinance had popular backing in the Transvaal, if only to appease critics in Britain. Milner resisted a referendum, making the untenable claim that the Legislative Council was in fact representative of popular opinion in the colony. Milner regarded the importation of labor as an imperial imperative, and he was not, at any rate, concerned with winning popular approval. In a memorandum to the Cabinet in early November, he had stated, "My own view is that our necessity is so great that Asiatic labour will in the long run have to be brought in, whatever the popular outcry against it."[32]

By late 1903, Milner could afford to be bullish toward his home government. In October, Chamberlain had been replaced as Colonial Secretary by Alfred Lyttelton, a suave admirer of Milner's who readily deferred to Milner's judgment in South African affairs. In November and December, the Colonial Office discreetly authorized the Transvaal government and the mining industry to establish the bureaucratic machinery in both China and South Africa for the importation of Chinese laborers.[33]

"Chinese Slavery" as British Class Politics

The proposal to import Chinese laborers into the Transvaal had surfaced in British public debate by early 1902, even before the settlement of the South African War in May.[34] By late 1903, the Liberal Party was watching the controversy develop and evaluating its political advantages.[35] When the Liberals attacked the government on this issue in January 1904, they highlighted the Conservatives' previous claims that the South African War would create jobs for all British citizens. The unspoken assumption in these attacks was that a large number of British laborers would gladly migrate to work in the gold mines of the Transvaal, an assumption that was never tested. This assumption did not, however, undermine the most powerful feature of the Liberals' rhetoric. The government's policy of apparent discrimination against white laborers in the Transvaal was presented as a reflection of its deference to elite capitalist interests in general and its disregard for the working classes at home in particular. In a speech in Glasgow on January 27, 1904, Campbell-Bannerman, the leader of the Liberal Party, declared: "When the British workman is promised more employment, let him compare South African promises with South African fulfillment."[36]

The Liberal leadership saw Chinese labor as a vulnerable point in the government's policies, but they did not regard this as a major issue in its own right. Opposition was mobilized from lower in the Liberal ranks. Herbert Samuel, who was already a leading advocate of Congo reform in the House of Commons, was seeking additional issues with which to define his early parliamentary career. He met Creswell on January 25 in London, and he subsequently established the parliamentary Transvaal Labour Committee, with which he would organize debates in the Commons.[37] According to Samuel Gordon, however, these early Liberal initiatives had little effect beyond London, and "the speed and intensity of the public's reaction to the policy initially owed little to [the Liberal Party's] political groundwork."[38]

It was Britain's trade unions that drove popular opposition to indentured Chinese labor in the Transvaal and raised the specter of slavery in British public debate. In likening indenture to slavery, labor leaders played upon a simile that abolitionists had established in the middle of the nineteenth century, generally with regard to Indian and Chinese indentured laborers in the Caribbean. James Ramsay MacDonald, the Secretary of the Labour Representation Committee (LRC), opposed the Chinese immigration scheme just as he had previously criticized a proposal to import indentured Indians to the Transvaal. Both schemes, according to MacDonald, would only "add to the troubles of the white workman" in the Transvaal.[39] Between February and March 1904, the LRC organized numerous protest meetings throughout the country, and it began to publish attacks against the government under MacDonald's direction.[40] An LRC leaflet titled "Slavery in the Transvaal" supported the accusation of slavery on two grounds. First, the LRC asserted (incorrectly) that under the Importation Ordinance the Chinese could be sold from one master to another against their will. Second, the LRC claimed (correctly) that the Chinese had no rights to property and, third, that their movement would be forcefully restricted. The Chinese would freely enter into their contracts and receive payment for their work, but they would forfeit all property rights in land, produce, and even their own bodies. "If this is not slavery," the LRC asked, "what is?" This condemnation of slavery augmented the LRC's criticism of the government for presenting the South African War as a means "to open up new fields for the employment of British labour." Supposedly, the mines did not want to hire whites because "British and colonial workmen take an interest in politics and trade unionism." "At home the unemployed increase in numbers," observed the LRC, "but South Africa is barred against our workmen."[41]

Another LRC leaflet, advocating voter registration, anticipated the central role of "Chinese slavery" in labor's campaign strategy. The leaflet concluded:

At the next General Election
you will be asked to vote to give justice
to trade unionism,
to prohibit Chinese slavery,
to reduce the taxation of the poor,
to put the burdens of municipal and national government upon the
right shoulders....[42]

Nonconformist ministers also entered the "Chinese slavery" controversy after February 1904, under the leadership of the National Council of Evangelical Free Churches. These nonconformists had already criticized Conservative policies on the South African War, and, on a separate front, they were now attacking the government's education policies.[43] The dominant theme in the Council's protests against "Chinese slavery" was the "un-Christian" nature of the government's labor policy. In February, the Council circulated a letter to the evangelical Free Churches of England and Wales, calling upon congregations to condemn this "new slave trade" for the sake of Christ's honor and the good name of Great Britain. The Council enclosed a resolution criticizing the proposed policy as a moral affront not only to the Christian nation of Britain, but also to the Chinese and the unrepresented white South African people. Numerous congregations across the country endorsed this resolution on Sunday, February 28, forwarding the texts of their criticism to the government.[44] It is noteworthy that while nonconformist ministers did not exert as much influence as trade union leaders in the "Chinese slavery" controversy, their participation may have helped to lay the groundwork for their dramatic entry into the Congo reform campaign two years later.

Labor and nonconformity joined hands in opposition to Chinese labor, mobilizing a mass demonstration in Hyde Park on March 26, 1904. The *Daily News* had called for such a demonstration to display public outrage over this reintroduction of slavery on British imperial soil. Trade unions organized the meeting, which was a preview of theatrics to come. The opening procession displayed approximately 500 trade union banners and included 21 labor organizations. Slavery was the overriding theme. One banner declared, "Slavery abolished 1833: Revived 1904." Twelve speakers' booths featured, among others, the labor leader John Burns and the leading nonconformist minister in Britain, Dr. John Clifford. The *Manchester Guardian* estimated that the attendance at this rally reached 80,000.[45]

Although the Chinese labor controversy had assumed the humanitarian discourse of an anti-slavery crusade in Britain, the nation's traditional anti-slavery lobbyists did not influence its progress. The British and Foreign Anti-Slavery Society covered the controversy in the *Anti-Slavery Reporter*, but generally stayed clear of the fray. Due to a long-standing and informal allotment of philanthropic territory, the APS took responsibility for South African affairs. Fox Bourne spoke out against Chinese labor, invoking the hallowed names of the abolitionists Clarkson and Wilberforce while decrying the threat of "a new slavery under new names."[46] Yet the APS was not particularly concerned with the enslavement of the Chinese. Fox Bourne warned that the Chinese would take jobs from whites in the Transvaal and threaten the health of the white community at large. The most important danger, however, would face the Transvaal's African population. Fox Bourne warned that the Chinese would decrease the wages of Africans by undermining their bargaining power in the labor market. Also, the Chinese would "contaminate" African culture with their "Asiatic customs," and they would "contaminate" Africans themselves with their notorious lack of hygiene. Although Fox Bourne shied from explicit predictions, he implied that the Chinese would encourage a breakdown of sexual mores among Africans. Reports published in the *Aborigines' Friend*, for example, suggested that the conditions of "enforced celibacy" in the mine compounds would drive the Chinese to sodomy.[47] "Whatever his merits," Fox Bourne declared, "the Chinaman has habits and methods which render his influence on the 'inferior' races of other lands altogether pernicious."[48]

The APS shared much with the broader campaign against "Chinese slaves," but the feeble voice of this organization was lost in the din of trade union demonstrations and sermons by nonconformist ministers. The political strategies of the APS were dull, if methodical, and certainly too restrained to win attention in the raucous world of British party politics after the third expansion of the franchise in 1884, the rise of trade unionism, and the appearance of mass-circulation newspapers at the turn of the century. The isolation of the APS had already been recognized in official circles. Chamberlain had remarked in a minute to Milner: "Do not let us make more than is absolutely necessary of this Society which is run by a single man and is composed of men many of whom are not very wise or well informed."[49]

As noted in the preceding chapter, the leadership of the new humanitarian lobby in Britain, the CRA, regarded the "Chinese slavery" scandal as a threat to its own publicity. Moreover, the CRA did not have substantial ties to British labor before 1906, so it had no easy means of coordinating with the anti-Chinese campaign.[50] There were some in the CRA who believed that the government would be deterred from condemning the Congo Free State for fear that King Leopold might accuse it of hypocrisy in countenancing "Chinese slavery" in South Africa. Indeed, the Congo State's propaganda machine made occasional use of the Chinese labor controversy in attacking the moral authority of its British critics, but it did not dwell upon this issue at length. It is possible that Leopold chose not to dwell upon "Chinese slavery" because his main Consul in Liverpool, Sir Alfred Jones, had already imported Chinese indentured laborers, without success, to Sierra Leone.[51]

There were those who participated in both the "Chinese slavery" and Congo reform campaigns before the 1906 general election. The most prominent of these people were Samuel, in Parliament, and Clifford, in the pulpit. Less conspicuously, the Cadbury family also drove these campaigns forward by funding both the CRA and one of the newspapers that led the media's opposition to "Chinese slavery," the *Daily News*. George Cadbury had purchased the *Daily News* during the South African War to voice his criticism of the Conservatives' imperialist policies, and he subsequently promoted the "Chinese slavery" controversy as an extension of his campaign against the government. Meanwhile, *Cadbury Brothers* was attempting to stifle increasing criticism of its purchases of cocoa from alleged slave plantations in Portuguese West Africa. When the "cocoa controversy" broke in 1906, the conservative press would exact unrestrained vengeance for the Cadburys' previous attacks against the Conservative government, as discussed in the next chapter.

The Transvaal Labour Importation Ordinance was introduced to the House of Commons on January 19, 1904, and the first debate on the Ordinance occurred on February 16 and 17. This and subsequent debates focused primarily on the issues of wartime promises and postwar unemployment. In the face of

Liberal attacks, the government managed to block attempts to scuttle the Ordinance. In a defiant gesture, Campbell-Bannerman then moved to censure the government, but he fell short by fifty-six votes. To the dismay of the Conservative leadership, many of its party members broke ranks to join in Campbell-Bannerman's censure. More important, although British labor did not yet have a substantial contingent within the Commons, popular protests beyond the walls of Parliament set an ominous tone for the upcoming election. When a Conservative MP, Major Coates, attempted to speak in favor of Chinese labor during a meeting at Forest Hill, he was heckled by men in the audience who cried, "Now for the Chinaman!" and "Get a little pigtail!" Lyttelton, the Colonial Secretary, remarked to Milner in April 1904, "We should all lose our seats just now over Chinese."[52]

The British advocates of indentured Chinese labor were few and far between. Although Balfour and Lyttelton stood by their policies in Parliament, Conservative politicians generally dodged the issue in public, or they preferred to let the Conservative Publication Department speak on their behalf. The main pressure group in favor of Chinese labor for the Transvaal was the Imperial South African Association (ISAA), chaired by Sir Gilbert Parker, a Conservative MP. It appears that the ISAA generally confined its work to the greater London area, defending importation on several fronts. First, it argued that indentured Chinese laborers were necessary to sustain the economy of the Transvaal and to prevent further impositions upon British taxpayers. The ISAA also asserted that British workmen should not be degraded by working beside blacks, that the Transvaal was too expensive for white unskilled laborers to make a living wage, and that Chinese laborers would create more places for skilled and highly paid white workers in the mines. Finally, proponents of Chinese labor argued that critics were cynically exploiting the issue in petty, partisan attacks upon the government.[53] Parker flatly rejected accusations of slavery, pointing out that slaves could not freely enter into contracts. "The Chinaman comes to South Africa with his eyes open," Parker maintained, "agreeing to do no skilled work, knowing that he cannot remain... and is permitted to do nothing save the work which he has come to do."[54]

The ISAA and the Conservative Party foresaw not only material benefits but also moral improvement for the Chinese. Both groups publicized a resolution passed by the Transvaal Free Church Council on April 7, 1904, refuting the charge of slavery. The Council had stated that the restrictions upon the Chinese were fair on the whole, and certainly necessary to prevent the "contamination" of the white community.[55] Some nonconformists in the Transvaal even anticipated opportunities for proselytization within the mine compounds. The Conservative Party published a resolution passed by the Witwatersrand Church Council on March 5, 1904, which "deprecated" the British Free

Church Council's agitation against Chinese labor. "The meeting suggests," according to the resolution, "that the [British] Free Church Council's efforts should be directed to securing perfect freedom for Christian work among the Chinese."[56] While the British nonconformists continually refused to support their South African brethren, the Archbishop of Canterbury, representing the Church of England, came out in support of Chinese labor on the Rand.[57]

British labor leaders and ministers dismissed such moralistic defenses of Chinese labor. Burns criticized "indentured yellow labour" as "a rich man's euphemism for slavery." He also attacked the would-be evangelists in the Transvaal, and especially the British Anglican establishment. "No one suspected" Burns declared, "…that we should witness the degrading spectacle of Primate, Bishops and clergymen condoning chattel slavery…in return for proselytizing facilities for converting Mongolian Confucians in capitalistic compounds." Although Burns and other labor politicians readily cooperated with British ministers in opposing "Chinese slavery," they did not address the issue in sectarian terms. Labor activists focused upon the rights of labor, and specifically the rights of British labor. This mingling of rights and race created an unstable discourse of protest. The presumed universality of basic rights, even "human rights," conflicted with ideas of racial difference and, more specifically, the interests of British labor. Most often, critics of Chinese labor indicted the Chinese along with the Conservative government. Very rarely, however, British labor would strike a paternalistic view toward the Chinese. As Burns stated:

> This evasion of human rights and national duty, apart from perversion of our noblest tradition, is a denial of our responsibility to inferior races, whom we can only claim to govern because in so ruling we substitute for the slavery of savages the free consent of the kindly governed.[58]

Chinese on the Rand

Before the arrival of indentured Chinese laborers on the Rand in May 1904, there had been only 981 Chinese residents in the Transvaal, most of them living in Johannesburg.[59] By the end of the year, thirteen shipments would bring 20,918 additional Chinese to the Transvaal.[60] A total of 63,695 indentured Chinese would arrive by 1907, and the number of Chinese employed on the Rand would peak at 53,828 in January of that year.[61] Over three years, only five women and thirty-one children accompanied their husbands and fathers to the Rand, although in 1904 some 22 percent of indentured men claimed to be married.[62] The importer had been obligated under the Transvaal Labour Importation Ordinance to pay all transportation costs for wives and children under age ten, but it appears that most men did not attempt to bring their families. They had no hope of settling in the Transvaal, their living conditions were uncertain, and the presence of families would have diminished their savings.[63] The absence of wives from the immigrant pool would fuel controversies in Britain, but a dearth of women was certainly nothing new to other unskilled workers in the mine industry. With regard to white workers, Robert Davies observes that "the majority…were bachelors or had their family ties outside South Africa."[64]

The recruitment of Chinese laborers was handled by three Transvaal emigration agents in cooperation with Chinese inspectors at Hong Kong, Chinwangtao, and Chifu. "Their most important duty," wrote William Evans, the Superintendent of the Foreign Labour Department, "is to ensure that every labourer who comes here under the Ordinance does so of his own free will after full explanation and thorough understanding of the terms of the indenture or contract."[65] It is likely that the agents downplayed the hardships of mine labor. The experience of working underground was, furthermore, difficult to convey to the majority of the recruits, who had previously worked only in agriculture. Each applicant underwent a physical examination, received vaccinations, and was photographed before being placed in a depot for at least forty-eight hours to await shipment. Prior to embarkation, the agents or their representatives asked each man if he still wished to proceed to South Africa. If so, the man signed a contract of service and received a badge with his shipping number.

Upon arrival at Durban, recruits proceeded to the reception depot at Jacob's Camp. The depot consisted of two large quadrangles, with accommodations for 4,000 men. Each man entered the registration office, answered questions to confirm his identity, and was compared against his photograph. Having confirmed the man's identity, the official then asked if he was "a willing emigrant" and if he had received the monetary advance for travel entered under his name. The registration process was completed by taking the man's fingerprints and providing him with a passport.

The system of recruitment and importation for Chinese laborers was logistically efficient, but difficulties soon arose due to unforeseen language problems. The first shipment of 1,052 laborers was drawn from Kwangtung Province of southern China. The mines had initially favored this region because its populace was supposedly accustomed to international labor migration. Consequently, the mines initially staffed their Foreign Labour Department with people who spoke Cantonese or had experience in southern China. This first shipment was, however, virtually the last from southern China, largely because the mines were dissatisfied with the health and endurance of laborers from the region.[66] In July 1904 the mines began recruiting in northern China at Chinwangtao and Chifu. This recruiting campaign was aided by economic instability in the area caused by recent flooding and the Boxer Rebellion, both of which had interrupted the migrations of agricultural laborers.

Of the 63,695 total Chinese emigrants to the Transvaal, 62,006 embarked from ports in the north.[67]

Superintendent Evans was on leave from his regular post as Protector of Chinese in the Staits Settlements. He had twenty years of experience in managing Chinese laborers, but he had generally worked with laborers from southern China. The Foreign Labour Department had few, if any, Mandarin interpreters, and it quickly encountered language problems as more Chinese arrived from the north. Generally, the Chinese could not communicate with either government officials or their mine managers. It was not until June 1905 that Evans was replaced as head of the Foreign Labour Department by James William Jamieson, who could converse in Mandarin. Still, the Foreign Labour Department was understaffed, and it was another six months before the government gave Jamieson the authority to make employers hire European managers who could communicate with their Chinese employees.[68]

The difficulties caused in the mines by poor communication often provoked frustration and violence between whites and Chinese. In Jamieson's opinion, for most mine managers, "a blow or the application of a heavy boot are thought to be the most efficient means of conveying to a coolie an idea of what his white boss wants."[69] This would become an acute problem in 1905, when Chinese laborers rioted at several mines. Lord Selborne, who had recently succeeded Milner as the High Commissioner of South Africa, informed the Colonial Secretary that the language barrier was the primary cause of these disturbances, and he blamed white overseers for their rough handling of the Chinese.[70] On July 2, 1905, a deputation of white miners petitioned the High Commissioner to act to stop the obscene language which Chinese miners were directing toward them. In reply, Selborne asked where the Chinese had learned these epithets in the first place, and he let the matter drop.[71]

As per their contracts, all Chinese performed rigorous "unskilled labour," most often underground. In the first year of their work on the Rand, approximately 40 percent of the Chinese were engaged in hand-drilling, while the remainder did jobs such as shoveling and tramming. They worked ten hours a day, six days a week. They initially received fixed daily wages, but many, especially the hand-drillers, chose the option of piecework. On average, the Chinese were paid less than Africans. For example, in 1905, the average Chinese monthly wage was 37s.7d., while Africans received 51s.9d.[72] Although mine labor was dangerous, the Chinese, like Africans, were more prone to death by disease than by accident. Their mortality rates were, however, far less than those of their African counterparts.[73]

When off the job, the Chinese could apply for permits to leave their compounds for up to forty-eight hours. Within the compounds, they were housed in large, ventilated rooms with stoves, windows, and, sometimes, electricity.

There were fully staffed hospitals available to the men, as well as kitchens with Chinese cooks, and stores on the premises where the men could buy items such as blankets and cigarettes. Given the lack of Chinese women, critics had predicted that the Chinese men might resort to raping African and white women. In 1906, the Transvaal Chamber of Mines observed that no evidence existed of Chinese assaults on white women.[74] The Chinese did employ African prostitutes, which the Colonial Office regarded as "a natural and comparatively harmless solution to the difficulty."[75]

Labor unrest did not take long to appear among the Chinese on the Rand. From the beginning, there were conflicts between Chinese and white miners. These conflicts originated most often from miscommunicated instructions, disputes over wages, or racist aggression by whites. Unrest was also provoked by the extortionate practices of the Chinese police, who had been selected from the recruits to help the mine managers to maintain order. It is probable that the Foreign Labour Department never heard about the vast majority of altercations and reprisals that occurred in the mines. The government authorities were mainly concerned with "riots and disturbances," those acts of violence which prompted the mines to call in the police to restore order. The first such disturbance occurred on July 22, 1904, at the East Rand Proprietary Mines. As Evans explained:

This disturbance arose from the alarms caused by a mine explosion in which two men were killed. It culminated in the men of the night shift refusing to turn out. Stones were thrown at some of the mine officials when they tried to induce them to go to work. A number of men were arrested and sentenced to varying terms of imprisonment.[76]

Between July 1904 and July 1905, there were twenty-eight riots and disturbances on the Rand. The parties involved included Chinese laborers, Chinese police, Africans, and whites. The causes ranged from poor-quality food to disputes over wages, but in many instances the authorities could not determine the specific subject of the original conflict. Several of the incidents resulted in deaths. One of the largest riots occurred on April 1, 1905, at the North Randfontein Mine, where coolies and the mine's management clashed in a wage dispute. After a two-day strike, managers attempted to arrest the supposed ringleaders. When the police moved in, over 1,000 coolies attacked them with stones and spades.[77]

The authorities were apt to trivialize these disturbances as isolated events provoked by a few "bad characters" among the Chinese. Yet in a quieter manner many laborers were rejecting the control exercised by the mine management. Rather than engaging in large public outbursts, laborers commonly walked away from the mines, seeking either a break from their work or passage home to China. Some men were found as far away as Swaziland, while others chose to follow the railway lines back to the sea. Donald Denoon observes:

> By mid-1905 a total of 21,205 unlawful absences had been reported to the government, and 1,735 cases had resulted in conviction for desertion. These figures do not represent the total number of absences, since by no means were all cases reported to the government. Even these figures, however, indicate that almost half of the Chinese working population had been unlawfully absent on one occasion or another.[78]

Although these Chinese were initially conspicuous only in their absence, they soon became known to white South Africans and the British alike as a public menace. Selborne observed, "That the coolies have had legitimate grounds for complaint as to their treatment is, unfortunately, not to be denied."[79] Nonetheless, the Chinese would soon be cast as "a yellow terror" in British domestic and imperial politics.

"Chinese Slavery" and the British General Election

As unrest mounted on the Rand in 1905, the Liberal Party in Britain continued to press the issue of "Chinese slavery" in its by-election campaigns. In the Everton campaign of February 1905, six men in Chinese makeup were taken around the constituency in a wagon, displaying a placard that read: "You English fight in South Africa. Welly good! The Chinese come there and get work—Welly good indeed!" Two British workmen followed the wagon, carrying placards which announced, "After the war, British not wanted, Chinese preferred."[80]

The Liberal leadership still did not treat Chinese labor as a major issue in itself. On November 23, 1904, when Campbell-Bannerman had instructed his chief campaign manager, Herbert Gladstone, to establish special committees to clarify the party's positions on key subjects, Chinese labor was not among his priorities. Instead, Campbell-Bannerman listed his political priorities as follows: (1) Ireland, (2) education, (2a) education—feeding children, (3) licensing, (4) unemployed.[81] Campbell-Bannerman and Gladstone's correspondence between mid-1904 and mid-1905 displays their confident views toward the next general election and a shrewd focus on domestic issues. The Liberal strategists recognized that working-class politics would play a major role in the election, and they also perceived that British labor was not invested in the aggressive patriotism of British imperialism, as Richard Price has demonstrated in his study of the South African War.[82] The electoral significance of imperial issues would be determined by their relevance to life at home. Accordingly, the Liberals used indentured Chinese laborers as provocative symbols of the Conservatives' commitment to capitalist interests at the expense of the average British citizen.

The debate over "Chinese slavery" fell into a predictable pattern by early 1905. Trade unionists and Liberals asserted that the importation of the indentured Chinese reflected the government's indifference to the British working class and, secondarily, that this "new slavery" violated the abolitionist traditions of the Empire. While attempting to refute the charge of slavery, the government further argued that the Chinese would strengthen the South African economy for the benefit of Britons at home and abroad. On April 15, Evans, the Superintendent of the Foreign Labour Department, arrived in England after thirteen months of work in the Transvaal. When questioned about the Chinese by a Reuters correspondent, Evans replied:

> The coolies on the Rand were never so well off, as they are well housed, well fed, and well paid, and have excellent hospitals, with qualified European doctors. The manner of their treatment leaves nothing to be desired.[83]

The focus of public debate in Britain soon shifted, however, when reports reached the House of Commons that Chinese laborers were being flogged. On May 15, 1905, the *Daily News* published a letter that claimed that Chinese laborers on the Rand were being flogged for refusing to work. In this particular case, Chinese men had been allegedly thrashed while tied to a pole by their "pigtails," with only their toes touching the ground.

Over the next two days, Maurice Levy, a Liberal MP, asked the Colonial Secretary in the Commons for more information about this incident. Lyttelton instructed Selborne, the High Commissioner, to investigate, noting, "I presume that the allegation is without foundation."[84] Lyttelton had previously dismissed charges of illegal flogging in the absence of confirmation from Milner.[85] Although Selborne could not find evidence about the particular incident recounted in the *Daily News*, he revealed systematic practices of flogging that shocked the Conservative government, provoking fears that such revelations would bolster cries against slavery on the Rand. The punishment of flogging was actually sanctioned under the law of the Transvaal Colony, but the punishment could not be legally administered without the approval of the Supreme Court. The main legal issue at hand was how the authority to flog Chinese laborers had been delegated to mine officials. In a pre-emptive measure, the Lieutenant Governor, Arthur Lawley, issued a memorandum to all of the mine owners on June 13, 1905, prohibiting "the infliction of corporal punishment of any kind whatsoever upon Chinese coolies" by mine officials or Chinese police.[86]

Upon investigating the issue further, Selborne spoke with the Lieutenant Governor and discovered a damaging claim. According to Lawley, Evans had told him in March that he had, with Milner's approval, "delegated certain powers to Compound Managers to deal summarily with minor offences." He had authorized the use of "slight corporal punishment" in accordance with two limitations: punishment had to take place in the presence of the manager, and "such punishment was strictly limited in degree to punishment of such nature as is permitted in schools and similar institutions in England."[87]

The government in London tried to suppress these revelations of flogging sanctioned by its own colonial officials. Nevertheless, Liberal and labor politicians took hold of this issue and used it to illustrate the state of slavery in which the Chinese worked on the Rand. In addition to reports of flogging, the government also found itself assailed by news that Chinese deserters were tormenting the Transvaal's Afrikaner community. On August 17, a farmer named P.J. Joubert was murdered by a group of Chinese at Moabsvelden in the Pretoria District. Subsequently, on September 6, Botha, the leader of the newly formed Het Volk political organization, led a delegation of Afrikaners to speak with the Lieutenant Governor. Botha complained to the Lieutenant Governor that roving bands of Chinese were stealing from farms, slaughtering cattle, and generally terrifying the Afrikaners. In response to this and other complaints, the imperial regime provided the Afrikaners with rifles for the first time since the conclusion of the South African War and posted bounties for the return of wandering Chinese men.[88] On September 18, Selborne reported that 275 South African Constabulary officers had been stationed around the mines, in addition to the ordinary postings of police. The stations were five miles apart, and there were constant patrols on the perimeters of the mines.[89] Despite these security measures, however, disturbances continued. On October 2, 1905, a storekeeper named Jacob Herman died when a group of Chinese used dynamite to blow up his shop near Boksburg.

It appears that the Conservative defense of Chinese labor shifted in the wake of the revelations of flogging and the reports of marauding Chinese. Henceforth, the government skirted discussion of the conditions under which the Chinese worked, and instead emphasized the absolute increase in white employment in the Transvaal which had accompanied the Chinese. In October 1905, there were 45,901 Chinese at work on the Rand. Between May 1904 and October 1905, white workers had increased from 13,127 to 18,359, a rise of 5,232. Conservatives also emphasized an increase in British exports of machinery to the Transvaal.[90]

With the general election in sight, the Liberal MPs Samuel, Seely, Charles Trevelyan, and T.J. Macnamara began to muster a strong partisan attack on the issue of "Chinese slavery." Their points of leverage were the incidents of flogging and the many labor disturbances on the Rand. The anti-Chinese lobby outlined its position on November 20, 1905, in a memorandum to the Prime Minister, Arthur Balfour, signed by twenty representatives of labor and nonconformist and radical politics. The memorial attributed riots and desertions among the Chinese to "the forfeiture of their liberty" and alluded to "grave outrages" perpetrated by the Chinese against the local white community. The memorandum advocated a renewed reliance upon African and white mine laborers, which would promote "economic progress free from social dangers." Finally, it asserted that the British nation at large had earned a right to "a voice in the settlement of this problem" through its sacrifices in the South African War.

In reply, Balfour asserted that Liberal estimates of Chinese unrest were exaggerated and that the Chinese played a crucial role in filling a shortage of unskilled labor. Also, Balfour emphasized the absolute, rather than the proportional, increase in skilled white labor on the Rand, and he stressed that the Transvaal would soon hold a referendum on the issue. Finally, Balfour was careful to condemn slavery in principle, even as he defended the use of indentured labor on the Rand:

> The system of indentured labour, whether coolie or native, must therefore be treated as a whole; and if, indeed, those critics be right who identify it with slavery, it must ruthlessly be extirpated from every colony where it has insidiously taken its root. This, however, is not the view of His Majesty's present Government.

Balfour observed wryly that, upon assuming power, his political opponents would no doubt come to share his view.

On December 4, 1905, Balfour announced his resignation, and on the following day King Edward invited Campbell-Bannerman to form a government. On December 16, Campbell-Bannerman announced the dissolution of Parliament, and the campaign for the general election began. In the carnivalesque atmosphere of the 1906 election, "Chinese slavery" figured prominently. According to A.K. Russell, "After Free Trade... Chinese labour was probably the most important single issue of the election which many Unionists later seized on as a convenient explanation of defeat."[91] In fact, the Conservatives were defeated on separate, though related, issues in the Liberal program. Russell explains that the main points of this program were support for free trade and opposition to imperial preferences, which presumably would have impoverished the working classes.[92] Chinese labor was exploited by Liberal and labor politicians as a more general indication that the Balfour government was in the pocket of elite capitalist interests. In these terms, the specter of the South African War again appeared in anti-Chinese propaganda. One widely distributed image (Figure 3.1), used on both leaflets and posters, showed a line of Chinese being shepherded by a fat plutocrat, while Tommy Atkins, the symbolic British soldier, asks a sleeping John Bull: "Is THIS what we fought for?"[93]

Fig. 3.1 Political poster, Liberal Party Publication Department, 1905. (Reprinted with permission of the London School of Economics. Collection reference 519/51.)

Although it was easy for Liberals to criticize the Balfour administration's previous policy on Chinese labor, it was difficult to construct an alternative policy to resolve the issue. Proponents of Chinese labor warned that its cessation would destroy up to a third of the mine industry. In formulating their policy, the new Liberal Cabinet attempted to weigh their previous declarations of a moral imperative to end "Chinese slavery" against their concern for the Rand's mine industry, the economic stability of the Transvaal Colony, and the burden upon British taxpayers which immediate repatriation might entail. The government knew that some 14,700 licenses had already been issued to laborers still in China, and that these could be revoked only through *ex post facto* legislation. In view of the upcoming elections, the Cabinet came to a partial decision on December 20. The new Colonial Secretary, Lord Elgin, informed Selborne that "pending decision as to grant of responsible government [to the Transvaal]," all recruitment, embarkation, and importation of Chinese indentured laborers should cease.[94]

On the next day, Campbell-Bannerman gave his first major speech of the campaign at Albert Hall before an audience of 9,000 people. Among other statements regarding the Liberal Party platform, he pledged "to stop forthwith—as far as it is practicable to do it forthwith—the recruitment and embarkation of coolies in China and their importation into South Africa."[95] The partisan crowd erupted in wild cheers of approval. Conservatives dismissed this pledge as hollow and opportunistic, but their complaints fell upon deaf ears. David Lloyd George subsequently incited audiences by suggesting that the Conservatives might next import Chinese laborers to the mines of Wales. The Chinese Labour National Protest Committee distributed leaflets claiming that Tory votes would lead to indentured Chinese in London. "By the new year," Russell observes, "pigtailed and manacled Chinamen were already as familiar on the streets and at Liberal meetings as big and little loves."[96]

Meanwhile, the Cabinet was resolving its policy on Chinese labor. Lord Elgin reflected the general tone of discussion in stating that "the matter is one which affects peace, order and good government, and ought to be dealt with on that basis, not from philanthropic motives."[97] Samuel had earlier proposed a tactic to free the Liberal government from accusations of slavery. In December he had suggested that the government arrange to subsidize the repatriation of any coolies who desired to go home. On this basis, the government could claim that it was not holding the Chinese against their will. "It would take the sting out of the slavery argument," Elgin concurred.[98] With regard to the licensed laborers still in China, the government decided simply to blame their contracts on the previous administration and claim that its hands were tied. As Campbell-Bannerman had anticipated, the public accepted this explanation. On January 3, the Cabinet decided to honor current licenses, reject future applications, and submit the issue to the future Transvaal government, to be settled by referendum.

Liberal and labor politicians enjoyed a massive victory in the general election of January 1906. The Conservatives dropped from 334 to 157 seats, and the new government had a majority of approximately 400 Liberal and "Lib–Lab" MPs. Campbell-Bannerman declared in a speech on January 16: "The policy and spirit which would govern the action of the present government would be the very antithesis of that of their opponents. It would be based on justice and liberty, not privilege and monopoly."[99] After the election, however, British imperial policy exhibited more continuity than change. Fortunately for the Liberals, the British public's interest in Chinese slavery quickly diminished after the election. With the election behind them, and the burden of government upon their shoulders, the Liberal leadership moved to distance themselves from their previous condemnations of slavery in the Transvaal, as Balfour had predicted they would. Campbell-Bannerman now explained that the Chinese were not enslaved, but merely "servile," and Elgin expressed his regret that the term "slavery" had ever been used with reference to the Transvaal.[100]

The Liberal government pursued its policy of repatriation, prompting a wave of protests from mining interests on the Rand. As of January 31, 1906, there were 18,582 whites, 93,933 Africans, and 47,166 Chinese employed in the mines. A mass exodus of Chinese would have been devastating, but this exodus never occurred. Notices of the offer of subsidized repatriation were posted on the Rand in May 1906, and by January 1, 1907, only 1,550 applicants had come forward, of whom 766 were repatriated. In view of these numbers, the mine owners calmed their fears.[101]

In February 1906 the Liberal government declared its intention to grant self-government to the Transvaal. The colony's first postwar election took place in early 1907. The platform of the Afrikaner party, Het Volk, was characterized by political compromise and economic caution. There would be no more indentured Chinese admitted to the Transvaal, but those Chinese who were already present would serve out their contracts as the number of African laborers was systematically increased. The Progressive Party, representing the mine interests, advocated continued importation, but Het Volk was able to cast the Progressives as self-serving "capitalists" and establish an alliance with the moderate British constituency of the National Association. After the polling on February 20, 1907, Het Volk emerged with an overall majority. The party then fulfilled its campaign pledge regarding Chinese labor by passing the Transvaal Indentured Labour Laws Temporary Continuance Act. The Liberal government in London had wavered on this issue, fearing accusations of hypocrisy from Conservatives and continued pressure from radicals. Yet the government, and especially Elgin and Churchill, had remained flexible on the issue, giving priority to two related factors. First, the government recognized the economic importance of sustaining the Transvaal's gold mines. Second, it did not want to promote conflict with the new Afrikaner regime. In the end, Samuel Gordon observes, "The desire to maintain good links with the new Transvaal administration outweighed any inclination to maintain a moral stand on the issue of 'slavery.'"[102]

In approving the continuance of indentured Chinese labor on the Rand in November 1908, the Colonial Secretary made suggestions for improvements in the labor system and expressed his confidence that Botha's government "will readily and of its own motion remove all that is objectionable in practice, so far and so soon as public convenience will permit."[103] Like the previous Conservative regime, the Liberal Party and Het Volk now subordinated the present conditions of Chinese labor exploitation to the future economic growth of the white community in the Transvaal. "Chinese slavery" would continue in the Witwatersrand gold mines until the last indentured laborer was repatriated in 1910.

Conclusion

The critics of indentured Chinese labor in the Transvaal conveyed little, if any, sympathy for the plight of the Chinese. The condition of indentured servitude was condemned as slavery, but the enslaved Chinese were primarily portrayed as a threat to the employment of whites and to the morality and social stability of Africans. British opposition to "Chinese slavery," an affront to the British abolitionist tradition, demonstrated how racial biases determined the measure of pity that oppressed groups could actually receive in Britain and the Empire. In the wake of the general election, it is remarkable that the former critics of "Chinese slavery" were prepared to countenance the same conditions of indentured servitude in the interest of the white community's economic progress.

This is not to say that all of the critics of "Chinese slavery" had a comparatively benevolent view on black Africans in the Transvaal. Trade unionists believed that Africans had constituted a threat to the employment and wage scales of white workers long before the Chinese arrived.[104] After the Chinese were gone, Creswell became the head of the South African Labour Party and led trade unionists on the Rand in turning their defensive aggression back upon Africans. White South African laborers had a number of grievances, but, as Hyslop emphasizes, "The underlying theme of the work of the union movement was the demand for the protection of white workers' monopoly of skilled jobs."[105] In a telling account, Hyslop explains that on March 1, 1914, the largest British labor demonstration of the early twentieth century convened in Hyde Park to support white South African trade unionists who demanded the exclusion of black and Asian workers from skilled jobs in the mines on the Rand.[106]

The Chinese indentured labor scheme played a pivotal role in imposing a legal "colour bar" upon the South African workforce. Granted, the Transvaal mine industry had made previous concessions to white workers who demanded privileges over blacks. Yet the Labour Importation Ordinance of 1904, designed to appease white workers in the face of Chinese competition, laid out a detailed list of skilled jobs upon which whites would build their economic dominance over, and political distance from, blacks long after the indentured Chinese left. It is no exaggeration to say that the apartheid regime in South Africa was built after 1948 in large part upon legal precedents, such as the segregation of work and living spaces, established under the British to manage South Africa's migrant labor force.[107] In this respect, the ramifications of the "colour bar" established by the Labour Importation Ordinance played out until the end of the apartheid regime, and arguably thereafter.

Class politics were inextricably linked to racial politics in the "Chinese slavery" controversy, jointly defining the political groups involved in both Britain and South Africa. Liberal politicians may have used "Chinese slavery" in their campaign rhetoric, but popular interest in the controversy was driven by the domestic agenda of Britain's trade unions. In a basic sense, this was not a scandal over imperial policy, but rather a vehicle for domestic class competition. In criticizing indentured Chinese labor, the British working class was advocating its own rights to fair employment and condemning the Conservatives for catering to privileged, capitalist interests. In these respects, the "Chinese slavery" controversy culminated the popular resentment against the Balfour government for its handling of the South African war and the war's aftermath.

The Congo reform campaign simultaneously criticized the influence of "capitalists" on government and, more specifically, imperial policy. Yet, in ideological terms, the differences between the protests against "Chinese slavery" and the Congo Free State appear to outweigh the similarities. Most important, the grassroots discourse of the Congo reform campaign was distinctly evangelical, while the critics of "Chinese slavery" generally dwelled in secular terms on economic inequity and class solidarity. While a leading faction within the Congo reform campaign preferred to dwell upon rights, these rights were distinct from those invoked by trade unionists with regard to the Chinese. While Morel dwelled upon the mutual rights of Africans and British merchants, trade unionists clearly subordinated the rights of the Chinese to their own rights to employment and welfare.

These two campaigns were nonetheless linked by strategic alliances, as well as the idiom of slavery. The leadership of the CRA built alliances with nonconformist ministers during and after the 1906 general election. These ministers were already cooperating with trade unionists to bring down the Conservative government, decrying slavery in the Transvaal as both a cause in itself and a means to topple an administration that had instituted education policies which were the nonconformists' primary concern. The nonconformist leaders introduced Morel and his humanitarian allies to leaders of the British labor movement, especially MacDonald. As British labor rose to national political power during and after the 1906 election, MacDonald and others recognized that they needed to expand their political repertoire beyond domestic issues.

MacDonald thus agreed to chair the Parliamentary Congo Committee, not because he saw this as an extension of the "Chinese slavery" debate, but because he needed credentials as an imperial statesman. Unfortunately for the Congo reformers, their newfound access to political power, whether through the Labour Party or through allies in the new Liberal government, did little to advance their cause. The Liberals, for all of their rhetoric, were equally averse to action on the Congo question and the issue of "Chinese slavery."

In addition to strategic alliances, the idiom of slavery joined the Congo question to the "Chinese slavery" controversy. This chapter has shown how different groups in Britain manipulated the definition of slavery to suit their political purposes. While trade unionists and Liberals argued that slavery could be defined by the conditions of labor, the Conservative government asserted that slavery could not exist under a contract into which both parties had freely entered, and that the conditions of the Chinese were essentially humane. Ironically, when the Liberals took power in December 1905, they invoked the sanctity of contract to defend their continuance of Chinese indentured labor in the Transvaal. Some might argue that this change in perspective exposed the insincerity of the Liberals' use of anti-slavery discourse to bolster their electoral campaign. Be that as it may, the "Chinese slavery" controversy elucidates the dynamic, popular currency of anti-slavery politics in Edwardian Britain.

CHAPTER 4

Calculating Virtue: *Cadbury Brothers* and Slavery in Portuguese West Africa, 1901–1913

Cadbury Brothers, Ltd., manufactured cocoa, fine chocolate, and a wholesome image of paternalistic management and benevolent public service. Beginning in 1878, the company constructed its famous "factory in the garden" at Bournville, in the countryside near Birmingham, where it promoted industrial productivity through Christian ethics, a healthy environment, and mutual respect between employers and their employees. In addition to their innovative labor policies, the Cadbury family devoted itself to philanthropy, social reform campaigns, and political leadership in Birmingham. On the national stage, the Cadburys were influential members of the Society of Friends and, after the turn of the century, prominent advocates of the Liberal Party and strong critics of the foreign and imperial policies of the Conservative government of Arthur Balfour.

The Cadbury fortune in the cocoa industry was closely tied to imperial economics and politics. It was therefore not surprising that George Cadbury, who became the Chair of the company in 1900, drew the family into Britain's partisan politics through the controversies over the South African War of 1899–1902. The Balfour government had justified this war as a fight for the rights of British subjects abroad, as a fight for lucrative territories that would generate jobs and other economic benefits for the British working class, and, finally, as a crusade to save Africans from enslavement by the Afrikaners. Critics of the war argued that it primarily served the interests of international financiers who wanted to monopolize South Africa's gold industry. Toward this alleged end, politicians spent the lives of approximately 25,000 of Britain's soldiers and £223 million of British taxpayers' money—after early predictions of a quick and decisive victory. Critics of the war also highlighted reports that British forces had perpetrated atrocities against the Afrikaners under General Kitchener's "scorched earth policy." The civilizing mission of the Empire had apparently degenerated into what the leader of the Liberal Party, Henry Campbell-Bannerman, called "methods of barbarism."[1]

Appalled by this state of affairs, George Cadbury purchased the *Daily News* and transformed the paper into a leading liberal organ of opposition to the imperialist policies of the Balfour government. In the aftermath of the war, the *Daily News* expressed outrage over the government's plan to import "Chinese slaves" to the Transvaal in order to save the colony's failing gold mines. Cadbury's attacks on the Balfour government would eventually provoke counter-attacks against *Cadbury Brothers* by the conservative press, which accused the company of complicity in another new slavery in Africa, this time on the West African plantations from which *Cadbury* purchased a substantial portion of its cocoa.

It was not unusual for the Cadburys to be involved in anti-slavery campaigns. Several members of the family were subscribers to the British and Foreign Anti-Slavery Society, and Joel Cadbury had been on the Anti-Slavery Society's Committee since 1893. As an extension of the Cadburys' opposition to the new slaveries of European imperialism, George Cadbury's nephew, William, would declare himself a supporter of the newly established Congo Reform Association (CRA) in 1904. William Cadbury was, at this time, on the board of *Cadbury Brothers*, with responsibilities ranging from production to purchasing. Just as George Cadbury was prepared to spend large sums in his campaign against "Chinese slavery" in the Transvaal, William Cadbury readily spent large sums in support of the Congo reform campaign. In June 1905, when the CRA was teetering on the brink of financial ruin, William Cadbury made a startling donation of £1,000 to the Secretary of the CRA, E.D. Morel. In the next few years, he and other members of the Cadbury family would donate hundreds of pounds to the CRA, make gifts to Morel and his family, and place the *Daily News* at the service of the Congo reform campaign.

By 1906, the Cadburys had established themselves as public critics of imperialistic exploitation and specifically of the new slaveries of imperial regimes in Africa. Ironically, in this year, *Cadbury Brothers* itself was embroiled in a scandal over its use of cocoa produced by slaves on the plantations of São Tomé and Príncipe in Portuguese West Africa. The board of directors, and especially William Cadbury, had been watching this scandal take shape for over five years, and they had taken tentative steps to pre-empt it. The Cadburys were accustomed to the British press offering positive coverage of their paternalistic management of factory laborers, and they did not want their benevolent image tainted. Their worst fears had been realized, however, when a British journalist, Henry Nevinson, traveled to Portuguese West Africa in 1904 and then published a series of damning articles, titled "The New Slave Trade," in *Harper's Monthly Magazine* between August 1905 and February 1906. Subsequently, Nevinson published a book titled *A Modern Slavery*. Nevinson's findings prompted the *Daily Mail*, among other British newspapers and periodicals, to criticize "large Quaker houses who largely advertise their preparations of cocoa but singularly enough never mention that the main ingredient is obtained by slave labour."[2]

The cocoa controversy sheds light on several aspects of British humanitarianism and imperial politics in the late Victorian and Edwardian eras. As in the Congo scandal, missionaries were the primary sources of information about slavery, but they commonly muted their protests in deference to the Portuguese government, which sanctioned and supported their evangelical work. Also similar to the Congo controversy was the aversion of the Foreign Office to any interference in Portugal's imperial policies. The Foreign Office was determined not to alienate Portugal after the South African War, because it was attempting to recruit laborers from the Portuguese colony of Mozambique to help resolve the labor crisis in the gold mines of the Transvaal. This factor remained important as the cocoa controversy reached its peak between 1906 and 1910, the same period in which the British government was attempting to replace the Chinese laborers who were leaving the Transvaal at the end of their indentures.

The cocoa controversy also exposed divisions within Britain's humanitarian community. Missionary societies, the Aborigines' Protection Society (APS), the Anti-Slavery Society, and the leaders of the Congo reform campaign all agreed that slavery existed in Portuguese West Africa, and that this slavery had a further, direct effect on Africans in the Congo Free State. It was common knowledge among humanitarians that slave traders from Angola purchased and abducted Africans from the territory of the Congo Free State for export to the cocoa plantations of São Tomé and Príncipe. Yet humanitarians divided over whether to criticize *Cadbury Brothers* for purchasing cocoa from these plantations. While H.R. Fox Bourne of the APS called for a boycott of the cocoa plantations, Morel supported William Cadbury's choice to continue purchasing slave-grown cocoa.

The most intriguing features of this controversy in Britain are the machinations of the Cadbury family, and particularly William Cadbury. It appears that the latter deftly exploited the humanitarian campaign against the Congo Free State to distract attention from his company's own slavery scandal in West Africa. Moreover, Cadbury recognized in Morel the skills of a brilliant propagandist and the character of a potential political leader. They began to correspond regarding labor conditions in Portuguese West Africa during 1903, and they met for the first time in 1905. Cadbury's subsequent relationship with

Morel combined sincere friendship and admiration with generous financial patronage. Cadbury contributed funds not only to the Congo reform campaign but also to Morel's family and, later, to Morel's parliamentary career. At the same time, Morel acted as Cadbury's private adviser in the cocoa controversy and publicly supported the controversial purchasing policies of *Cadbury Brothers*. There is evidence that Cadbury and Morel attempted to conceal their alliance in the cocoa controversy, perhaps having recognized the problematic ethics of choosing to combat one new slavery while perpetuating another. When, for instance, *Cadbury Brothers* came under increasing public criticism from the British press and commercial adversaries for its role in Portuguese slavery in 1907, Cadbury discreetly resigned from the Committee of the CRA with Morel's consent.

In 1909, *Cadbury Brothers* sued the *Evening Standard* for libel after the paper accused the company of purposefully exploiting slavery in West Africa. In the trial, *Cadbury v. Standard*, the defense accused *Cadbury Brothers* of bold-faced hypocrisy, arguing that the company had selectively ignored slavery in Portuguese West Africa for its own profit. The defense emphasized the Cadburys' keen awareness and intolerance of slavery on other fronts, recounting the Cadburys' financial support for the Anti-Slavery Society, the APS, and the CRA, as well as the attacks by the *Daily News* against "Chinese slavery" and the Congo Free State.[3] Although *Cadbury Brothers* won its case against the *Standard*, historians have continued to puzzle over the issues raised in the trial, trying to reconcile this imperial scandal with the firm's pristine reputation for meticulous and paternalistic management at Bournville. Charles Dellheim admires Cadbury's industrial management, observing, "The Cadburys practiced benevolence without autocracy and pursued efficiency without turning workers into living tools." Yet in his brief reference to Portuguese slavery he concedes, "Their judgement was dubious and their actions were slow....It is difficult to avoid the conclusion that commercial interests constrained their actions." Geoffrey Nwaka also puzzles over "the embarrassing inconsistency of indirectly subsidizing a system of slavery while professing philanthropy." James Duffy, by contrast, chooses to emphasize Cadbury's cooperation with both private humanitarian organizations and the Foreign Office in combating slavery in Portuguese West Africa. According to Duffy, the Cadburys were uncertain of their course of action and naively agreed not to boycott Portuguese cocoa at the request of the Foreign Office, "not knowing that they were being used to help guarantee a labor force for the South African mines."[4]

While this chapter presents evidence that refutes Duffy's generous portrayal of the Cadburys' uncertainty and naïveté, the objective here is not to reopen a past trial. Historians have had difficulty in situating the cocoa controversy in *Cadbury's* history because they have chosen to accept *Cadbury's* benevolent, carefully crafted image as a realistic measure of ethical conduct in its business dealings. In fact, the significance of the cocoa controversy lies in the Cadburys' efforts to reconcile their aversion to slavery with sound business policy. More specifically, this chapter illuminates how William Cadbury made strategic use of humanitarian politics and thus displayed a common tension between commercial interests and the principles in anti-slavery protest. Cadbury's role in the cocoa controversy makes sense only in relation to other humanitarian controversies over new slaveries in Africa, and only with due consideration of the company's domestic priorities, which extended beyond simple profits. *Cadbury Brothers* was certainly successful from the standpoint of its profits, as sales rose from £1,057 million in 1905 to £2,346 million in 1914.[5] But William Cadbury's calculations involved more than these numbers. It must be said that Cadbury did not regard the labor conditions on São Tomé and Príncipe as a form of slavery comparable to the atrocities on the Congo or the conditions in the gold mines of the Transvaal. Moreover, in evaluating acquisition policies in West Africa, he consistently prioritized production at home. *Cadburys* required cocoa of specific grades, and they did not have an alternative, sufficient supply that compared in quality with the cocoa of Portuguese West Africa.

Clearly, an immediate boycott would have had a detrimental effect on the works at Bournville, prompting the company to lay off several hundred employees on a temporary basis. Given these considerations, William Cadbury chose to bide his time and seek alternative sources of cocoa. By 1907, he had found a viable alternative in Britain's Gold Coast Colony, where *Cadbury Brothers* had already begun to nurture young cocoa plantations that came to maturity in 1909. That same year coincidentally witnessed a sudden drop in the prices of raw cocoa worldwide, and *Cadbury* seized this moment to initiate a boycott of cocoa from Portuguese West Africa, replacing this significant part of its supply with cocoa from the Gold Coast.

Slavery in Portuguese West Africa

The small, volcanic islands of São Tomé and Príncipe lie off the West Coast of Africa in the Gulf of Guinea. Portugal laid claim to these islands in the fifteenth century, and the islands subsequently served as supply centers for Portuguese merchant vessels and as sites for sugar plantations cultivated by slaves from the mainland. By the seventeenth century, the Portuguese devoted the islands entirely to provisioning the heavy traffic of slave ships *en route* to Europe and the Americas. Two centuries later, the plantation owners turned to the production of coffee in response to the decline in slave traffic, which had been caused by Great Britain's abolition of the slave trade in 1807. After Portugal signed an anti-slave trade treaty with Britain in 1842, coffee production became all the more important, and in the 1850s a handful of plantations began to experiment with the production of cocoa. Cocoa remained a minor commodity in the islands' economy until the 1880s, when lucrative markets for this product developed in Great Britain, Germany, and the United States.[6] This increasing demand for cocoa in the late nineteenth century created a booming economy on São Tomé and Príncipe, far out-stripping exports such as coffee and rubber from Portugal's traditional West African stronghold, Angola. As Gervase Clarence-Smith observes, the cocoa from these small islands made them "the pearls of the empire in this period," but these same islands also became political liabilities as revelations of slavery strained Portugal's international relations.[7]

The Portuguese government had declared slavery to be illegal in its colonial territories in 1869, largely in response to international humanitarian pressure. The government had no intention, however, of undermining its colonies' economies, and its abolitionist policies over the next forty years exhibited more semantic dexterity than practical affect. It is noteworthy that the government was further deterred from an aggressive abolitionist policy by a major economic depression that hit Portugal in 1873. By the 1890s, the government was struggling to avoid bankruptcy and to save the country's industrial and shipping firms from ruin. In these difficult circumstances, cocoa from the islands of São Tomé and Príncipe, and rubber from Angola, provided significant relief to the nation's economy.[8]

After 1869, slaves in the Portuguese empire were to become *libertos*, but their liberty was to be suspended until formal emancipation on April 29, 1878. An official decree on April 29, 1875, abolished the legal category of *liberto*, effective in 1876. Africans were still to remain subject to governmental "tutelage" until April 29, 1878, when they would become *serviçaes*, or contract laborers. British consular officials in Portuguese Africa did not find that these legal reforms provoked any actual changes in the labor conditions and lives of Africans.[9] "Lisbon thus played a double game," Clarence-Smith comments, "pacifying international philanthropic pressure groups by a facade of abolition, while saving the planters and fishermen from ruin by allowing *de facto* slavery to continue."[10]

Slavery remained the dominant mode of labor in Portuguese West Africa from 1878 until 1911, a year after the seizure of power in Lisbon by a reform-minded republican government. In the meantime, Africans were bound to their previous conditions of enslavement in three ways. First, emancipated slaves were required to sign labor contracts with their "redeemers" for a maximum of five years. "This provision of the law," Clarence-Smith explains, "was used not only to bind ex-slaves to their former masters, but also to enable the continued buying of slaves from African dealers, the price of purchase being now described in humanitarian terms as the cost of redeeming slaves from barbaric servitude."[11] These contracts were to be voluntary, but slaves commonly refused to sign, demanding instead their certificates of manumission. Slave resistance to the contract system escalated between 1877 and 1879, breaking into open violence and finally prompting imperial officials to impose contracts without signatures of acceptance.[12] The second method which employers used to keep their laborers was a process of automatic recontracting at the end of five years. Although this process was illegal, the imperial regime permitted it to continue. Likewise, the regime was complicit in perpetuating slavery through a third method: an illegal system of subcontracting.[13]

Portuguese and African labor agents traveled up to 800 miles inland through Angola to purchase slaves. These slaves were often drawn from the territory of the Congo Free State known as the Garenganze, or the Katanga District. Africans would be obtained from chiefs or rebel soldiers in exchange for guns, ammunition, and cloth, despite the opposition of Congo Free State officials.[14] Slaves were then marched to the coast, passing through the Portuguese fort at Mashiko, then across the Hungry Country, a sparsely inhabited region stretching approximately 250 miles to the Luanza River. After crossing the Luanza, the caravans followed one of the oldest slave routes in West Africa through the Bié district and finally to the port at Benguela.[15] Here the slave agents sold the Africans as "contract laborers," and the Africans signed mandatory five-year contracts of service.[16]

Prior to embarkation for the islands, each slave received a tin disk with his or her registration number, the initials of the agent, and sometimes the name of the island to which he or she was bound. Each slave also received a tin cylinder with a copy of his or her registration form, listing the year of contract, his or her number, name, birthplace, chief's name, agent's name, and miscellaneous observations.[17] Finally, Portuguese officials distributed cotton clothing, usually patterned with distinctive blue and white horizontal stripes.

An estimated 70,000 people were purchased for export to São Tomé and Príncipe between 1880 and 1908.[18] There were more men than women, but planters attempted to achieve balanced sex ratios among their laborers for procreation.[19] On São Tomé and Príncipe these Africans joined thousands of other laborers from central Africa. At the turn of the century, the population of São Tomé was approximately 35,000, of whom 18,000 were men and women from Angola and the Congo Free State. There were 2,500 Europeans and 3,500 free Africans, called Angolares and Gregorianos, who had been emancipated or were the descendants of emancipated African migrants. There were also over 11,000 indigenous inhabitants of the islands, who did not work on the plantations, as well as an assortment of migrant laborers from Dahomey, Gabon, the Cape Verde Islands, Mozambique, Liberia, British West Africa, and southwestern China.[20] The ratio of European administrators to Africans on the islands was always low, and even in the late 1800s it was only about 1 to 30. Poor whites generally managed the work gangs on the plantations; the foremen were African contract laborers, often of different ethnic origins than those whom they supervised.[21] While the great majority of laborers from these other locations departed at the conclusion of one-to-three-year contracts, those from central Africa remained on the islands indefinitely as their contracts were automatically renewed. Moreover, the children of these laborers were born into servitude, making the system, as Clarence-Smith observes, "even more akin to straight slavery."[22]

Labor conditions on the islands improved over time, but the work remained difficult in the hot, damp climate, which rendered Africans and Europeans prone to diseases such as malaria and sleeping sickness. Prior to the growth of the cocoa industry, and even after it came to dominate the islands' economy, Africans produced a variety of exports including coffee, sugarcane, vanilla, rubber, coconuts, and cinchona trees (the bark of which was used to make quinine, an anti-malarial drug). In the early years of the cocoa plantations, the hardest work for laborers was transporting heavy sacks of cocoa on their heads and constructing the islands' infrastructure of light railways and roads. The completion of the railways served to alleviate much of the worst labor, so after 1900 the hardest work for most people was digging holes for new plants. Laborers generally worked 9.5 to 10.5 hours a day, and several hours on Sunday, though this was supposed to be a day of rest.[23]

The planters claimed to pay their laborers monthly wages, but in fact they devised numerous means to avoid paying these meager wages in full. They imposed fines for supposed misconduct, they deducted money for illness, and they often did not pay laborers in currency, but in tokens redeemable at stores owned by the planters themselves.[24] Until the 1890s, rations were often poor in quality, with inadequate protein. Also, plantation owners did not provide adequate clothing to their laborers—although they were required to do so by law—and housing was commonly overcrowded and unsanitary. Fortunately, the planters began to remedy the latter three problems at the turn of the century by distributing adequate rations and clothing, and by providing laborers with small houses built of wood, with concrete floors and corrugated iron roofs. It appears that the planters were prompted to take these measures by the high death rates of laborers on the islands, a trend that planters also tried to counter by fostering the growth of families, following marriages commonly arranged under the planters' authority.[25]

At the same time that these changes occurred in the living conditions of laborers on São Tomé and Príncipe, health care remained inadequate and education was nonexistent, except for boys whom the planters chose to become artisans. Religious instruction in Catholicism was a legal duty of the planters, but most were ambivalent if not opposed to this. There were no missionary stations on the islands at the turn of the century, and laborers generally pursued their own religious practices.[26]

Restrictions on movement and land rights, as well as tyrannical modes of law enforcement, were also regular features of the laborer's life. Laborers had to get permission to leave their estates, and planters commonly locked workers in their dwellings at night, even on the large estates which were patrolled by dogs and surveyed by guards in watch towers. Authority on the plantations was regularly enforced by corporal punishment, ranging from kicks and punches to flogging and torture.[27] Clarence-Smith concludes:

> Labour conditions altered markedly over the period 1875 to 1914, but the planters did not make an effective transition to free labour, and changes were not always seen as improvements by the workers....Although the evidence is fragmentary, it would seem that workers would have preferred more leisure time, more access to land, more control over their labour, and, above all, a measure of real personal freedom.[28]

British Views on Slavery in Portuguese West Africa

Stories of Portuguese slavery had long since circulated in Britain. In the middle decades of the nineteenth century, missionaries and explorers such as Dr. David Livingstone and Lieutenant Verney Lovett Cameron published critical reports on Portuguese slavery in both East and West Africa.[29] Cameron observed that the Portuguese slave trade was still proceeding at the outset of the scramble for Africa in the 1870s:

> Indeed, the cruelties perpetuated in the heart of Africa by men calling themselves Christians and carrying the Portuguese flag can scarcely be credited by those living in a civilised land; and the Government of Portugal cannot be cognizant of the atrocities commited by men claiming to be her subjects.[30]

At the same time, the Foreign Office was specifically investigating Portugal's exportation of slaves to the coffee plantations on São Tomé. The Foreign Office abandoned its inquiries in May 1878, however, when its legal advisers determined that Britain had no grounds for intervention under the treaty of 1842, since the laborers were no longer technically slaves, but *serviçaes*. "The lead on this issue," observes James Duffy, "now passed out of the Foreign Office into the hands of the philanthropists, never to be regained."[31]

In subsequent decades, the Foreign Office displayed no interest in revisiting the issue of slavery in Portuguese West Africa. In 1894, Joseph A. Pease, a member of the newly established Friends' Anti-Slavery Committee, informed the Foreign Office that he had heard from a Liverpool firm that slaves were being exported from Angola to São Tomé.[32] The subsequent Foreign Office inquiry produced a damning report on forced labor by the British Consul at

Luanda, W. Pickersgill. One of the minutes on this report states, "The question is whether we should now in any form renew our efforts in favour of the natives. Slavery is nominally abolished in the Portuguese colonies, and I think for the present we had better leave it alone." The Foreign Secretary, Lord Kimberley, wrote simply, "I agree."[33]

The British and Foreign Anti-Slavery Society had made complaints against Portuguese slave trading and slavery throughout its existence, and continued to do so well into the twentieth century. On these abolitionist grounds, the society opposed the Anglo–Portuguese Treaty of 1884, joining merchants and missionaries who had their own interests at stake. As discussed in chapter 1, British merchants opposed Portugal's protectionist trade policies, while missionaries were wary of Portugal's sectarian discrimination. All critics of the treaty used anti-slavery rhetoric to enhance the moral authority of their claims, and São Tomé figured prominently in the ensuing debates. The Reverend William Holman Bentley of the Baptist Missionary Society (BMS) published an indictment of Portuguese slavery in *The Times* of April 14, 1884. In his private correspondence, Bentley's calculated use of slavery was exposed by his preoccupation with Portugal's sectarian policies, which had already caused problems for the BMS at San Salvador.[34] The reader might also recall Bentley's comparatively complacent view toward slavery on the Congo at this same time.

Over the next thirty years, the British abolitionist attacks against Portugal would depend increasingly upon the evidence provided by missionaries.[35] In the mid-1880s, it was common knowledge among the small number of British missionaries in central Africa that Portugal sanctioned a slave trade to the plantations of São Tomé and Príncipe. Although the BMS was the most vocal critic of Portugal at this time, it was the missionaries of the Plymouth Brethren who would have the most contact with Portuguese slavery in the years ahead.

The pioneering missionary of the Plymouth Brethren in Africa was Frederick Stanley Arnot, who arrived in South Africa in 1881. Three years later, he traveled through Angola to the coast at Benguela, then returned inland to establish a station in the Garenganze region of the Congo Free State in 1886.[36] In December 1887, Arnot was joined by Charles Swan and W.L. Faulknor, and over the next ten years he coordinated the arrivals of dozens of other male and female missionaries, who established a thin string of stations between Garenganze and the Angolan coast. Like the missionaries on the Congo River, the Brethren perceived and responded to slavery in terms of their evangelical priorities and their logistical dependence on others. It appears, however, that their logistical concerns were more complicated, since they depended on four different groups: local African leaders in Garenganze, the Congo Free State, the Ovimbundu traders of Bié in Angola, and the Portuguese imperial regime.

Arnot's first mission station in Garenganze was based at the court of Msiri, the most powerful ruler in the region. As Robert Rotberg demonstrates, the missionary's role was often that of a trading liaison, clerk, doctor, and token of Msiri's power, rather than that of an evangelist.[37] Arnot and other Brethren stood by in silent disgust as Msiri meted out brutal punishments to his subjects and distributed slaves as the spoils of his wars. In an attempt to combat slavery on a small scale, Arnot would occasionally purchase children, as on one occasion when he bought a little girl, paying for her with a young goat.[38] On the whole, however, the missionaries did not contradict Msiri, and they struck a neutral posture when the Congo Free State challenged Msiri's authority. After a state official murdered Msiri in December 1891, the Brethren immediately shifted their loyalties. "No longer were they beholden to the great chief," observes Rotberg, "but with his death, and with the dismantling of his kingdom, anarchy prevailed in Katanga [Garenganze]. The missionaries therefore looked to the Belgian military establishment for the restoration of order."[39]

In traveling to Garenganze, the Brethren required the assistance of porters to carry their supplies. A standard missionary caravan consisted of 200–300 porters, and porters were in chronically short supply. One major obstacle to obtaining porters was the fact that the Ovimbundu traders in Bié used most of the available porters to carry rubber and ivory from the interior. Arnot and other missionaries hired the Ovimbundu traders to provide porters for their trips into the interior, although the great majority of these porters were slaves—a fact that the Brethren overlooked in their publications. Whether due to inconvenience or conscience, the Brethren looked forward to the construction of railways and steamers, which only the Portuguese imperial regime could provide.[40]

Occasionally, one finds a letter highly critical of Ovimbundu slavery in the Brethren journal, *Echoes of Service*, such as that by Dugald Campbell, who wrote from Chilonda in Bié on September 16, 1893:

> The Ovimbundu have large numbers of slaves in their villages, whom they buy with cloth in the far off Luba and Lunda countries. These do most of the work, at least, the dirtiest and hardest. The big and strong are usually taken to Benguella, and are there sold to the white men and shipped elsewhere like so many head of cattle. It has saddened me at different times to see a large caravan of slaves coming from the far interior....Our hearts rise to God in prayer that the day may be near when He shall have put an end to this vile practice of one man selling another for gain.[41]

For all of his outrage, Campbell did not advocate missionary interference in Ovimbundu slave traffic, but rather God's intervention.

As time passed, the Brethren became increasingly frustrated with the interference of the slave trade in their evangelical work. Their frustration focused on both the slavers and the enslaved. For example, William Lewis in Bié complained that his meetings were poorly attended because Ovimbundu villagers went off to the interior for slaves. By contrast, Lizzie Brayshaw complained that slave raids in the interior made it difficult to establish relations with the Africans there. Recounting her travels with a missionary party, she remarked that it was difficult even to buy supplies from local communities. She and other women went to a village to reassure the people of their benevolent intentions, but, she recalled, "they fled into their huts and shut the doors, the children screaming: that is owing to the white man's doings."[42]

"Labour of the Very Best Kind": *Cadbury Brothers* and Slave-Grown Cocoa

In 1913 the Reverend John and Alice Harris, the Joint Organizing Secretaries of the British and Foreign Anti-Slavery and Aborigines' Protection Society, published a book titled *Portuguese Slavery: Britain's Dilemma*. Looking back on the controversy over slavery in Portuguese West Africa, the Harrises observed: "It is somewhat difficult to discover the exact date when the three principal cocoa firms of England had serious misgivings upon the methods by which much of their raw cocoa was produced." At one time, the Harrises explained, "an acrimonious controversy" had centered upon this issue.[43]

One can actually say with certainty that in the 1890s the Foreign Office, the Anti-Slavery Society, the APS, the Friends' Anti-Slavery Committee, the BMS, and the Plymouth Brethren all perceived that slaves worked on the cocoa plantations of São Tomé and Príncipe. Yet the Cadburys, who began to purchase cocoa from São Tomé and Príncipe in 1886, claimed that they had no "definite knowledge" of slavery on the islands prior to the turn of the century.

This controversy eventually faded in the British humanitarian community and the press, but it was never resolved. Over the course of more than forty-five years, William Cadbury gave inconsistent accounts about how he and his company became aware of labor problems on São Tomé and Príncipe. For example, in July 1904, Cadbury explained to Harry Johnston, a former imperial official and prominent Africanist, that slavery on the islands had been brought to his attention in 1902 when a missionary from Angola, M.Z. Stober, visited Bournville to discuss the issue.[44] Two years later, Cadbury informed his company's international sales staff that his attention had been directed to the "unsatisfactory labor conditions" on the islands by a Foreign Office report of 1902, followed by the meeting with Stober.[45] Finally, in a peculiar document written in November 1949 and titled "A Private Inside History of the Connection of *Cadbury Bros., Ltd.,* with African Slavery," Cadbury explains that he reported rumors of labor problems on the islands to *Cadbury's* board of directors after his return from a business trip to Trinidad in 1901. In the following year, according to Cadbury, they received definitive proof in the form of a sales catalog for an estate on São Tomé that listed 200 African laborers for sale with the land, machinery, tools, and cattle of the estate.[46]

Cadbury's papers indicate that he received the offer of the estate on São Tomé in mid-April 1901. He raised this issue with the board of directors on April 30, and the board responded by approving the following minute: "S. Thome, conditions of labour on Cocoa Estates. We agree to assist in the investigations, and if need be the publication of the facts of the case, through the Anti-Slavery Society or otherwise, and W.A.C. is directed in the first place to see Joseph Sturge or Wm. A. Albright and seek advice in the matter." On the next day, Cadbury wrote a letter to Sturge, the scion of a famous family of abolitionists, in which he remarked upon the labor situation on São Tomé:

> One looks at these matters in a different light when it affects one's own interests, but I do feel that there is a vast difference between the cultivation of cocoa and gold or diamond mining, and I should be sorry needlessly to injure a cultivation that as far as I can judge provides labour of the very best kind to be found in the tropics.[47]

Given Cadbury's ambivalent view toward slavery in Portuguese West Africa, he chose to delay the company's action upon the issue, while at the same time entering into dialogue with the Secretary of the Anti-Slavery Society, Travers Buxton. It appears that in the first half of 1902, Buxton arranged a meeting between Cadbury and Stober, who was in charge of the Angola Evangelical Mission, a small and relatively poor mission that practiced evangelism through faith healing.[48] Stober had been in contact with Buxton since at least 1900, and he likewise provided Cadbury with his eyewitness accounts of the slave trade to São Tomé and Príncipe.[49]

Cadbury was reluctant to take action upon Stober's testimony. Contrary to the conviction that was displayed in the board's minute of April 30, 1901, Cadbury remarked to Buxton:

> I do not feel myself called upon to take any initial step in the matter, though I am willing to help in any organized plan that your Society may suggest for the definite purpose of putting a stop to the slave trade of this district. I should think that the Scotch missionary from Angola [Stober] would be more probably a help to you, and if there are sufficient missionaries settled in the district, their own quiet work is perhaps the best means of attaining the end.[50]

At odds with Cadbury's desire for "quiet work" toward labor reform in Portuguese West Africa, his missionary informant, Stober, was intent on publicizing his cause in Britain. Perhaps in response to Cadbury's reticence, Stober sought out Fox Bourne of the APS for an interview in early June 1902.[51]

On the basis of his conversation with Stober, Fox Bourne sent a memorandum to the Foreign Office, urging the Secretary of State to demand labor reforms in Portuguese West Africa on the grounds that many Portuguese slaves were obtained from the Congo basin, in violation of the Berlin Act. Fox Bourne linked Portuguese slavery to his previous protests against slavery and atrocities in the Congo Free State, expressing his hope that "the abuses now referred to will be regarded by His Majesty's Government as furnishing additional reason for the enquiry into violations of the international obligations which have been the subject of recent appeals from the Aborigines' Protection Society."[52] The Foreign Office forwarded Fox Bourne's letter to its consular official on the Congo, Roger Casement, who confirmed that Africans were purchased or abducted from the Congo Free State territory to become slaves in Angola, São Tomé, and Príncipe.[53]

The Foreign Office did not investigate labor policies in Portuguese West Africa more closely, given its priorities elsewhere. As discussed in the preceding chapter, Britain's newly acquired Transvaal Colony was struggling through a labor crisis in the aftermath of the South African War. In cooperation with the Colonial Office, the Foreign Office was at this time attempting to secure access to African laborers in the Portuguese colony of Mozambique. The Foreign Office was fully aware that a dispute over Portuguese labor policies in West Africa would interfere with its efforts to secure labor from Mozambique for the benefit of the Transvaal.[54]

Although the British government declined to pressure the Portuguese government for labor reforms in West Africa, the Colonial Ministry in Lisbon remained sensitive to private humanitarian and commercial protests from Britain. After June 1902, slavery on São Tomé and Príncipe became a regular feature of protests by the APS and the Anti-Slavery Society. At the same time, protests arose from Portuguese colonists in Angola, who were motivated by a combination of moralistic indignation over the continuance of slavery on Portuguese soil and resentment over the loss of labor to the islands. In early 1903, the Portuguese Governor-General in Angola responded with a highly publicized crackdown on slavery, indicting twenty-seven colonial officials and merchants.[55] In the same period, the Colonial Ministry in Lisbon made several legal reforms to discourage the abduction and coercion of laborers and to secure repatriation from São Tomé and Príncipe to the mainland. The enforcement of these reforms was weak, however, because the Ministry gave the administrative control over the reforms to the plantation owners.

In the light of the Portuguese reforms of 1903, and under pressure from the APS and the Anti-Slavery Society, William Cadbury traveled to Lisbon in March with Stober to consult with the Portuguese Colonial Minister and the plantation owners, who assured him that the Portuguese would improve conditions on the islands and institute a reliable system of repatriation. Cadbury sought the advice of the British minister in Lisbon, Sir Martin Gosselin, who advised him to wait and see what effect the promised reforms might have. Gosselin shared Cadbury's desire not to alienate the Portuguese, for just as Cadbury wished to maintain his company's supply of raw cocoa, Gosselin had been instructed by the Foreign Office to persuade Portugal to allow the Transvaal mine owners to recruit laborers from Angola.[56] Gosselin suggested that Cadbury could best exert influence for reform as a large purchaser of cocoa. Gosselin and Cadbury agreed that *Cadbury Brothers'* leverage lay in its threat to boycott Portuguese cocoa, and they overlooked the diminishing returns of a threat that would never be exercised.[57]

In May 1903, following his return from Lisbon, Cadbury began to search for a man to travel to Portuguese West Africa and assess the effects of Portugal's labor reforms. It is curious that he did not choose Stober for this task, since Stober had the languages and experience that would have enabled him to conduct an informed inquiry. Clearly, Stober was one of the few missionaries prepared to criticize the Portuguese regime, and it was probably for this reason that he and Cadbury parted ways. It appears likely that Stober became suspicious of Cadbury when he watched him interacting on friendly terms with plantation owners and officials in Lisbon, and Cadbury was no doubt annoyed by Stober's skepticism and impatience. In searching for a more tractable emissary, Cadbury consulted with Fox Bourne, the Liverpool merchant John Holt, and, for the first time, Morel.[58]

In October 1904, the journalist Henry Nevinson contacted Cadbury and explained that he had been commissioned by *Harper's Monthly Magazine* to travel to Angola, São Tomé, and Príncipe to investigate reports of slavery. He offered to serve as Cadbury's commissioner as well. Cadbury declined the offer, on the grounds that he wanted an investigator with knowledge of the Portuguese language, which Nevinson did not have, and that Nevinson's proposed trip of six months was too brief.[59] It is also likely that Cadbury recognized Nevinson as an opportunist who would likely produce a report of a sensational nature.

Cadbury sought a commissioner who would comply with his dilatory strategies, be acceptable to the Portuguese plantation owners, and yet be able to produce a cogent report that would spare *Cadbury Brothers* from accusations of a cover-up. With these objectives in mind, he selected Joseph Burtt, a fellow member of the Society of Friends and a personal friend for twenty years. Cadbury explained to Fox Bourne:

> We think it is extremely important that he should go as the friend of the planters, with the fullest introductions to all parts of the islands, and his visit will not be hurried. We think in this way he will see very much more than it would be possible for a representative of any philanthropic Society, who would be treated on arrival as a spy.

In view of Burtt's impending investigation, Cadbury implored the APS and the Anti-Slavery Society to suspend their public protests against Portuguese slavery, "as we fear it might seriously prejudice the planters to him and lessen the value of his visit." Yet Cadbury had already arranged Burtt's visit to West Africa in full cooperation with the cocoa proprietors, who still regarded Cadbury as a reliable business associate rather than a political adversary. Perhaps to demonstrate his humanitarian solidarity with Fox Bourne, Cadbury enclosed with his letter a subscription of £15 for the APS.[60]

As Burtt departed for Portugal to begin several months of language training, Cadbury turned his attention to countering Nevinson's imminent report on Portuguese West Africa in *Harper's*. He found an ally in Morel, with whom he had been in correspondence for almost two years. Morel opposed any public controversy over Portuguese slavery, just as he opposed agitation against "Chinese slavery" in the Transvaal, because he believed that these controversies would undermine his own Congo reform campaign. Moreover, in Morel's opinion, the cases of slavery in Portuguese West Africa and the Congo Free State were not comparable in their gravity, so he had no interest in linking them together, as Fox Bourne wished to do. Morel's desire to stifle the Portuguese slavery scandal fit perfectly into Cadbury's own agenda. In publicizing the Congo reform campaign, Cadbury could simultaneously engage in a moral crusade and distract attention from the controversy growing over his own company.

Beginning in February 1905, Cadbury took an active role in bolstering the Congo reform campaign. Initially, he introduced Morel to prosperous members of the Society of Friends, including his fellow cocoa magnates, the Rowntrees and Frys, and he orchestrated the first coverage of Congo Free State atrocities in the journal *The Friend*. Morel recognized Cadbury as a potential benefactor, and he complained pitifully to Cadbury in early 1905 about the inadequate funding of the CRA. In the first week of April, Morel told Cadbury that he had informed the CRA Committee that he required £500 to cover the costs of the organization's expenses for the current fiscal year.[61] On June 26, as the CRA stood on the verge of collapse, and as *Cadbury Brothers* anticipated the publication of Nevinson's damning exposé, Cadbury met with Morel for the first time and donated a staggering £1,000 to the CRA.[62] Less than two weeks later, Cadbury promised to pay Morel "as editor of the *West African Mail*, the sum of £50 per quarter for the next two years," a salary which accounted for more than one-third of Morel's personal income during this period. Cadbury remarked, "It will be a private understanding between you and myself, and I do not wish my name mentioned to anyone outside."[63]

Cadbury's largesse would continue throughout the remainder of Morel's life. In 1908, for example, Cadbury gave Morel £100 for the education of Morel's eldest son, Roger (who had been named after Roger Casement).[64] In 1911, Morel received a public testimonial of £5,000 for his work in the

Congo reform campaign, of which Cadbury donated over £1,000. In April 1912, Cadbury encouraged Morel to run for Parliament and promised a personal income of £800 a year, plus £400 for each electoral campaign. In the event of Morel's death, Cadbury promised to provide Morel's wife, Mary, with an annual income of £500 until their youngest son turned twenty-one, and £300 a year thereafter.[65]

Fox Bourne, unaware of the growing rapport between Cadbury and Morel in the summer of 1905, continued to encourage Cadbury and the Foreign Office to link the Congo and Portuguese slavery controversies, and thus demand reforms from the Portuguese regime under the terms of the Berlin Act.[66] By this time, however, Cadbury had already secured Morel as a strong ally against this strategy. Morel wrote to Cadbury in August 1905:

> I hope the Portuguese inquiry will not lead people off the Congo State scent; bad as the plantation business may be in Portuguese Congo, San Thome etc; it is as nothing compared with the situation in the Congo State…. People will not understand the difference between (I) plantation servitude or slavery if you like (II) slave raiding for those plantations (III) the enslavement of the African in his own home under the Congolese system—which is infinitely worse than the others; in fact cannot be mentioned in the same breath with them.[67]

In the years ahead, Morel would privately urge Fox Bourne, Nevinson, John Harris and others not to criticize *Cadbury Brothers*, and he occasionally took public stands on *Cadbury's* behalf.[68] The Cadburys simultaneously provided Morel with funding and placed the *Daily News* in the service of Congo reform.

Nevinson published a series of articles, under the title "The New Slave Trade," in *Harper's* between August 1905 and February 1906, followed quickly by the publication of his book, *A Modern Slavery.* "In this account," Nevinson explains, "I only mean to show that the difference between the 'contract labour' of Angola, and the old-fashioned slavery of our grandfathers' time is only a difference in legal terms."[69] Nevinson then recounted the system of slavery in Portuguese West Africa and the regime's threats and methods of control which had deterred protests by some missionaries. "How can missionaries of either division [Protestant or Catholic] risk the things they have most at heart by speaking out upon a dangerous question? They are silent, though their conscience is uneasy."[70] Nevinson recalled that at Benguela he had passed forty-three men and women being escorted by armed guards to the port for shipment to São Tomé and Príncipe:

> Thus it is that the islands of San Thomé and Principe have been rendered about the most profitable bits of the earth's surface, and England and America can get their chocolate and cocoa cheap.[71]

Nevinson's exposé provoked humanitarian declarations in Parliament and calls for a British boycott of slave-grown cocoa. With pressure mounting, George and William Cadbury met with the Foreign Secretary, Sir Edward Grey, on October 27, 1906. Grey urged them not to join in the public protest against Portuguese West Africa, and certainly not to boycott Portuguese cocoa, until they had received Burtt's report and permitted the Portuguese government to respond. It is noteworthy that Grey had every incentive to conciliate Portugal. The new Liberal government was struggling to fulfill its promise to offer repatriation to the indentured Chinese in the Transvaal, and it was attempting to replace the Chinese with laborers from Portuguese territories in East, and now West, Africa. George Cadbury wrote later on the same day, "We should be glad to agree to such a suggestion."[72]

Burtt had departed for Africa in June 1905, and received a warm welcome from the Portuguese cocoa proprietors and colonial officials. He stayed at over forty *roças* on São Tomé and Príncipe for over five and a half months, then spent four months in Angola, traveling 800 miles inland. He next proceeded to southern Africa, where he completed the draft of his report before returning to England in April 1907. William Cadbury submitted Burtt's report to the Foreign Office, which then forwarded it to the Portuguese government, which delayed its response until October.[73] Burtt confirmed the existence of slavery on São Tomé and Príncipe and concluded his report by observing:

> I am satisfied that under the serviçal system as it exists at present thousands of black men and women are, against their will, and often under circumstances of great cruelty, taken away every year from their homes and transported across the sea to work on unhealthy islands, from which they never return. If this is not slavery, I know of no word in the English language which correctly characterizes it.[74]

Burtt's findings prompted an investigation by the Portuguese themselves. The Colonial Minister, Augusto de Castilho, sent Lieutenant-Captain Francisco Paula Cid, a former governor of Benguela and São Tomé, to conduct the inquiry. Neither the British Foreign Office nor the colonists in Angola had faith in Paula Cid's objectivity and judgment.[75]

Burtt's report provoked a shift in Cadbury's approach to slavery in Portuguese West Africa. Although Cadbury and the Foreign Office withheld Burtt's report from publication throughout 1907, Burtt's findings could not be ignored. *Cadbury Brothers* could not reasonably continue to support a labor system which both the British government and its own investigator had identified as slavery. Cadbury had no reason to anticipate a wave of substantial reforms from the Portuguese regime, and so, in the near future, the company would have to stop purchasing cocoa from São Tomé and Príncipe or face public condemnation.

Cadbury began to search in earnest for an alternative source of cocoa in Africa in 1907. Holt pointed Cadbury toward the Gold Coast, and Cadbury dispatched one of his company's cocoa experts, William Leslie, from Trinidad to evaluate the potential for cocoa plantations on the Gold Coast in September 1907. Meanwhile, in Britain, *Cadbury Brothers* invoked its deference to Foreign Office policy in explaining why it had not boycotted slave-grown cocoa from Portuguese West Africa. This explanation apparently satisfied British humanitarians until the early summer, when voices of discontentment began to rise within their ranks, inspired by the continuing protests of Nevinson and Stober. In June, Fox Bourne of the APS proposed to begin a public agitation, explaining to Cadbury that five years was long enough to wait for real reforms.[76] Buxton of the Anti-Slavery Society was also becoming restless, and Cadbury found that his deference to the Foreign Office was beginning to appear disingenuous.

In view of the remarkable revival and success of the Congo reform campaign, Cadbury had reason to fear a "public agitation" against his own company. He was especially concerned about the influence that Nevinson and Stober might exert through the British press and commercial circles. In late July 1907, Cadbury began to confer with the other British cocoa manufacturers, *J.S. Fry and Sons* and *Rowntree and Company*, about a recent rumor that Nevinson was preparing another critical article about Portuguese West Africa for publication in the *Fortnightly Review*. Within a week, *Rowntree* sent its solicitor, who was a personal acquaintance of Nevinson's, to attempt to convince the journalist not to criticize the cocoa manufacturers in this piece, which was due to be published in September.[77]

Late in the summer, Holt informed Cadbury that Stober was consulting with the Liverpool shipping magnate Sir Alfred Jones about Portuguese slavery.[78] Jones was the President of the African Section of the Liverpool Chamber of Commerce and the most important Consul of the Congo Free State in Great Britain. Cadbury must have been alarmed by this news, given his disintegrating support among the humanitarian community and the imminent publication of Nevinson's article in the *Fortnightly Review*. The prospect of a public attack by Jones and the Liverpool Chamber of Commerce prompted Cadbury to write to Morel on September 14, 1907:

> I want you to get me relieved from the Congo Committee [i.e., the Executive Committee of the CRA] when the right time comes. I can do more good quietly just now, particularly with folk interesting themselves in the Angola matter.[79]

Two weeks later, Jones called a meeting of the Liverpool Chamber of Commerce to hear testimonies regarding slavery in Portuguese West Africa by Stober and Nevinson. The Chamber passed a resolution calling for a boycott of slave-grown cocoa. Cadbury remarked afterward, "Sir Alfred Jones will do all he can to boom the Angola affair with a view of quieting interest in the Congo," and he blamed Stober for bringing Jones into the controversy.[80] Indeed, the Liverpool resolution did provoke renewed attention to *Cadbury Brothers* and Portuguese slavery in the British press. On October 3, 1907, the *Daily Graphic* published an article titled "Slave Grown Cocoa, Responsibility of the Quaker Manufacturers." *Cadbury Brothers* threatened a libel suit, and the *Daily Graphic* published an apology on October 24.

Cadbury met with the Liverpool Chamber of Commerce on October 22 to refute the charges by Stober and Nevinson and to offer his own explanations. Morel had already prepared the ground for Cadbury with the cooperation of Holt, who gave an impassioned speech, which Morel had written, in Cadbury's defense.[81] Despite the continuing criticism from Jones, the Chamber withdrew its previous resolution, expressing support for *Cadbury Brothers*, although Cadbury himself saw this as a Pyrrhic victory.

With his company under increasing pressure, Cadbury returned to Lisbon and met with government officials and cocoa proprietors in late 1907. The extent of *Cadbury's* previous cooperation with the proprietors was reflected in their indignation over the critical nature of Burtt's report on their activities. As Cadbury reported, the proprietors were angry that he had given "our report" to the government, turning "a private investigation into an international matter." Cadbury explained that his company was under growing humanitarian pressure, and the cocoa proprietors relented. On the whole, according to Cadbury, the conference was characterized by "pleasant personal understanding."[82] Upon his return to Britain, Cadbury made a press release of his statement to the cocoa proprietors, a statement in which, for the first time, *Cadbury Brothers* threatened to boycott Portuguese cocoa. The company stated that it would initiate a boycott, regardless of the cost, unless it was assured that in the future its raw cocoa would be produced by free labor. Once again, both the Portuguese government and the proprietors offered their assurances that labor conditions would improve.[83]

The public pressure on *Cadbury Brothers* was lifted in February 1908, not due to its own actions or any reforms by Portugal, but because the Portuguese King and Crown Prince were assassinated, throwing the Portuguese government into a political crisis. The Cadburys were relieved to discover that neither the most aggressive journalists nor idealistic humanitarians expected reforms in West Africa to be instituted in these circumstances. Cadbury therefore took advantage of this lull in the humanitarian storm to break with Fox Bourne and the APS over the issue of the boycott, declaring to Morel, "They are not to be trusted."[84]

By early 1908, Cadbury had received favorable reports about cocoa cultivation on the Gold Coast from his expert investigator, Leslie. On the basis of Leslie's findings, Cadbury asked Morel to publish positive articles about the prospects for cocoa in the British colony.[85] Until the late summer, the controversy over slavery in Portuguese West Africa remained at a standstill in Britain. By the end of the year, most British humanitarians were calling for a boycott, but they were also resigned to wait until Portugal resolved its domestic political crisis. In September, Cadbury and Burtt departed for West Africa on a trip that was publicized as a final investigation of labor practices on São Tomé and Príncipe. The itinerary also included Cadbury's tour of his new sources of cocoa on the Gold Coast. In November, *Cadbury* bought 137 bags of cocoa from the Gold Coast which it judged to be even better in quality than the cocoa from São Tomé and Príncipe. An alternative supply had thus been established, although the Gold Coast plantations still could not produce sufficient volume to meet *Cadbury's* requirements.

On September 26, 1908, the *Evening Standard*, a staunchly conservative paper, published an article that accused *Cadbury Brothers* of exploiting slavery in Portuguese West Africa for its own profit. The article commended William Cadbury for his present journey of inspection, noting with irony that Cadbury had previously been sensitive to slavery in South Africa and the Congo Free State, but not, somehow, in Portuguese West Africa. The *Standard* cast Cadbury as a self-serving hypocrite, mocking his reputation for benevolent treatment of company employees. "Mr. Cadbury," the *Standard* observed, "might have been expected to take some interest in the owners of those same grimed African hands whose labour is also so essential to the beneficient and lucrative operations of Bournville."[86] As in the case of the *Daily Graphic* a year earlier, *Cadbury* threatened to bring libel charges against the *Standard*, but the *Standard* refused to back down. The paper had long since attacked the Cadburys for their criticism of the Balfour government's policies in South Africa, and it now welcomed the opportunity to face the Cadburys' threats in court. Remarkably, having thrown down the gauntlet, William Cadbury proved himself reluctant to face the full force of the *Standard's* charges of hypocrisy. When Cadbury was asked in his deposition to present an account of donations by *Cadbury Brothers'* board of directors to the APS, the Anti-Slavery Society, and the CRA, he chose not to report his gift of £1,000 to the CRA in 1905.[87]

As *Cadbury Brothers* and the *Standard* marshaled their forces for a legal battle, three major developments in the spring and summer of 1909 broke the status quo that had thus far characterized the Portuguese slavery controversy. First, on March 19, following William Cadbury's return from Africa and a significant drop in the price of cocoa on world markets, *Cadbury Brothers* announced to the British press that it was now boycotting slave-grown cocoa from São Tomé and Príncipe. As suggested above, and as *Cadbury's* own statistics confirm, the company also made this decision in view of alternative sources of cocoa on the Gold Coast (see Appendix). The second development came in April 1909, when the Portuguese investigator in West Africa, Francisco Paula Cid, filed a report that recommended reforms in Portuguese colonial labor policies, such as the direct regulation of recruiting agents by the colonial government. Finally, in a move that surprised everyone in the British humanitarian community, the Portuguese Colonial Minister, Manuel da Terra Vianna, suspended labor recruitment in Angola on July 29, 1909.

Portuguese Slavery and British Partisan Politics on Trial

In the wake of these events, the trial of *Cadbury v. Standard* convened in Birmingham between November 29 and December 6, 1909. The lawyers for *Cadbury Brothers* included Rufus Isaacs, the future Attorney General of the Liberal government of Herbert Asquith, and John Simon, the future Solicitor General. The principal advocate for the *Standard* was Sir Edward Carson, an arch-conservative who would subsequently lead the Unionists in the north of Ireland to the brink of war in 1914 over the Irish nationalists' bid for self-government.

The central legal issue in this case was whether *Cadbury Brothers* had willfully ignored and concealed slavery in Portuguese West Africa in order to maintain its profitable business. The *Birmingham Daily Post* reported that after the closing arguments,

> [Mr. Justice Pickford] asked the jury was this a dishonest plot to delay the matter being brought before the British public in order to enable the plaintiffs to go on buying slave-grown cocoa which they ought to give up. That was the matter for the defendants to prove, and that alone was the issue to be tried.[88]

From a partisan political standpoint, this case also called into question the moral integrity of the Liberals' attacks on the Conservatives' foreign and imperial policies during and after the South African War, attacks that had helped to bring down the Balfour government in the general election of 1906. The *Daily News* had been at the forefront of these attacks, and Conservatives had accused the paper of cynicism and hypocrisy. Now the *Standard*, a champion of conservative politics, would seek vengeance, or at least the humiliation of the Cadbury family.

In his opening remarks, Cadbury's barrister urged the jury to put partisan sentiment aside and overlook the Cadburys' previous condemnation of "Chinese slavery" in South Africa. As Isaacs explained to the jury, the Cadburys were known throughout Britain "as a firm who cared for the social welfare of their employees." Under these circumstances, Isaacs emphasized, "the libel became of a more serious character."[89] In response, Carson followed a strategy of straightforward and unrelenting attack. He set out to demonstrate that the Portuguese plantations used slaves, that Cadbury knowingly purchased cocoa from these slave plantations, and that Cadbury had waited to initiate its boycott until prices fell to a low point in the cocoa market. To sustain his claim that Cadbury had delayed its boycott of these plantations, and even concealed information, Carson could produce no hard evidence. Instead, he highlighted the coverage of "Chinese slavery" in the *Daily News* and juxtaposed the Cadbury family's self-promotion as paternalistic employers with their support for slavery. Yet neither of these approaches proved Cadbury's deceit. The Cadburys themselves corroborated Carson's claims regarding slavery in Portuguese West Africa, but they defended their purchases as humanitarian acts to maintain leverage against the Portuguese regime, under orders from the Foreign Office.

In retrospect, and with the benefit of William Cadbury's personal papers, one can see that Carson misdirected his attacks on two fronts. He dwelled on the partisan issue of "Chinese slavery," when he might have made more of the Cadburys' participation in the Congo reform campaign. Had Carson been aware of William Cadbury's donation of £1,000 to the CRA in 1905, he certainly would have hammered home this point. Second, Carson emphasized that the Cadburys wished to avoid a boycott of their cocoa and chocolates by the British public. In fact, Cadbury had been primarily worried about maintaining its supply of raw cocoa. Carson asked William Cadbury:

If the "Daily News" had carried on the same agitation in regard to this slave-grown cocoa as they did in connection with indentured labour in the Transvaal do you doubt that you would not have been able to sell a shillingsworth of your cocoa?

Cadbury responded, "I doubt that," and he was probably being sincere.[90]

The jury found in favor of *Cadbury Brothers*, but awarded the company only £1 in damages. This meager award suggests that although the jury felt compelled to find for the plaintiff on technical grounds, it also believed that *Cadbury Brothers* was not above reproach by standards of conscience, if not of law. Soon after the trial, William Cadbury published a book, *Labour in Portuguese West Africa*, offering a clear criticism of the Portuguese plantation owners, a methodical chronicle of labor exploitation, and a rehearsal of the main issues in *Cadbury Brothers'* successful suit against the *Standard*. Duffy comments, "It was the most meticulously proper and restrained statement to be written by an English philanthropist during the whole controversy."[91] More important, it was a brilliant piece of propaganda, rendering Cadbury an author of protest, rather than a dubious victim of libel. Cadbury himself was not a gifted propagandist, but he had a shrewd eye for talent and strategic alliances. Consequently, Morel had edited Cadbury's manuscript of this book and rewritten the final chapter.[92]

Conclusion

On January 27, 1910, the Governor-General of Angola decreed that the recruitment of laborers from the colony could recommence on February 1. This recruitment did not resume, however, for another three years. In the meantime, cocoa proprietors on São Tomé and Príncipe obtained migrant laborers from the Cape Verde Islands and Mozambique. The inconsistencies and delays in Portugal's colonial labor policies and practices might be attributed in large part to the ongoing political instability of Portugal itself, where a revolution culminated in the establishment of a republican government in October. One month later, John and Alice Harris, the Joint Organizing Secretaries of the amalgamated British and Foreign Anti-Slavery and Aborigines' Protection Society, led an anti-slavery delegation to meet with ministers of the new government in Lisbon. The delegation was received cordially and provided with effusive assurances that labor reforms would finally be realized in Portuguese West Africa. The delegation departed with skepticism, and in 1911 the Anti-Slavery Society dispatched the Harrises to West Africa in order to evaluate the progress of reforms in both the Portuguese and the Belgian colonial territories. Upon their return in 1912, the Harrises published *Dawn in Darkest Africa*, which recounted the continuing slavery on São Tomé and Príncipe.[93] Public protest against Portuguese slavery continued in Britain, led largely by the Anti-Slavery Society and its ally, John St. Loe Strachey, the editor of *The Spectator*. There were questions in Parliament, and meetings and resolutions by religious groups and commercial interests. Yet after 1909, as Duffy observes, the protests lost focus and became a "shouting match" between humanitarians and the Foreign Office.[94]

In 1913 there were 1,008 laborers imported from Angola to São Tomé and Príncipe. According to British consular officials newly posted at Benguela and on São Tomé, the conditions of laborers had been improved in two important respects. Coercion appeared to be on the decline, and repatriation was now the rule. In the same year, the Anti-Slavery Society conceded that repatriation was taking place, and turned its attention to labor exploitation in Angola itself. Although the British humanitarians claimed victory, the positive influence of their campaigns was short-lived. The Portuguese regime in West Africa readily returned to forced labor after the First World War. The Anti-Slavery Society once more attempted to mobilize public protest in Britain, but without success.[95] As discussed in the next chapter, John Harris then took his protests against Portuguese labor policies to the League of Nations, which had held out the promise of a new, more humane era in imperial labor practices under the revived principle of trusteeship. In a tragically ironic turn, Harris found his recourse to international government blocked by a combination of Portuguese and Belgian officials, who occupied key positions on the League's Temporary Slavery Commission.

The controversy over slavery in Portuguese West Africa has faded into the background of British humanitarian politics in the Edwardian era. Yet it remains a specter in the business history of *Cadbury Brothers*. The company's own historians, A.G. Gardiner and Iolo Williams, have dismissed the accusations as slanderous, while, most recently, Charles Dellheim has treated the event as a conundrum which reveals nothing substantial enough to tarnish *Cadbury's* good name.[96] Yet it is clear that this controversy weighed heavily on the mind of its central player, William Cadbury. He was subsequently perceived as an author of protest due to his book *Labour in Portuguese West Africa*, and his humanitarian efforts were later valorized in Morel's classic book, *The Black Man's Burden*, which Morel dedicated to Cadbury and his wife, Emmeline. Cadbury continued to lead a distinguished life, serving as the Chairman of *Cadbury Brothers* and the Lord Mayor of Birmingham, among other positions. However, despite these various distinctions, in the last several years of his life, Cadbury chose to write a brief document titled "A Private Inside History of the Connection of *Cadbury Bros., Ltd.*, with African Slavery." In explaining his purpose in writing this history, Cadbury stated that he wished to respond to the lingering belief that his company had been driven to action by Nevinson's book, *A Modern Slavery*.[97] Cadbury's history, although "private," is composed almost entirely of information that Cadbury had made public at one time or another in the past. At first glance, it appears to be a personal vindication, a decisive claim to integrity for the benefit of his family. Yet there is one important revelation in this document: Cadbury's simple admission that he turned to Morel, throughout the controversy, for consultation and advice.[98] It is this understated acknowledgment of Morel's role which displays the tension between Cadbury's humanity and his hard-nosed business sense.

Cadbury and Morel had at least one common interest in stifling the controversy over slavery in Portuguese West Africa. Neither, apparently, perceived that labor conditions on the cocoa plantations were comparable to the atrocious conditions in the Congo Free State. Consequently, the two men saw themselves cooperating in a humanitarian effort to publicize the worst, if not the only, new slavery in Africa. On a personal level, the two men became very close, perhaps due to their beleaguered ethical positions. Their correspondence suggests that by 1912 each was among the most intimate friends of the other. Among all of Morel's correspondents, Cadbury was the only one besides his wife, Mary, who addressed him by his Christian name, George.

Both men recognized the problematic ethics of their financial relationship, but it seems that Morel carried the lighter burden of conscience. His decision to undermine the Portuguese slavery controversy in Britain was dictated by his overriding commitment to Congo reform. He sincerely believed that the Congo Free State posed an incomparable evil, and he accepted the fact that humanitarian campaigns had to compete to survive. Consequently, he became Cadbury's ally, and ultimately admired Cadbury for contributing to his cause.

Like Morel, Cadbury did not think that slavery in Portuguese West Africa was as bad as labor in the Congo Free State or elsewhere in Africa, but he furthermore chose to exploit slavery on the plantations of São Tomé and Príncipe to meet his company's need for raw cocoa. Cadbury's objective was to delay a boycott of slave-grown cocoa so that his company could avoid a major shortfall in its supplies, and a consequent crisis in domestic production, at the same time that he assured the British public that the company was conscientiously proceeding toward an ethical stand. The Foreign Office encouraged this course of action for the sake of its own interests in supplying labor from Portuguese colonies to the mine industry of South Africa, particularly given the departure of "Chinese slaves" after 1907. When Cadbury saw the opportunity to boycott slave-grown cocoa and simultaneously sustain his cocoa supply, he promptly redeemed his company and himself, having calculated the costs and benefits of virtue.

CHAPTER **5**

British Anti-slavery and the Imperial Origins of International Government and Labor Law, 1914–1926

In the early days of the First World War, British anti-slavery activists looked forward to peace on their own terms. This humanitarian lobby was represented primarily by the Reverend John and Alice Harris, the Joint Organizing Secretaries of the British and Foreign Anti-Slavery and Aborigines' Protection Society, a dynamic organization that brought together missionary societies, the Society of Friends, merchants, and various other groups who interested themselves in international labor policies and opposition to slavery "in all its forms." Over the previous dozen years, these groups had participated in widely publicized campaigns against the so-called new slaveries, ranging from forced labor to indentured servitude, in colonial Africa and elsewhere. The most prominent of these campaigns, orchestrated by the Harrises and E.D. Morel under the auspices of the Congo Reform Association (CRA), had exposed slavery and atrocities in the Congo Free State, fueling the largest humanitarian controversy in British imperial politics since the age of emancipation in the nineteenth century.

In response to Britain's declaration of war against Germany on August 4, 1914, the Anti-Slavery Society suspended much of its work, as its members turned their attention and energy to the conflict in Europe. Four days later, the British government instituted security measures under the Defence of the Realm Act that restricted the Society's access to its standard channels of public influence through the media and Parliament. Nonetheless, while the Society limited its activities and accepted the government's wartime measures in support of the national cause, leading humanitarians kept their own long-term objectives in view. Within the first month of fighting, John Harris began to confer with philanthropic groups about a postwar, international conference regarding imperial policies on "native races."[1] "The whole question of native races," Harris remarked to his American ally, Booker T. Washington, "will take a different aspect after the war."[2]

The question to which Harris referred was made up of a multifaceted set of issues involving Europe's methods of imperial administration in tropical Africa. These issues focused fundamentally on the discrepancy between the professed, benevolent principles of European expansion and prevailing practices of imperial labor exploitation. John and Alice Harris, and other prominent humanitarians such as Morel, anticipated that the war would destabilize imperial administrations, creating opportunities for reform in the course of reconstruction. The general objective of British humanitarians in this period was to reform imperial labor policies in Africa to ensure that commercial development would simultaneously promote Africans' moral and material improvement and create a more efficient workforce to enhance European prosperity. The humanitarian community was divided, however, in its paths toward this goal.

British humanitarians had previously been split between the ideologies of evangelical philanthropy and human rights, as seen in the Congo reform campaign. Evangelicals prioritized Christian conversion and the social reform of Africans. Human rights activists prioritized Africans' ownership of land and the fruits of their labor, and they believed that imperial administration should take into account the essential racial differences that presumably defined African cultures. Whereas the political strength of the evangelical agenda still rested with missionary societies and nonconformists, Labour Party leaders had become vocal supporters of human rights politics, declaring that there must be humane limits on the exploitation of imperial subjects. In asserting the rights of peoples from "the temperate zones" of Europe to "free trade" in the tropics, James Ramsay MacDonald explained, "This right of the Temperate Zone populations to enjoy the products of the Tropics does not override the superior right of the Tropical peoples to be treated as human beings."[3]

During the First World War, the debates over these distinctive ideologies were augmented by the issue of political sovereignty. The war involved imperial subjects and territories around the world, opening the door to numerous demands for self-government, if not independence, in the aftermath of the conflict. A growing number of British radicals and Labour Party leaders had begun even to question the traditional structure of the British Empire, asking whether imperial sovereignty actually promoted or undermined the welfare of foreign peoples. As an alternative, radicals proposed a new system of international government, "a league of nations," to oversee the anticipated redistribution of Europe's imperial possessions at the war's end. Humanitarians found themselves engaged in these debates over the proposed league of nations, seeking to determine which system of sovereignty might best combat new slaveries in the postwar era. In debating the shape of international government, all parties looked back to the Berlin Act, the central document of the European scramble for Africa, as their legal and ideological precedent.[4]

Humanitarians attempted to strike a balance between their advocacy of "native interests," international government, and their commitment to the national interests of Britain in its military crisis. In the short term, the Anti-Slavery Society assisted the British war effort through propaganda that highlighted the brutalities of Germany's imperial administration and legitimized the seizure of Germany's empire by Britain and its allies. In this respect, the Anti-Slavery Society was primarily concerned with the German colonies in Africa, including Togoland, the Cameroons, German South West Africa, and German East Africa. In published propaganda and wartime lectures, John and Alice Harris advocated "Christian imperialism," recalling the dominant discourse of evangelical philanthropy in the Congo reform campaign.

They then expanded upon this Christian discourse after the armistice by supporting British imperial officials in defining the ethical authority of the British Empire and, in turn, the League of Nations, as a "sacred trust." Clearly, this discourse of trusteeship must have resonated with the well-known declarations of Edmund Burke, despite the fact that the discourse of trusteeship had slipped into abeyance for much of the nineteenth century. Yet the precise meaning of trusteeship had changed in significant respects by the postwar era, and it had come to mean distinctly different things to imperial officials and humanitarians.[5] While the Harrises, as evangelicals, were slow to recognize these differences, Morel, as an advocate of human rights, was deeply skeptical of this revival of trust, as we will see below.

Following the lead of President Woodrow Wilson and Prime Minister David Lloyd George, John and Alice Harris argued that Germany's colonies in Africa should be parceled out to Britain and other responsible states as "mandates" under a new, international governing body. The sovereignty over these mandates would rest with their indigenous peoples, but, since these peoples presumably were not ready for self-government, the mandates would be held as a "sacred trust" by Europeans for the benefit of their inhabitants. Although imperial territories would be demarcated by European political boundaries, there would be no form of political preference or economic protectionism within each territory. Although the various mandates would be subject to international oversight, there would be no international means to punish a regime for violating mandatory principles. Instead, violations would be overcome by the weight of official censure and public opprobrium.

The Anti-Slavery Society did not regard this proposed mandates system as an abdication of imperial authority, but rather as an innovation in European imperialism in general, on the basis of the best traditions of the British Empire in particular. The Harrises declared in one of their many public lectures during the war: "The great upheaval which is now taking place must shake to their very foundations all governments on our planet and should spell a new era in colonial expansion."[6]

Morel, the former Secretary of the CRA and now a Vice President of the Anti-Slavery Society, claimed that Germany's imperial record was being distorted by British propaganda. In 1914, Morel became a founding member of the Union of Democratic Control (UDC), a group committed to the democratization of British foreign policy and the promotion of free trade among Europe's colonies. As the Secretary of the UDC, Morel helped to define the foreign policies of Britain's political left during the war. He denied that Germany was solely responsible for the conflict, which he attributed to the capitalist competition and avarice of all the European powers, both at home and abroad.

Morel split from the Anti-Slavery Society to argue that Germany should participate in the creation of an unprecedented, international sovereign state in Africa. He argued that simply seizing Germany's imperial possessions, and especially those in Africa, would only promote future tensions by depriving Germany's growing population and economy of vital resources. "An African cancer," wrote Morel, "the product of bad European administration, infects the political body of Europe. An attempted monopolisation of the raw material of Africa by this or that European Power in the interest of its own nationals has its repercussion upon the international relations of Europe."[7] Morel believed that Africa would remain a source of friction for Europe unless *all* of the imperial regimes agreed to neutralize the greater part of its tropical and subtropical regions under an international administration. The principles of this administration were the same that Morel and others had advocated for the Congo: protection of human rights through free trade and African ownership of land and labor, and respect for cultural relativism, based on the recognition of essential racial differences. MacDonald, a fellow founder of the UDC and the future Labour Prime Minister, had articulated this radical agenda in his book *Labour and the Empire* in 1904. In condemning imperialist "exploiters," MacDonald stated:

> They have begun by uprooting native civilizations, by destroying the economic expressions of these civilizations—such as tribal lands, by forcing the native mind into new grooves which that mind does not fit and never can fit. One hears the British official condemn the tribal system because it does not produce British virtues, and he points to native specimens of self-help and British individualism, who are tragic grotesques.[8]

While such views on imperial policy were merely unpopular during the war, the UDC's views on Germany provoked intense hostility from the general public and the government. Morel had been hailed in 1913 as a hero for his humanitarian battle against the Congo Free State, but his critical assessment of the war soon alienated him from many of his supporters and landed him in prison in September 1917.

At the beginning of January 1918, Prime Minister David Lloyd George informed his War Cabinet that he regarded Germany's colonies as the most difficult point in defining Britain's war aims.[9] Lloyd George and the Cabinet were determined to retain Germany's empire if the allies won the war, but they had difficulty in legitimizing this seizure of territory in Britain's current political environment. British humanitarian politics, coupled with the labor movement, had played a significant role in creating a common antipathy to "imperialist conquest." During the past two years of the war, radicals and labor leaders had carried forward Morel's humanitarian agenda of rights and free-market commerce, propagating the suspicion that the war was being fought for imperial territory and the profit of international financiers and businessmen. The same political coalition of radicals and labor had previously driven the "Chinese slavery" controversy after the South African War, and now it had significantly more power with which to push its claims.

This domestic pressure on the government was compounded in January 1918 when President Wilson presented his Fourteen Points to the U.S. Congress, calling for the political self-determination of small nations. The United States had entered the war in April as an "associate" power, and Lloyd George was intent on building at least the façade of an ideological consensus with Wilson, despite his personal frustration over the president's meddling in Britain's imperial affairs. Lloyd George thus felt compelled to define Britain's acquisition of Germany's colonies in a manner that would appease *both* his critics at home and an "associate" in the ongoing fight against Germany and the Ottoman Empire. Given these political imperatives, Lloyd George acquiesced to President Wilson's proposal to create a system of "mandates" to manage the redistribution of European imperial territory after the war. Wilson had derived this idea from his reading of a treatise titled "The League of Nations: A Practical Suggestion," by the Afrikaner war hero and politician Jan Smuts, who was a member of the British Imperial War Cabinet.[10] Although the British government was initially resistant to the idea of mandates, as opposed to traditional colonies, it soon realized that it could manipulate the proposed mandates system to serve its own ends. Moreover, Smuts subsequently provided the government with a discourse through which it could legitimize its imperial machinations, a discourse that President Wilson adopted wholeheartedly in drafting the Covenant of the League of Nations. Smuts described the mandates system as a "sacred trust."[11]

In its origins, Britain's "sacred trust" had been deeply imbued with Protestant theology, and it had entailed the Christian duty to educate and discipline the imperial "ward" for the ward's own benefit. After the First World War, however, imperial officials conveyed little recognition of the theological origins of trusteeship, and they redefined trust as a duty to ensure the imperial ward's material welfare. Apart from this important change in the politics of trust, there were other aspects of trust that remained consistent with the Burkean tradition discussed in chapter 1. Most important, the presumed immaturity of the ward, and the ward's incompetence to manage his own affairs, were measured against a cultural hierarchy of civilization. As Smuts explained, "The German colonies in the Pacific and Africa are inhabited by barbarians, who not only cannot possibly govern themselves, but to whom it would be impracticable to apply any ideas of political self-determination in the European sense."[12] This cultural hierarchy would be subsequently reflected in the ranking of A, B, and C mandates, ranging from those peoples who presumably could be educated in the principles and skills of self-government to those peoples whose barbarism was virtually irremediable.[13]

It was the duty of the "civilised" trustee to raise the "savage" ward to a comparable level of civilization through paternal tutelage. In principle, the ward retained his or her natural rights to property and sovereignty, while the trustee managed the ward's affairs. The trustee's authority to manage the ward's property and sovereignty was to expire at such time as the ward learned to emulate civilized society, but the trustee alone possessed the ability to determine when the ward had achieved a level of education sufficient to justify independence.

Article 22 of the Covenant of the League of Nations characterized the mandates system as a "sacred trust." Smuts, among other influential figures, regarded this ethic as something new, but in fact it did not mark a qualitative shift from empire to a new vision of international government. Smuts himself had claimed in 1918: "Today the British Commonwealth of Nations remains the only embryo League of Nations because it is based on the true principles of national freedom and political decentralization."[14] In the latter regard, Lloyd George even went so far as to embrace President Wilson's principle of national self-determination, though he noted privately that "precisely how the principle was to be applied need not now be discussed."[15]

The British government's opportunistic use of trusteeship was exposed in its subsequent treatment of the Anti-Slavery Society. The Society had contributed to British propaganda against Germany, endorsed the government's rhetoric of "trusteeship" as part and parcel of its own "Christian imperialism," and even cooperated with the War Office in caring for African troops in France.[16] John and Alice Harris were then surprised when the government attempted to block John Harris's passage across the English Channel to lobby on behalf of the Anti-Slavery Society at the peace conference at Versailles. Morel, on the other hand, was not surprised by this action, recognizing that the British government regarded humanitarians as unreliable, though humanitarian discourse was a useful tool. The mandates system, wrote Morel, "is an attempt…to reconcile the altruistic pronouncements of President Wilson with what is substantially a policy of imperialistic grab at the expense of the beaten foe."[17]

John Harris called upon the British government to enact new abolitionist legislation after the war, but he soon realized that his petitions were falling upon deaf ears. Consequently, he attempted to bypass British officials and appeal directly to the League of Nations. As discussed below, Harris's lobbying efforts began the process through which the League enacted the Slavery Convention of 1926, a process in which British imperial officials would take a leading role. However, like Morel during the war, Harris could provoke the government to take action, but he could not dictate the precise nature of that action. In the end, as the discourse of trusteeship floated upon the air, a former colonial governor, Sir Frederick Lugard, and officials in the British Foreign Office would tailor the Slavery Convention to suit the objectives of British foreign policy and the preferences of imperial administrators.

Humanitarians and the War Effort

At the outset of 1914, the Anti-Slavery Society was a healthy and active philanthropic body with ambitious goals. Abolitionist politics in Britain had been waning at the turn of the century, but the controversies over the new slaveries of imperialism had then renewed popular interest in the subject and rejuvenated the anti-slavery lobby. The experience of these anti-slavery campaigns served to train and consolidate an influential group of activists stretching from Plymouth to Glasgow, with their center of operations in London. This humanitarian lobby was well-connected among politicians, nonconformist leaders, businessmen, and the press. John Harris, in particular, maintained close relations with the editors of *The Spectator*, the *Manchester Guardian*, the *Daily News*, the *Contemporary Review*, and other publications. He and his wife, Alice, also maintained strong links with the Society of Friends, the National Council of Evangelical Free Churches, and several missionary societies. Finally, the Anti-Slavery Society was closely allied with the Liverpool merchants and British cocoa manufactures who were involved in the West African trade.

There had been significant changes in the organization of British anti-slavery activists in the past several years. Following the death of H.R. Fox Bourne in 1909, the Aborigines' Protection Society had amalgamated with the British and Foreign Anti-Slavery Society, and the Congo Reform Association had disbanded in 1913. The subsequent consolidation of humanitarian efforts in the Anti-Slavery Society had been directed by John and Alice Harris, who had assumed their posts as the Society's Joint Organizing Secretaries in early 1910.

The Anti-Slavery Society had increased its funding in the next few years and branched out through new auxiliaries in Britain and Africa. The Society fulfilled the role of a traditional pressure group by lobbying Parliament, the Foreign Office, and the Colonial Office, but it also conducted extensive grassroots campaigns to educate the general public about its work and aims. John and Alice Harris had begun their philanthropic careers as missionaries, and they continued to propagate the message of "Christian imperialism" through lectures, drawing room meetings, and "home visits" by missionaries on furlough. Alice Harris, the principal lecturer for the Anti-Slavery Society, had begun her career as a public speaker in Britain in 1906, testifying to her experiences as a missionary on the Congo. By 1914, she had given hundreds of lectures on Africa, primarily to Christian organizations and women's groups in Britain. She had also lectured in the United States, France, and, most recently, Switzerland.[18]

Following Britain's declaration of war against Germany, the Anti-Slavery Society suspended its campaigns to secure labor reforms in Portuguese West Africa and land rights for Africans in Rhodesia. Like many people in Britain, the members of the Committee of the Anti-Slavery Society did not anticipate a long war, and they believed that the suspension of their work was a short-term measure. In the interim, the Society chose to pursue private initiatives, as in late 1914, when John and Alice Harris traveled to South Africa on an inquiry into colonial land policies.[19] After the Harrises returned from South Africa in February 1915, it was obvious to all but the most deliriously optimistic that the war had not "ended by Christmas." Neither the Harrises nor the Committee of the Anti-Slavery Society was willing to suspend their philanthropic work indefinitely, so in 1915 they adapted the program of the Society to the war effort. They began this process by recasting their philanthropic efforts, for public and official consumption, as important contributions to Britain's strategic interests. Posturing as the motive force of humanity in the Empire, the Anti-Slavery Society took credit for the loyalty of Britain's African and Asian colonies, which presumably had rallied to support their benevolent regimes.[20]

At the Anti-Slavery Society's annual meeting in April 1915, John Harris proposed an agenda to increase the organization's funding during the war and build closer alliances with members of Parliament.[21] The Society subsequently dropped any pretense of political impartiality and built its wartime strategies on the simple premise that the nation's enemy was its own. British anti-slavery activists had never before singled out the German empire for extensive criticism. John Harris had previously believed that the Germans were second only to the British as imperial administrators, and during the Congo controversy Morel and other humanitarians had actually considered the merits of annexing the Congo Free State to Germany. This respect for the German empire was an extension of Britain's general respect for German culture before the war. The Kruger Telegram of 1896, the Anglo–German naval arms race, the Moroccan crises of 1905–1906 and 1911, and increasing economic rivalries had provoked political tensions, but these tensions had not prompted Britain to question Germany's fundamental sense of humanity. "These feelings died forever on the British side in August 1914," Jean Stengers observes, "when the Germans became the Huns." Britain's representation of the Germans as a barbarian race began with the infamous "rape of Belgium" and continued through numerous testimonies to German atrocities that British propagandists publicized throughout the war.[22] In the years ahead, both the British government and the Anti-Slavery Society were quick to extend the humanitarian politics of outrage and moral authority to Germany's empire. "Huns," as Stengers concludes, "could not be entrusted with the sacred task of civilizing other peoples."[23]

In the spring of 1915, the Anti-Slavery Society targeted the German empire for critical scrutiny.[24] The Society quickly assembled a file on Germany's punitive colonial expeditions, as well as allegations of forced labor. In July the Committee appealed to the Colonial Secretary, Andrew Bonar Law, for an inquiry into German imperial policies, referring to the massacres of the Hereros in German South West Africa in 1904, reprisals against rebellious Africans in Togoland in 1911, and the current use of forced labor on the plantations of South West Africa. The Anti-Slavery Society offered to assist in any inquiry that the government might undertake, but the Colonial Office declined even to acknowledge the Society's proposal.[25]

The Colonial Office was not indifferent to evidence of maladministration in Germany's African colonies; in fact, it had begun to assemble its own evidence on this subject to combat Germany's charges that British forces were mistreating German military prisoners and missionaries in the Cameroons. The Colonial Office was concerned about official German propaganda and, particularly, a pamphlet titled "The Martyrdom of the Evangelical Missionaries in Cameroons, 1914. Narratives of Eyewitnesses," written by Pastor W. Stark, Director of the Evangelical Press Union for Germany. In June 1915, the Colonial Office had established a Committee on Alleged German Atrocities and initiated discussions with the Foreign Office regarding the publication of reports on German atrocities in Africa. As the Undersecretary of State for the Colonies, H.J. Read, observed: "It seems desirable to consider again the question of publishing those reports, especially as the German press is spreading false reports to the effect that the British authorities in the Cameroons have been inciting the natives by money rewards to murder Germans."[26]

The reluctance of the Colonial Office to work with the Anti-Slavery Society in an inquiry into German imperial policies might be explained by several factors. First and foremost, the Colonial Office generally perceived the Society as a collection of amateurs interfering in official business. Also, the Colonial Office could not be certain how it would use the findings of a full inquiry, since Britain's imperial goals had not been clarified. Finally, the Colonial Office suspected that the Anti-Slavery Society might turn on the British government to publicize improprieties in Britain's own empire.

Although the Colonial Office dismissed the inquiries of the Anti-Slavery Society, John and Alice Harris found other means of participating in the war effort. In the early autumn of 1915, the Anti-Slavery Society cooperated with the YMCA to present lectures on imperial issues to the British troops stationed in camps in the greater London area. These lectures were produced with a view toward promoting "sound principles of colonial development." As John Harris explained, "We feel the enormous importance of educating the young men of the country in problems affecting native races." It was not John, however, but Alice Harris who gave most of the lectures in the camps, incorporating these talks into her regular calendar of engagements. She was already presenting up to three lantern lectures a week in and around London on the subject of her travels in Africa.[27] Over the next year, she also lectured in the army camps, giving talks on her travels and on other topics such as "Britain's Coloured Colonial Children," "The Triumph of Christian Imperialism," and "Native Races and the Peace Terms." In November 1916, she received requests from the army for lectures on the German colonies, so in the next few months she wrote an additional lecture titled "Germany's Lost Colonial Empire."

These lectures were testimonies to the benevolence of the British Empire, peppered with statistics and colorful anecdotes. The general tone is reflected in Harris's declaration, "The cardinal principle of British colonization is that of sacrifice and service, whereas that of other Powers has been primarily and very largely colonization in the material interests of the motherland." The lectures had a strong religious tone, whether in discussing the foundations of the British Empire by "Christian statesmen" or in emphasizing the role of missionaries in the moral progress of foreign peoples. Furthermore, the war became the final measure of the success of Britain's Christian principles of governance. "There are three tests," Harris explained, "which may be applied as to the soundness of British colonial policy....There is first the test of social regeneration, secondly the economic test and finally the test of loyalty to the British Crown." The Anti-Slavery Society touted loyalty, above all, as the measure of its own success and usefulness to the British nation. In April 1916, at the annual meeting of the Society, Victor Buxton declared in his presidential address that Britain's African subjects had rallied to the flag in this time of crisis, "and this showed the value of the work that the Society was doing."[28]

While the Harrises and the Anti-Slavery Society had fallen into line behind Britain's wartime government and its propaganda campaign, Roger Casement and Morel followed dissident political paths that led to their collisions with the government and British society at large. Casement, an important participant in the Congo reform campaign, had been knighted by the British Crown in 1911 for his humanitarian work as a British consular official in South America. Without the knowledge of his humanitarian colleagues, however, Casement had become involved with militant Irish nationalists before the war, and, after the outbreak of hostilities, he had traveled to Germany to mobilize Irish prisoners of war into a regiment to fight the British forces. He also became involved in securing arms for the Easter Rising of April 1916. After being captured in Ireland by the British prior to the Rising, Casement was prosecuted for high treason and hanged at Pentonville Prison on August 3.

Morel came into conflict with the government as the Secretary of the UDC. At the instigation of Charles Trevelyan, Morel had helped to establish the UDC with several other radicals and labor leaders, including Norman Angell and MacDonald. The primary purpose of the UDC was to democratize British foreign policy and remove it from the control of elitist statesmen, financiers, and their exclusive bureaucracy of policy makers. The UDC also advocated free trade as a panacea for colonial conflict. Morel had laid the conceptual groundwork for this egalitarian and occasionally paranoid approach to foreign policy through his recent works on "secret diplomacy" in the Moroccan crises. Looking back to the Congo reform campaign, it is easy enough to see the origins of Morel's suspicious view toward Europe's foreign policy establishment. Not only had Morel regarded the Congo Free State as an avaricious scheme to fill the pockets of King Leopold II, he had also faulted the British government, and especially the Foreign Secretary, Sir Edward Grey, for the dilatory and disingenuous manner in which they had handled the Congo controversy. By mid-November 1914, the UDC had established several branches and adopted a constitution drafted by Morel. According to Marvin Swartz, "E.D. Morel dominated the Union of Democratic Control," and he established a close alliance with the Labour Party on foreign policy issues.[29]

The UDC refused to define the war in terms of Germany's guilt, opting instead to portray it as an international, "imperialist" conflict. The UDC critique was initially unpopular in Britain, and Morel, as the Secretary of the UDC, suffered the brunt of the nation's resentment. It is noteworthy that the UDC's views were drawn directly from the prevailing radical critiques of imperialism as an exploitative machine driven by monopoly capitalists. The view of the war as a cynical imperialist ploy drew upon the earlier discourses of protest leveled against the South African War by J.A. Hobson and against the Congo Free State by Morel. These views would increasingly gain currency in Britain after the horrendous casualties sustained on the western front in 1916. Initially, however, Morel faced a nationalist backlash that entailed even a popular revision of the history of the Congo reform campaign. One year before the war, the CRA had been praised as an example of humanitarianism in the finest tradition of British anti-slavery politics. Less than one year after the war began, the British media attacked Morel and, by extension, the CRA as tools of the German state.[30]

The Anti-Slavery Society found itself implicated in the scandals surrounding Casement and Morel. Although the Harrises gave personal assistance to both men, the Society publicly distanced itself from these two political liabilities. On July 6, 1916, for example, the Committee of the Anti-Slavery Society declined to act on William Albright's request to issue an appreciation of Casement's services to "native races."[31] Morel, a friend and avid admirer of Casement for over ten years, later refused to visit Casement in prison prior to his execution. Morel claimed that such a meeting would only have fueled suspicions of their cooperation in a treasonous conspiracy, and thus alienated the British public further from the UDC.

The new coalition government of David Lloyd George, which had every intention of seizing Germany's empire, had been watching Morel with increasing distrust and looking for an excuse to silence him. The government found its opportunity in August 1917, when it learned that Morel had sent some political literature from the UDC, via Ethel Sidgwick, to Romain Rolland in Switzerland, in violation of the Defence of the Realm Act. Morel was arrested on the morning of August 31, 1917, and then tried between September 1 and 4. He was found guilty and imprisoned at Pentonville, where Casement had been executed a year earlier. This incarceration took a serious toll on Morel's health, but his physical difficulties were nothing compared to his mental state of bitter resentment. Morel was released on February 2, 1918, and soon thereafter he turned his back on the Liberals to join the Labour Party, in which he had already assumed considerable authority.

Humanitarians and the Postwar Imperial Settlement

The early proponents of an international system of government were primarily concerned with the prevention of wars among European states. The Hague Conventions of 1899 and 1907 attempted to provide a forum for the adjudication of disputes, but the authority of the Hague Tribunal had been weakly defined. The principle of an international system of government nonetheless appealed to an influential group of political theorists and officials in Britain. Their search for a lasting peace was spurred by the First World War, and lively debates ensued between various factions of the labor movement, the Liberal Party, and the Conservatives. The term "league of nations" was coined by Lowes Dickinson in the first month of the war, and in May 1915 the League of Nations Society became the first British pressure group devoted to developing a postwar, international administration.[32] The Asquith government had already begun to discuss the issue of a league in April 1915, and the subject arose for the first time in the House of Commons in October 1916.

Although most debates over a league of nations centered upon the negotiation of peace, a small number of British writers saw such a federation as a means to alleviate the deeper sources of conflict in economic competition, particularly imperialist competition. Hobson had raised this idea in his seminal work, *Imperialism: A Study*, in 1902, and he returned to it in 1915 in his book, *Towards International Government*.[33] British labor soon took the political lead in conceptualizing the postwar system of imperial administration, unifying behind the general concept of colonial mandates in early 1918.[34] Henry Winkler explains, "It was the labor movement and its supporters which gave the widest circulation to the twin demands for protection of native rights and for machinery to ensure equal economic opportunities—all under international supervision."[35] Morel was the main advocate of "native rights" within the labor movement, but his radical views had limited influence. When push came to shove in the postwar settlement, Arthur Henderson and the majority of the labor leadership did not prioritize the land rights or the human rights of Africans, as Morel would have wished. Labour and Conservatives alike found a satisfactory solution to the colonial question in the mandates system and the principle of trusteeship.

After the spring of 1915, John and Alice Harris joined in the public debates over the organization of postwar empires in Africa. Although the war in Europe remained at a stalemate, Britain and its allies would easily seize most of Germany's African empire by the end of 1916. Togoland had fallen to British forces in August 1914, South West Africa would fall in July 1915, and the Cameroons in February 1916. Only the German troops in East Africa would hold out against the British until the armistice in 1918.[36] In looking toward the postwar settlement in Africa, the Anti-Slavery Society called for a continuation of the work started by the Berlin Act of 1885 and the Brussels Convention of 1890, which, though ineffective, "raised to a higher level than before the accepted administrative and commercial standards for the treatment of native races." Apart from humanitarian concerns, an ethical administration was necessary to sustain the supply of African labor and raw materials upon which Europe's industrial growth would increasingly depend. The "ideal step" in any postwar territorial settlement would be to give Africans a voice in their own destiny. "We admit, however," the Anti-Slavery Society Committee conceded, "that so far as most territories are concerned, this would not be a practical proposal."[37]

With the support of the committee, in March 1917 John Harris published *Germany's Lost Colonial Empire and the Essentials of Reconstruction*, a book apparently based upon the lecture that Alice Harris had written in February. The Harrises characterized "the dominating factor" in British expansion as "a genuine desire to seek first the good of the inhabitants over which Britain's flag was hoisted." By contrast, they explained, "in motive and administrative activity German policy has been the very anti-thesis of British policy; it has been confessedly a selfish motive."[38] They accused the Germans of managing a system of forced labor in East Africa, and they condemned atrocities against the Hereros during the 1904 punitive expeditions in South West Africa and also in Togoland between 1903 and 1913.[39] The Harrises displayed rebellion and lack of economic productivity as the failures of German colonialism, which had contributed to the instability within Germany that had provoked the present war.[40]

According to the Harrises, the German colonies had rich resources waiting to be tapped by a more effective and just British administration. Borrowing a page from Morel, they argued that the best means to this end was the education of Africans to develop their own economy. "The indigenous producer...," they asserted, "...will then reap abounding harvests, which he will sell to the white merchant who stands in his proper relation of middleman between the producing and consuming community."[41] The Anti-Slavery Society's first major treatise on the war found a receptive audience in the British government, probably due to the book's unrestrained indictment of German imperial practices. Within the year, the War Propaganda Bureau bought 5,000 copies of the Harrises' book and distributed it in allied and neutral countries.[42]

In July 1917, Morel responded to the Harrises' book with a pamphlet titled "The African Problem and the Peace Settlement," expanded later in 1917 into a book, *Africa and the Peace of Europe*. Morel's objectives were the resolution of European imperial rivalries in Africa and the creation of a prosperous and ethical imperial administration that would prohibit the exploitation of Africans in the future. He envisioned most of Africa as a peaceful free-trade zone in which the economy would be run by African agriculturalists catering to a European export market. "The means to this end," Morel explained, "are plainly indicated. They would consist in neutralizing the greater part of Africa, and in internationalizing commercial activities within the neutralized area.... These proposals," Morel added, "are substantially an amplification and precision of the purposes of the Berlin Act."[43]

In observing the purposes of the Berlin Act, Morel put his finger on the inadequacy of the means which that Act had provided for the realization of its principles. Fundamentally, the Berlin Act lacked both the power of enforcement and a mechanism for reconciling internationalism with state sovereignty. As Morel observed:

> The failure of the Powers has, therefore, been a moral failure, not a violation of international law. The policy they sought to promote is not invalidated by that failure. The policy in question was not enshrined in international law as a policy binding upon the parties, but merely as a pious hope which it was left to the option of the signatories to consummate.[44]

Morel's answer to this shortcoming of the Berlin Act was the creation of an international state to administer most of Africa. This state would have a prerogative to punish violations of Africans' rights because these violations would occur within the scope of its sovereignty. Morel did not, however, clearly define the balance of power within the state's administrative structure.

Morel's proposal was radical, but what made it provocative was his insistence on including Germany in the postwar governance of Africa. Morel saw Germany's continuance as a imperial power as a practical step toward a lasting peace. Stripping Germany of its colonies would, Morel warned, provoke animosity due to Germany's "sentimental" attachments to its empire. Furthermore, Morel asserted that Germany, as one of the most rapidly expanding "white peoples," needed Africa's resources to fuel its growth, which would promote stability and pacify its drive for European expansion.[45]

In the months before Morel's arrest in September 1917, the British government had decided to attempt to retain Germany's imperial territories after the war. This decision to take over Germany's empire had been set in motion on the day after Britain's declaration of war, when the government decided to attack and seize Germany's colonies. In fact, the first engagements of British forces in the war commenced in Togoland on August 7, 1914, a week and a half before the British Expeditionary Force landed in France.[46] While the British government took an immediate strategic interest in Germany's empire in 1914, it had not yet determined its postwar objectives. The process of clarifying Britain's postwar territorial goals was begun on August 8, 1916, when Prime Minister Herbert Asquith appointed the Subcommittee on Territorial Changes.[47] This group met for eight months and filed four reports, the last of which was completed on July 17, 1917. As this group concluded its work, the new Prime Minister, David Lloyd George, appointed the Committee of the Imperial War Cabinet on Territorial Desiderata. Both of these committees contributed to a prevailing opinion within the Cabinet, the Foreign Office, and the Colonial Office after 1917 that Britain had major strategic interests in stripping Germany of its colonies. The Cabinet was particularly intent upon securing German South West Africa, due to its proximity to South Africa, and German East Africa, due to its proximity to the sea route to India. One might say that Lloyd George's War Cabinet was predisposed to assume this aggressive stance toward territories in Africa, given the presence of old-guard imperialists such as Lord Milner and Lord Curzon. John Gallagher has remarked, "Indeed it would be hard to find any more imperially minded government in British history than Lloyd George's."[48]

The government confronted formidable obstacles to its goal of imperial expansion. Most important, the war with Germany was far from decided in early 1918. Russia's withdrawal from the war at the end of 1917 had aggravated the allies' difficulties, and the British had not yet anticipated Germany's last great offensive of the war in March 1918. On the diplomatic front, the British government found itself catering to the idealistic pronouncements of President Wilson as it attempted to draw the United States farther into the war in France. Wilson condemned the prospect of territorial annexations after the war and advocated the political rights of small nations. On the home front, Lloyd George faced pressure from British labor not to engage in a "war of conquest" at the expense of the soldiers in the trenches.[49] With specific reference to Germany's colonies in Africa, the Labour Party declared:

> The British Labour Movement disclaims all sympathy with the Imperialist idea that these should form the booty of any nation, should be exploited for the profit of the capitalist, or should be used for the promotion of the militarist aims of Governments.[50]

Recognizing the resonance of this criticism in Britain, German and Bolshevik propagandists asserted that the British government was waging its war only to annex more territory.

When the Cabinet began to draft its declaration of Britain's war aims in late 1917, Lloyd George was primarily concerned with appeasing the Labour Party and refuting German and Bolshevik accusations of imperialism. In a Cabinet meeting on December 31, the Prime Minister reported that he had held a successful interview with a labor delegation regarding war aims. They had been in general agreement, and "with regard to the German colonies north of the Zambesi, they all agreed that they should not be handed back to the Germans, and advocated some super-national authority being established to administer them."[51] Lloyd George and his Cabinet were actually hostile to the idea of a "super-national" colonial authority, but they were ready to make concessions to the Labour Party in words, if not, subsequently, in deeds. On January 5, 1918, the Prime Minister gave his definitive speech on British war aims to trade union delegates at the Central Hall in Westminster. In a grand gesture that pre-empted Wilson's declaration of the Fourteen Points three days later, Lloyd George accepted the principle of political self-determination for small nations. He extended this principle to the German colonies, explaining that their political status should be determined by a postwar conference "whose decision must have primary regard to the wishes and interests of the native inhabitants":

> The governing consideration, therefore, in all these cases must be that the inhabitants should be placed under the control of an administration acceptable to themselves, one of whose main purposes will be to prevent their exploitation for the benefit of European capitalists or Governments.[52]

The Colonial Office continued to assemble evidence of maladministration in the German empire, enlisting assistance from the governments of South Africa and Australia, both of which would acquire German colonial territories in 1919. By displaying the brutalities of German rule, the government hoped to substantiate its claims that the transfer of colonial sovereignty to Britain would reflect the self-determination of Germany's subjects. The Foreign Office also participated in indicting German imperialists by publishing in the summer of 1918 "atrocity bluebooks" that contained, among other damning evidence, photographs of Africans hanged by punitive expeditions. These blue books, as William Roger Louis suggests, "provided evidence implying that the Germans had committed such atrocious acts that the natives could not help but have a pro-British attitude."[53] Although the Foreign Office records do not indicate how officials reached the decision to include photographs in the blue books, it is possible that they had been impressed by the effective use of photographic evidence of atrocities in the Congo reform campaign.

Looking toward the organization of the postwar settlement in Africa, the Colonial Office and most of the Cabinet favored annexation.[54] This path diverged, however, from the course of U.S. and British public opinion, which was increasingly enamored of Wilson's Fourteen Points. Under these circumstances, the British War Cabinet made a virtue of necessity by embracing the prospective league of nations and the mandates system, but only after calculating that imperial objectives could be secured through this experiment in international government. As the Colonial Office explained in a memorandum circulated in November 1918, the Berlin and Brussels Acts were the most frequently cited precedents for the mandates system, and these acts carried no enforceable guidelines. In the end, the mandates system would be only an ethical pretense.[55]

The Revival of Trust

President Wilson drew upon the work of a number of British and British imperial officials in conceiving the League of Nations and creating his influential draft of the League's Covenant.[56] Wilson and leading British politicians, including the grudging Lloyd George, saw the peace settlement as the foundation of a new era of Anglo–American cooperation and world leadership. Yet this cooperation depended upon reconciling Wilson's advocacy of the self-determination of small nations with the British government's commitment to empire.[57] In the end, Smuts provided the language of reconciliation in trusteeship. In a resolution of January 30, 1919, submitted to the Council of Ten, Smuts described the mandates system as a "sacred trust." Three days later, Wilson incorporated this language into his fourth draft of the League of Nations Covenant.[58]

The principle of trusteeship provided the British government with an ideological justification of its imperial expansion by means of the League of Nations. In accepting responsibility for overseas territory and peoples "in trust," British officials neither claimed sovereignty over the lands in question nor completely denied the peoples' right to self-determination. Instead, they would ostensibly prepare their imperial "wards" to determine their own political course in the future—and an indefinite future at that. While there is no evidence that the Imperial War Cabinet made a concerted decision to revive the discourse of trusteeship to support its aims, it is apparent that this particular discourse enabled them to navigate between domestic agitation against territorial aggrandizement and President Wilson's call for the self-determination of small nations.[59]

Addressing the House of Lords on May 13, 1920, Lord Milner, the former High Commissioner of South Africa and the current Colonial Secretary, stated:

> I may say…that I accept—I have repeatedly stated it myself—the principle of trusteeship with regard to our position as a nation in all these dependent Crown Colonies and Protectorates. I consider that wherever we are obliged, owing to the backwardness of the population of these countries, to keep the ultimate authority in our own hands, we have to exercise that authority in the interests of the people of those countries and not for our own advantage.[60]

In the light of the theological origins and strong Protestant connotations of trusteeship between the sixteenth and eighteenth centuries, as discussed in chapter 1, it is noteworthy that Milner did not explicitly define trust as a Christian duty. It is remarkable, in fact, how little the advocates of trusteeship in the 1920s knew of its theological origins.[61] Smuts, who played an important role in presenting the British Empire as a structural and ideological model for the "sacred trust" of the mandates system, regarded trusteeship as a recent idea. In a speech in Cape Town, South Africa, in 1942, Smuts recalled: "I remember from my young days that Cecil Rhodes used repeatedly to say that the proper relation between whites and blacks in this country was the relation between guardian and ward. This is the basis of trusteeship."[62] Having cited Rhodes as a source of trusteeship, Smuts went on to note that "[Trusteeship] is closely connected with our Christian ideals."[63] Smuts did not, however, elaborate upon the latter point.

Following the war, British officials revived the discourse of trusteeship with an overt emphasis not upon Christian duty, but on responsibility for "native welfare."[64] One might reasonably speculate that this discursive shift was a response to radicals who had emphasized an economic critique of imperialism since the turn of the century. More generally, imperial officials revived and recrafted the discourse of trusteeship after the war in ways that made ethical sense of their economic and political exigencies. Britain emerged victorious, but in a weakened state, from the war, and it soon confronted uprisings in Ireland, India, and Egypt by resurgent nationalist movements. At the same time, the government was attempting to restore the home front through social reform and welfare initiatives under the gaze of a strengthening labor movement. In its efforts to stabilize the Empire, and simultaneously recover at home, the government sought to delegate political responsibilities to loyal native authorities, particularly in West and central Africa, and avoid overseas social reform projects, which it saw as tangential to the business of empire. "As an exercise in retrenchment and redeployment rather than the prelude to Imperial retreat," Nicholas Owen comments astutely, "the reinvention of imperialism as trusteeship had more to do with financial stringency at home and crises of authority on the periphery than to any sudden triumph of liberal opinion."[65]

The thin veil of trusteeship and Lloyd George's declarations on political self-determination ultimately could not conceal the imperialist attitudes and objectives of the government. Lloyd George's declarations in favor of imperial reform were viewed with particular skepticism by other European governments and the United States. President Wilson, in particular, did not trust Lloyd George, and observed, "He is constantly turning somersaults. He is an impossible, incalculable person to do business with."[66] At home, the Labour Party also remained wary of Lloyd George, even though the government had apparently accepted the party's principles for reforms in both foreign and imperial policy. Indeed, the War Cabinet had its own imperial objectives, but it was now compelled to recast these goals to accommodate an economic and ethical critique of empire which had emerged through the humanitarian politics of the previous twenty years. Behind the Labour Party's call for imperial reforms stood Morel and his political allies, building upon their earlier campaigns against the Congo Free State. On the side of the government stood John and Alice Harris and the Anti-Slavery Society, defending the state's "sacred trust" over colonial mandates as an extension of their own "Christian imperialism." In the following year, even before the peace conference convened at Versailles, the Anti-Slavery Society would find itself alienated from the British government as these three groups debated the responsibilities of mandatory powers to their African subjects under the Covenant of the League of Nations.

Initially, the Anti-Slavery Society heralded the League of Nations as a "momentous event in the history of Africa," and applauded the foundation of the mandates system upon the *Christian* principle of trusteeship.[67] In 1919, John Harris defined trusteeship in the following terms:

Trusteeship means that the Government is to be in the interests of the governed; it means that when the ward has attained manhood the trusteeship will be surrendered; it means that it is the prime duty of the trustee to so foster the growth of the ward that upon reaching the state of manhood the capacity to manage his own affairs will not be denied or questioned.[68]

Harris suggested that trusteeship entailed social reform and economic intervention, thus opening the door for his own evangelical agenda. He advocated a renewed civilizing mission to Africa on the bases of "commerce and Christianity," now to be carried forward by self-sustaining "industrial missions." Harris asserted that the success of trusteeship required the recognition of customary African land tenure, but it is important to note that he regarded land tenure as necessary for the practical stability of Christian communities. The African's right to land remained contingent upon conversion.[69]

Harris further believed that the success of trusteeship depended not only on sovereign authority, but also on the selection of particular states that had proven themselves to be ethical imperial rulers. His wartime valorization of the British and denigration of the Germans suited the government, but Harris diverged from official policy in opposing Belgian mandates in Africa. During the war, Belgium had become a noble martyr in the eyes of the British nation, and—to Harris's dismay—the infamous brutality of the "Belgian Congo" had been largely ignored, although not forgotten. The war and its aftermath witnessed a reaffirmation of the Anglo–Belgian alliance on the basis of common strategic interests in Europe. This was clearly reflected in British support for the postwar Belgian mandate over Ruanda-Urundi.

In advocating trusteeship, Harris chose to emphasize its Christian connotations, but it soon became clear that his faith in this discourse had been misplaced. As in the eighteenth century, trust was the discourse of imperial government, and imperial officials remained wary of evangelical initiatives. Granted, the advocates of both trust and evangelicalism remained committed to capitalist development, but, as emphasized in chapter 1, evangelicals saw this development as an engine for comprehensive social reform, in the spirit of Livingstone's call for "commerce and Christianity." By contrast, Burke and, subsequently, Smuts argued that government should promote political economy, but avoid systematic attempts to assimilate the cultures of foreign peoples. This ideology suited the interests of the British government after the First World War, when imperial officials found themselves torn between their desire to hold the Empire and their realization that they had to do so with overextended resources, in the face of mounting nationalist opposition.

In resisting the initiatives of evangelicals, imperial officials privileged native welfare over the saving of souls as the standard of ethical imperialism. The idiom of "moral and material improvement" became longhand, in effect, for "material improvement." This shift arguably reflected the changing religious environment of Britain after the war, when evangelicalism dissipated dramatically. It is telling, in this regard, that the most important postwar treatise on empire, Sir Frederick Lugard's *The Dual Mandate in British Tropical Africa* (1922), makes virtually no mention of "Christian duty," but identifies Britain's "dual mandate" in terms of an imperial economy that is mutually, if not equally, beneficial to Britons and Africans. Lugard made the case for Britons "as trustees to civilization for the adequate development of their [the natives'] resources, and as trustees for the welfare of the native races."[70]

Lugard's *Dual Mandate*, to which we will return shortly, was a response to Morel's last comprehensive statement on European administration in Africa, *The Black Man's Burden*, published in 1920. In the course of his incarceration during the war, Morel had shifted decisively to the political left, joining the Labour Party in April 1918. He wrote *The Black Man's Burden* as a guide to colonial administration for "the producing masses" who would soon seize control of government from the propertied classes. "We stand on the threshold of a new era," Morel declared. "The moment is propitious for the birth of an international conscience in regard to Africa."[71] Morel believed that the League of Nations had the potential to promote this international conscience, but he was skeptical that European governments could ultimately overcome the burdens of their own imperial histories, and thus bring integrity to their "trusteeship."

Morel recognized that the Berlin Act was the primary precedent for the League of Nations' policies on colonial administration. Consequently, he focused his criticism upon those two basic elements of the League Covenant that perpetuated the errors of Berlin. First, Morel portrayed sovereignty as an obstacle to international administration, exposing the nationalist interests in territorial expansion that had characterized both the Berlin Conference and the peace conference at Versailles. "The 'mandatory system,'" Morel explained, "was introduced into the Covenant as a device to distribute Germany's dependencies in Africa between such of Germany's former enemies as were African Powers already."[72] According to Morel, international industrial capitalists, in cooperation with the ruling classes, had usurped the imperial policies of Europe's nation-states and now threatened to decimate tropical Africa in the same manner as the Congo Free State had before. The British had no monopoly on legitimacy, and the brutality of German imperialism had been in no way exceptional.[73] Morel declared that the League should override the capitalists who dictated the policies of imperial states, even if this required the League to cross sovereign boundaries. If the League did not possess the power to censure and regulate its members, Morel observed, the mandates system would be "a mere phrase."[74]

Turning to the principle of trusteeship, Morel raised the critical issue of African land rights. "As the African peoples were prefigured in 1884 so are they described to-day—the wards of civilisation."[75] While the taproot of imperialism was grounded in capitalist exploitation, Morel observed of Africans' human rights: "*The root is in the land.*"[76] He acknowledged that the endorsement of free trade under the Berlin Act afforded a promising precedent for the mandates system, but he also emphasized that the Berlin Act had "made no attempt to define native tenure" or to forbid the expropriation of African lands.[77] Morel suggested that Europe should "neutralize" tropical Africa, creating a massive free-trade zone under impartial League administration, based upon communities of African agriculturalists with customary rights to land and produce.[78]

Even as Morel's book went to press, Lugard was writing his classic text on colonial administration, *The Dual Mandate*, which would broadly refute Morel's arguments. Lugard had recently retired from the governorship of Nigeria, and he was one of the most famous and widely respected imperial officials of his day. Margery Perham has noted that contemporaries regarded *The Dual Mandate* as an answer to Labour's proposals for British imperial policy. Perhaps mistakenly, Perham suggests that Lugard had focused his rhetoric upon Leonard Woolf, whose book *Empire and Commerce in Africa* had appeared in 1921.[79] It is more likely, however, that Lugard was writing his rebuttals to Labour with Morel in mind. Apart from the fact that Morel had more influence than Woolf in Labour's policies toward Africa, Lugard and Morel had been in correspondence before the First World War. Moreover, Lugard had regularly read Morel's trade journal, the *West African Mail*, as well as Morel's book *Nigeria: Its Peoples and Problems*, published in 1911.[80] In this book, Morel expressed his great admiration for Lugard as an administrator and, more generally, for Lugard's system of "indirect rule" in Nigeria. It is also significant that Morel had been a familiar figure to Flora Shaw, Lugard's wife and the editor on African affairs at *The Times* between 1893 and 1900.[81] It appears that Morel's cordial relations with this formidable couple were disrupted by his views toward Germany during the Great War and his increased radicalism after his imprisonment.

Lugard treated slavery, in particular, as "an administrative problem" complicated by its variety of socio-economic formations. "Of all African problems," Lugard reflected, "there is none more engrossing than that of slavery, and...to assist in its solution has been the consistent object of my efforts since I first entered tropical Africa in 1888."[82] His main experience with slavery and abolition had occurred in the context of Islamic societies, but he generally regarded slavery as an "inevitable" feature of "the earliest stages of development." Whatever its form, slavery was "demoralising" to both masters and slaves, weakening their self-discipline and promoting indolence.[83] Lugard was careful to explain that in some colonial societies slavery could be beneficial to Africans, actually facilitating their transition to "civilisation" by enhancing the authority and, presumably, the constructive influence of their European masters.

In this relationship, according to Lugard, the European master had a paternalistic obligation to care for the slave. Moreover, Lugard specified that the status of slavery must not be recognized by law, "so that the slave, if ill-treated, can leave his master."[84]

In addition to advocating this transitional process from slavery to wage labor, Lugard warned against sudden and absolute emancipation, particularly in Islamic societies where slavery was incorporated into the socio-economic order. "It is clear," Lugard declared,

> that sudden emancipation would dislocate the whole social fabric. Men wholly unaccustomed to any sense of responsibility and self-provision would be thrown on the streets to fend for themselves. Slave concubines would become prostitutes. Masters, albeit with money in their pockets, would be ruined; industry would be at a standstill; and plantations would be wrecked before the new order could adjust itself.[85]

Lugard proposed a strategy for abolition that involved the imperial government's full control over a gradual transition from slave to wage labor. Rather than declaring an emancipation, the imperial government should simply abolish slavery as a legal category. In this way, the former "slave" would be provided with the option to assert his or her freedom from the former "master," who would therefore have to ensure that the laborer worked under satisfactory conditions. "A master is not compelled to dismiss his slaves," Lugard proposed, "and so long as the two work harmoniously together the law does not interfere."[86] It is noteworthy that Lugard was not introducing a new method of abolition; rather, he was endorsing a policy of legal disengagement that had been employed by British imperial officials for decades, as discussed in chapter 1.

Standing behind this renegotiation of labor relations was the coercive power of the imperial government. In fact, in Lugard's scheme, the former slave had to appeal to the government in order to change his or her employment. If the government faced a mass exodus from a particular kind of work, the imperial executive was supposed to temporarily reject the appeals of the laborers for the sake of socio-economic stability. "Such measures may seem to constitute an arbitrary interference with natural laws of progress," Lugard admitted. "They are suited only to a brief period of transition, which can be hastened by judicious explanations to master and slave alike. They will not arrest or defeat the operation of the law, but only make it more gradual."[87]

Although Lugard agreed in principle with Morel that Africans should be free to own and cultivate land, he also believed that Morel's vision of African economies based on independent agriculturalists was impracticable. Lugard did not want to extend universal land rights to Africans because this policy would undermine the needs of the imperial regime and European businessmen and farmers for wage labor. It was thus the occasional duty of the administration to impose "a temporary check" upon grants of land to Africans, compelling them to seek wage labor.[88] Aside from this indirect compulsion to labor, Lugard also believed that "forced labor" under governmental supervision was sometimes acceptable. "Compulsion is only justified," he observed, "where labour cannot otherwise be procured for public works of an essential and urgent nature."[89] In depriving Africans of land rights and sanctioning forced labor, Lugard advocated an imperial system no different from those of the "new imperialism" some thirty years before.[90]

Thus, in the early years of the League of Nations' mandates system, three distinct voices could be heard in British debates over abolition in Africa. John and Alice Harris, representing the Anti-Slavery Society, advocated evangelical philanthropy under the rubric of "Christian imperialism" and attempted to rearticulate the principle of trusteeship as an evangelical duty. While the Harrises' trust made little impression on imperial officials, other "Christian imperialists," such as J.H. Oldham in Kenya, kept this ethic alive in public debate, with mixed results.[91] Despite resistance from his own government, John Harris would soon instigate progress toward a convention against slavery in the League of Nations Assembly, but his influence over the convention would end there.

Morel helped to lay the groundwork for the slavery convention by framing British political debates over imperialism and human rights, but he would not participate in the actual creation of international labor legislation. Morel enjoyed a successful parliamentary career as a Labour MP after the war, defeating Winston Churchill for one of the parliamentary seats of Dundee in 1922, but he suffered from declining health and died on November 12, 1924. Prior to his death, he anticipated the contentious issues of imperial sovereignty and native land rights that would define the strengths and conspicuous weaknesses of the League of Nations' Slavery Convention of 1926.

Finally, there was Frederick Lugard, who emerged from his retirement as a colonial governor to take a leading role in postwar imperial policy. Lugard had little patience with the Harrises' evangelical agenda, though he was committed to the cause of abolition in principle. Likewise, he had little patience with Morel's belief in Africans' right to land as a guarantee of their human rights. Lugard's guiding principles were the profitable and stable development of imperial territories, coupled with the improvement of the welfare of African societies. "Let it be admitted," declared Lugard, "that Europe is in Africa for the mutual benefit of her own industrial classes, and of the native races in their progress to a higher plane; that the benefit can be made reciprocal; and that it is the aim and desire of civilised administration to fulfill this dual mandate."[92] Lugard's dual mandate would prove to be the model upon which the principle of trusteeship took shape under the League of Nations, constituting the imperial origins of international labor law under the Slavery Convention of 1926.

The League of Nations and Reluctant Abolition

Although the League of Nations was a new institution, it possessed the extensive procedures and bureaucracy of an older political body. The administration of the mandates system was outlined under Article 22 of the League Convenant. The League Council had primary authority to make decisions on mandates, with assistance from an advisory body, the Permanent Mandates Commission. Ostensibly, the members of the Permanent Mandates Commission acted only in a personal capacity, not as representatives of their national governments, but this principle had no reality in practice. Beyond this commission, the League Assembly could discuss issues concerning the mandates and submit resolutions to the Council.

By 1922, the Committee of the Anti-Slavery Society had become frustrated by the reluctance of the British government to sponsor new legislation against slavery. Moreover, it was disenchanted with the mandates system and specifically with Britain's acquiescence to the imperial aggrandizement of Belgium and France. Seeking a means to circumvent the policies of the government and its allies, the Anti-Slavery Society turned to the League of Nations in the hope of securing international legislation on the behalf of Africans. John Harris was already working as a lobbyist in Geneva in May 1922, when the Anti-Slavery Society began to raise funds for a campaign to bring the issue of slavery before the League Council. In pursuing this objective, Harris enjoyed assistance from several influential figures, including Sir Arthur Steel-Maitland, who was the League delegate for New Zealand, H.A. Grimshaw of the International Labour Organisation, and Lugard, who now sat on the Permanent Mandates Commission.[93] Although Harris did not have an ally on the Council, his contacts and supporters could guarantee that his initiatives would be presented to the Assembly, where they received ready support. Given the high expectations for idealism within the League, the British officials who held sway in the Council could not dismiss slavery in the face of the Assembly's concern.

The Anti-Slavery Society had established a working relationship with Steel-Maitland during the war, when he served on the Committee for the Welfare of Africans in Europe. As the delegate for New Zealand in the League Assembly, he cooperated with Harris in attempting to raise the issue of slavery for discussion. On September 6, 1922, Steel-Maitland informed the Assembly that there had been "a considerable recrudescence of slavery in Africa of late," and he referred specifically to reports of slavery in Abyssinia. He then proposed the following resolution: "The Assembly resolves to refer to the appropriate Committee the question of the recrudescence of slavery in Africa in order that it may consider and propose the best methods for combating the evil."[94]

The Assembly subsequently adopted the resolution in modified form, and the Council then agreed to act upon it. The Council instructed the Secretary-General, Sir Eric Drummond, to compile a report on slavery, soliciting from the governments of League members "any information they may see fit to communicate to it on the existing situation."[95] The League's subsequent request for information on slavery was received with annoyance by the British Foreign Office. The sentiments of the Foreign Office were well represented by E. Orde of the American Department, who minuted on October 14: "One wonders how much evidence the League is likely to collect from the Govts addressed. No Govt will testify against itself and few will care to produce evidence against others."[96] Accordingly, in December, the Foreign Office informed the Secretary-General that there was no evidence of "a recrudescence of slavery" in British territory.[97]

The Anti-Slavery Society became aware that the British government was withholding information on slavery from the League, particularly with regard to Abyssinia.[98] In fact, the Foreign Office was determined to withhold its files on Abyssinia because this was not a British territory, and the government had no intention of interfering in Abyssinia's labor practices.[99] The Anti-Slavery Society persisted nonetheless, and Harris sent a petition titled "Slavery and the League of Nations" to the League Council in July 1923. At this point, Harris was blocked by the mutual interests of Belgian and British officials in stifling private, humanitarian interference in their colonial policies. Perhaps recalling Harris's prominent role in the Congo reform campaign, the Belgian representative on the Council proposed that, henceforth, all documents from private organizations must pass through their respective governments. The proposal received support from the British delegate on the Council, Lord Robert Cecil, and Drummond, the General-Secretary.[100] In voting to approve this new policy, the Council compelled Harris to ask the British Foreign Secretary, Lord Curzon, to forward his petition to the League. Curzon predictably refused, on the grounds that the Anti-Slavery Society did not represent official policy.[101]

Recognizing that the British government had obstructed his direct access to the League Council, Harris attempted an end run through the Assembly. As leverage in his lobbying efforts, he publicized the poor results of the League's first inquiry into slavery. By April 1923, only fifteen of fifty-two members had responded to this inquiry, and these responses were not adequate for a report, as the British Foreign Office had anticipated. The majority of respondents discussed their laws against slavery rather than the conditions of labor in their overseas possessions. Of those few notes in which slavery was acknowledged, the Belgian response typifies the views of colonial administrators:

Although the Government…has done all in its power to promote the extension of individual liberty, it was neither possible nor prudent to abolish by a stroke of the pen a traditional institution, the sudden disappearance of which would have caused a profound disturbance in native life. The State, however, regards domestic slavery as contrary to the principles which the civil law describes as public and international.[102]

Harris' aggressive lobbying produced another resolution from the Assembly on September 28, 1923. The Assembly asked the Council to establish a separate, competent body to further the investigation of slavery, soliciting additional information from "individuals or organisations whose competence and reliability are recognised." In conclusion, the resolution conveyed "the desire that...the fifth Assembly receive a report showing the progress made in different countries with regard to the suppression of slavery in all its forms." The Foreign Office was incensed at this "distinct score" by the Anti-Slavery Society at its expense. Not only had the Assembly endorsed unofficial sources of information, but the Anti-Slavery Society had even incorporated one of its classic phrases, "slavery in all its forms," into the League's agenda. The Foreign Office reiterated to Cecil that it wished to keep the Anti-Slavery Society out of the Council's deliberations.[103]

The Council delayed its action on the Assembly's resolution of September 28. Finally, on December 11, it responded by formally postponing its decision on a separate body of experts until the next session. In view of the failure of its first inquiry, the Council now issued three more questions on slavery to League members, requesting answers by June 1, 1924. The Council asked what measures had been taken to suppress slavery, and what were the social and economic effects of abolition. Furthermore, the Council asked "whether they would see any objection to indicating any organisation or individual in their country who might be able to give reliable and valuable additional information on this subject." In view of these questions, a Foreign Office official, Alexander Cadogan, complained: "This is clearly inspired by the Anti-Slavery Society, whose activities have constantly led us into trouble."[104]

In deference to the Council, Harris led a deputation of humanitarians to the Foreign Office in February 1924 and requested that the Anti-Slavery Society be affiliated with any "competent body" commissioned to examine slavery for the League. The Foreign Office refused to support this proposal. Above all, the Foreign Office wanted the members of the Subcommittee on Slavery to be appointed directly by their own governments and to take instructions from the same.[105]

The Council decided, instead, to invite the Permanent Mandates Commission to select the members of the Temporary Slavery Commission. In order to exercise British influence, if not control, within the Slavery Commission, Secretary-General Drummond persuaded Lugard, a member of the Permanent Mandates Commission, to accept his nomination. As Drummond observed to Sir Eyre Crowe of the Foreign Office, Lugard had taken "the hint about the necessity of his consulting H.M.G. [His Majesty's Government] before attending the meetings of the Slavery Committee or taking action on points to be raised there."[106] Lugard was an excellent, if not ideal, member of the commission, having a long history of administrative experience in Africa. The only potential problem with his appointment was his famous resistance to orders from the bureaucrats of the central government in London. He had resigned the governorship of Nigeria due to his conflicts with the Colonial Office, and his initiatives on the Temporary Slavery Commission would eventually conflict with the dilatory policies of the Foreign Office. Nonetheless, Lugard's views would significantly shape policies toward slavery and labor under the League of Nations and, subsequently, the United Nations.[107]

The eight members of the Temporary Slavery Commission were named in June, and they then convened on July 9, 1924.[108] The Commission elected the Belgian representative, Gohr, as its Chairman, and the representative from Portugal, Freire d'Andrade, as its Vice Chairman. The former was the Director General in Belgium's Ministry of the Colonies, and the latter was Portugal's former Minister of Foreign Affairs and a current member of the Permanent Mandates Commission. Clearly, these men had situated themselves, with the consent of their allies, to protect the imperial possessions of their governments from criticism. The Belgian and Portuguese governments did not want to revive the prewar controversies over their imperial labor policies, and, as illustrated below, the previous debates over new slaveries in Africa would decisively influence the League's efforts to abolish slavery under international law.

Lugard took the leading role in outlining the issues that the Commission would address. He observed, "The lines on which we are instructed to proceed are very indistinct and nebulous—if not contradictory." To provide some basis for discussion at the initial meetings, he prepared and submitted a summary statement on topics, possible goals, and questions, the first of which was whether the Commission needed to define slavery as a prerequisite to its debates and possible recommendations. He emphasized that slavery was an amorphous subject, difficult to define on the basis of either law or particular conditions of labor. He observed, for example:

> Slave-trading and dealing in slaves by sale, gift, transfer or inheritance may be said to include the acquisition of slave concubines whose purchase-price has been disguised as "dowry," or of female children as "Mui-Tsai" in China. It may also include adoption, if undertaken with ulterior motives, together with "debt slavery," "peonage," and the pledging or pawning of persons.[109]

Lugard's question regarding a definition of slavery provoked disagreement among the commissioners. While a minority wanted to create a working definition, the Belgian Chairman led the majority in opposing this course.

The other fundamental question that Lugard raised was whether the Commission had the prerogative to discuss the imperial policies of particular sovereign states. The Chairman, Gohr, firmly rejected any such violation of state sovereignty.[110] Subsequently, the Commission often worried over the prospect of offending certain governments, and nationalist conflict within the Commission itself commonly stifled its dialogues and proposals.

Finally, with regard to the gathering of information, Lugard mentioned that the Anti-Slavery Society had asked to address the Commission, and he suggested that this would be acceptable if it were not regarded as a precedent. Lugard's colleagues, especially Gohr of Belgium, insisted, on the contrary, that all petitions from private organizations had to be sent through their respective governments. The Commission simultaneously acknowledged that governments were apt to reject these petitions in order to conceal their own offenses, as was their sovereign privilege.[111]

A year later, the Temporary Slavery Commission had not made significant progress in its work. The basic obstacles before it were a lack of information from members of the League and the nationalist conflicts among members of the Commission itself. The Portuguese Vice Chairman was incensed by overt and implied criticisms of Portugal's labor policies in Africa, and Portugal's reports to the Commission were defensive, if not shrill, in their denunciations of Portugal's foreign critics. Lugard wrote to Cecil:

> I think that this Slavery Commission of the League may at its best achieve a real step forward in the relations between European Employers and Native Labour (as well as in the eradication of slavery) [and] at the worst may degenerate not merely into a futile debate but into a source of friction and recrimination.[112]

Lugard complained that discussions were characterized by useless generalizations and criticism. In an effort to break this impasse, he proposed to "place before the Commission a definite and not too complex bit of constructive work" which might lead to results. Lugard urged, first, "a decision as to the action to be taken in regard to Abbysinia, Hedjaz and Portugal in respect of which countries there are precise accusations and data." Second, he wished to recommend to the Council a draft convention on slavery and forced labor, and, finally, a "Labour Charter" on principles of imperial administration. The initial proposal, Lugard observed, "will give opportunity for the garrulous to blow off steam and avow their devotion to the great cause of freedom and similar froth and incidentally to decide a course in regard to the three countries named."[113]

Lugard submitted his preliminary draft of the Slavery Convention for the British Crown lawyers to examine and revise. Not surprisingly, Lugard's superiors were alarmed by his call for decisive action, and they feared that he might place his draft convention before the Council before the British government could respond.[114] The Foreign Office promptly convened a meeting on July 7, attended by representatives of the Colonial Office, the India Office, the Admiralty, the Board of Trade, the Ministry of Labour, and the Sudan Government Office.[115] The discussions of this group focused upon tailoring the draft convention to suit Britain's interests in imperial and naval power. For example, the India Office and the Colonial Office asserted that slavery should be defined in such a manner that land tenure and labor conditions in India and Kenya would not qualify. The Admiralty received general support for its proposal to treat the slave trade as piracy, which would give British vessels the right to search foreign ships without prior treaty arrangements. Having revised Lugard's draft in accordance with these and other demands, the Foreign Office returned the convention for submission to the League Council.[116]

In introducing Britain's draft of the Slavery Convention to the Council, Cecil observed:

> We shall all recognize that in certain cases in the past the attempt to do away with slavery, and other similar conditions in an abrupt manner, although noble in its inspiration, has resulted in unforeseen and regrettable hardships for the individuals whose condition it was sought to alleviate, and even in grave social upheavals.[117]

In the future, Cecil added, abolition "could only be successfully brought about with due regard to the maintenance of order and the well-being of the peoples concerned."[118] The slavery convention reflected this desire of imperial administrators to reconcile freedom and welfare as a "sacred trust" of the state. As Lugard had observed in the *The Dual Mandate*, "The task of the administrative officer is to clothe his principles in the garb of evolution, not revolution."[119]

On September 29, 1925, the Council resolved to submit the draft Convention on Slavery for comment to the members of the League and other governments, including Afghanistan, Egypt, Ecuador, Germany, Mexico, Russia, Sudan, Turkey, and the United States. Harris observed of the Convention and the work of the Temporary Slavery Commission: "It is no exaggeration to say that these represent the biggest advance made by Anti-Slavery forces since 1885."[120] By June 1, 1926, only nineteen members of the League, as well as

Egypt, Sudan, and the United States, had commented upon the draft. The only major modification to the draft was the deletion of piracy by France and Italy, on the grounds that Britain might exploit this provision and its superior naval strength to harass foreign shipping. On June 9, the Council resolved to present a final version of the Convention to the Assembly. A month later, at the annual meeting of the Anti-Slavery Society, the Committee adopted a resolution in support of the Convention, thanking the British government for its contributions and offering to assist in strengthening the Convention before its ratification.[121]

Conclusion

The Slavery Convention was signed at Geneva on September 25, 1926. The terms of the Convention expressed a desire "to complete and extend" the work against slavery and the slave trade which had been initiated under the General Act of Berlin of 1885, the General Act and Declaration of Brussels of 1890, and the Convention of Saint Germain-en-Laye of 1919. It was an attempt to make "more detailed arrangements" toward the goals of these previous treaties and "to prevent forced labour from developing into conditions analogous to slavery."

Despite the grand aspirations announced in the Slavery Convention, this document extended previous international labor legislation in only one significant respect. Article 5 of the Convention introduced "forced labour" as an illegal condition of oppression. Although this unprecedented legislation against "forced labour" technically extended the scope of protection for laborers, it was actually specified as a means to legitimize the continued coercion of labor by the imperial state. As Lugard had asserted in *The Dual Mandate*, forced labor under official supervision was occasionally necessary for public works of the government's design. Echoing Lugard's earlier opinion, Article 5 stipulated that "forced labour" could be mobilized only by "the competent central authorities of the territory concerned" for public purposes. In such a case, coerced laborers were to receive just remuneration and not be removed from their places of residence.

Aside from this problematic extension of international labor legislation, the Slavery Convention replicated the main provisions of the Berlin Act with regard to labor. Most important, the convention featured those two aspects of the Berlin Act, state sovereignty and the subordination of African land rights to state policy, which Morel had criticized and which Lugard had perceived as necessary to the transition of Africans from slavery to freedom. While both the Berlin Act and the Slavery Convention were premised on the profitability and ethics of free labor, this ideological construct, as Frederick Cooper observes, "led its proponents to blind spots as well as insights into the uses and abuses of power in a colonial situation: they defined slavery or coercion in a narrow way, giving an aura of normality to other colonial practices."[122]

As Lugard and other imperial administrators had wished, the process of abolition under international law was left entirely to their discretion. Article 1 of the Convention defines slavery in general terms, as "the status or condition of a person over whom any or all powers attaching to the right of ownership are exercised." Article 2 refers to "slavery in all its forms," but none of these forms are specified. The privilege of colonial administrators to interpret these generalities was guaranteed under Articles 2, 6, and 9, which stipulated that the Convention would be enforced separately by the signatories within their sovereign borders, with no prospect of international intervention by land or sea. Moreover, the signatories could choose to commit only some of their territories to the Convention, and they were permitted to specify which territories would or would not adhere to specific parts of the Convention.

While the Convention observed the sovereignty of the imperial powers, it made no mention of indigenous land rights. As Morel had asserted, the preservation of African land rights was "the acid test of trusteeship."[123] Yet Lugard and others argued that in some cases slavery could facilitate a primitive society's education in "civilized" commercial exchange. More to the point, the expropriation of indigenous lands provided the imperial regime with a wage labor force. Without rights to the land and the fruits of the soil, Africans would not be able to sustain themselves, trade, or pay taxes, except through labor in the imperial economy.

The Slavery Convention reflected the firm grasp of European imperialists upon the League of Nations and its early experiments in international law and administration. The British government had welcomed the League as a new forum for its declarations of ethical authority, but it was careful to ensure that these declarations would not interfere with imperial administration. Slavery had long stood at the center of British humanitarian debates over the ethical authority of imperial rule in Africa, and it had posed complex dilemmas for British imperial officials who valued order over emancipation. In the 1920s, as in the previous thirty years, British officials did not choose to address the issue of abolition, but found it thrust upon them by abolitionists. Nevertheless, humanitarian politics reflected relations of power, and British officials could still dictate international legislation on slavery and imperial labor in the era of the League of Nations.

Epilogue

> Abolition in 1807, led to Emancipation in 1833. Thereafter, Britain, in the strength of a clear conscience, warred cease-lessly against the Slave Trade still carried on by foreign countries . . . . Finally, in our own day, the League of Nations has taken in hand "the abolition of slavery in all its forms," and put into words the great principle of trusteeship.
>
> —**John Harris,** *A Century of Emancipation* (1933)

John Harris, the Secretary of the British and Foreign Anti-Slavery and Aborig-ines' Protection Society, publicized the Slavery Convention signed at Geneva in 1926 as the culmination of an epic humanitarian campaign by the British nation and its abolitionists. The Convention was indeed the product of British initiative and craftsmanship, but if it manifested a tradition of British aboli-tion, this tradition was characterized by internal dissent. In fact, Harris pub-licly hailed the Convention in order to promote the Anti-Slavery Society on the centennial of Britain's Emancipation Act of 1833. Privately, he regarded the Convention as an extraordinary opportunity that his own government had undermined in the interest of British imperial labor exploitation.

The campaign for a League of Nations Convention on Slavery was a direct extension of British campaigns against the "new slaveries" of European impe-rialism in Africa, and particularly in the Congo Free State. The precedents for the League's anti-slavery legislation were found in the General Act of Berlin of 1885 and the General Act and Declaration of Brussels of 1890, both of which were amended by the Convention of St. Germain-en-Laye of 1919. The benev-olent principles articulated in the first two treaties had not only defined the legitimacy of European expansion in Africa, but had also provided the legal bases for British humanitarian protests against new slaveries in Africa from the 1890s through the First World War. Remarkably, several of the people who were instrumental in producing postwar anti-slavery legislation under the League of Nations—John and Alice Harris, E.D. Morel, and Frederick Lugard—had begun their careers in different fields of African affairs in the midst of the scramble for Africa. This steady, if sometimes turbulent, confluence of law, evangelicalism, commerce, imperial governance, and individual lives reveals that international government and international labor law have deep roots in the politics of empire.

Evangelical philanthropy, human rights, and trusteeship were distinctive humanitarian ideologies in Great Britain in the late nineteenth and early twentieth centuries, and different groups put them to a variety of uses in legitimizing their interests in European expansion in Africa. The advocates of humanitarianism represented different interests in Christianity, commerce, and partisan politics, as well as official interests in reconciling economic development with administrative stability. Despite the disparate nature of humanitarianism, each of these facets contributed in one way or another to legitimizing empire. All of the participants in the controversies over the new slaveries in Africa regarded "imperialism" as an egregious form of capitalist exploitation which was the exception, rather than the rule, in Europe's relations with its foreign subjects. Humanitarian activists were not committed to the end of empire, but rather to the reform of imperialistic regimes for the mutual, if unequal, benefit of Africans and themselves.

In seeking an ethical form of empire in Africa, all of the participants in British humanitarian politics shared two fundamental principles. First, they believed that free-market capitalism was a vehicle for constructive imperial development. Disagreements over the manner in which free markets in trade and labor should be instituted for Africans were shaped by the disparate goals of proselytization, commerce, and imperial administration. Second, British humanitarians generally conceived of foreign peoples in terms of a racial hierarchy, ranging from civilization to savagery, and they believed that one's position in this hierarchy was reflected in one's culture. There were two basic variations on this hierarchy, the first of which was based on the cultural relativism of Mary Kingsley and Morel. While Kingsley and Morel advocated respect for cultural difference, they also asserted that there were superior and inferior cultures, which were determined by essential racial characteristics. By contrast, both evangelicals and proponents of trusteeship in the 1920s rejected racial essentialism—at least in principle—and regarded the adaptation of western culture through commercial exchange and capitalist development as a measure of racial improvement. Both John Harris and Jan Smuts, for example, endorsed trusteeship on the basis of Cecil Rhodes's declaration: "Equal rights for all civilised men."[1] Of course, Harris and Smuts agreed that only the trustee possessed the authority to determine when the imperial ward had achieved a level of civilization sufficient to justify independence.

The participants in the campaigns against new slaveries in Africa recognized their shared principles, but they remained keenly aware of their ideological differences. The most significant ideological divide in British humanitarianism existed between the proponents of evangelical philanthropy and the proponents of human rights. Evangelical philanthropy was the more popular and powerful of these two ideologies until the First World War, and evangelicals would subsequently succeed in initiating progress toward the League of Nations' Slavery Convention. Beyond the 1920s, however, human rights would have progressively more influence on the avowed principles of British imperial administration and those of international government.

Morel articulated a human rights ideology that extended land rights and free trade to Africans while acknowledging the integrity of African cultures. He declared, "The maintenance of trade itself as the economic factor in the relationship between civilised and primitive communities...is synonymous with the recognition that the latter are possessed of elementary human rights. If that principle be set aside, slavery, which is a denial of human rights, must in some form or another necessarily take its place."[2] It is crucial to note that Morel was advocating a right to welfare, not a right to a political voice. In debating the rights of Africans through the 1920s, none of the leading figures in British humanitarianism gave serious thought to granting political representation to Africans. In advocating the property rights of Africans, radicals such as Morel sought to provide Africans with a greater measure of freedom from European control, but they still fundamentally conceived of Africans as laborers in the service of imperial economies.

It is further noteworthy, in this regard, that Africans found limited empathy, but no political affinity, in the British labor movement. It is certainly no coincidence that the British controversies over the new slaveries of imperialism coincided with the emergence of the labor movement as a national political power in Great Britain itself. British society had long grappled with the inequities of industrial capitalism, and by the turn of the twentieth century it could clearly perceive connections between the exploitative practices of "capitalists" at home and overseas.[3] Yet, even as labor leaders gained a voice in the British government and joined in protests against the new slaveries, they did not advocate suffrage for Africans in Europe's imperial territories. Without the component of political representation in British humanitarian debates over the new slaveries in Africa, all of these debates developed on the common ground of virtual representation and paternalism.

There were, however, important differences between the paternalism of Morel's human rights and the paternalism of Lugard's trusteeship. While Morel advocated native land rights and, in turn, a greater degree of freedom for Africans

within the imperial economy, Lugard rejected rights as the seeds of discontentment and political instability. Members of Britain's political left, and especially
the Fabian Colonial Bureau, continued to push Morel's agenda after his death,
calling for the incorporation of native land rights and cultural relativism into
the "sacred trust" of the mandates system.[4] They thus contributed to a remarkable change in the principles of British imperial administration, eventually
combining trusteeship and human rights into a single, coherent ideology which
presaged the terms of the United Nations Charter of 1945.

The proponents of this rights-based trusteeship portrayed their agenda as an
extension of lost imperial traditions. Leonard Woolf, for example, argued that
the complementary nature of trust and rights was evident in Britain's empire
until the late eighteenth century. Speaking of this earlier period, Woolf explains:
"There was…no attempt to dominate or control or to force one civilization to
adjust itself to the political or economic system of another. The adjustment of
one civilization to the other was on a basis of tolerance—religious, racial, political, economic tolerance. The contract between the continents and the peoples
remained mainly economic."[5] This approach to empire had presumably ended
in the nineteenth century, when industrialization provided Europe with the
power of conquest. Looking back to the era of Burke, Woolf urged the League
of Nations to fulfill its trust by respecting natives' customary rights, thus
enabling Europe's imperial wards to reclaim their freedom. The identification
of trusteeship and cultural tolerance, advocated from Locke to Burke, was thus
collapsed into the contemporary principle of cultural relativism. Like the
trusteeship of Lugard, however, this ideological combination of trusteeship
and rights remained invested in "welfare" and progress through capitalist
development. In this respect, the British left was in step with official policy
which, following the lead of postwar imperial officials including Lugard and
Milner, passed the Colonial Development Act of 1929, followed by the Colonial Development and Welfare Acts of 1940 and 1945.[6]

Unlike Lugard—and even Morel—however, advocates of trust on both
the left and the right now appreciated that capitalism entailed major social
reforms in African societies. By the 1930s, officials were increasingly concerned that capitalist development produced "detribalization," which Smuts
would characterize as "the greatest revolution" that had ever happened on
the African continent.[7] British officials acknowledged that capitalist development and nationalism were producing changes in African society that
they could not stop, but they still hoped to manage these changes under the
terms of their trust. In the interest of maintaining their authority, colonial
officials determined that they would have to make definitive commitments
to transform rights to welfare into rights to self-government.[8]

Colonial nationalism and the relatively weakened state of Britain's economy
and military between the wars were the main causes of this shift to a political

combination of rights and trusteeship. In rejecting the imperialist's trust, nationalists themselves invoked rights, which were based on liberal democratic principles *and* dissident concepts of culture and history. The rights claimed by colonial nationalists were not contingent on a historical ascent of the imperialist's cultural hierarchy, but rather on their own cultural traditions. Trust was a waiting game, but rights empowered political claims in the present—political claims which the British government tried to accommodate more often after the First World War, though not at the expense of ultimate political control.[9] In this context, British critics of empire and British officials developed the ideological tools to reconcile themselves to a new balance of power in the British Empire and under international government.

Influential members of Britain's political left, as well as colonial officials, were ready to conceive of imperial reforms on the basis of native rights in the 1930s, but the government in London was not yet ready to construct a new, comprehensive political order, particularly not after Winston Churchill became Prime Minister in May 1940. Churchill wanted to turn back the clock on the progress of Britain's imperial subjects toward self-government, but his views were out of step with a general turn in Britain toward the fulfillment of trusteeship through the recognition of rights, as would become evident at the war's end. In the meantime, Churchill, like Lloyd George before him, was forced to cater to the idealism of a U.S. president.

William Roger Louis observes, "Franklin D. Roosevelt...belonged to the epoch of the great European colonial empires and he held essentially the same outlook as Wilson two decades earlier. He also was a gradualist. He foresaw the possible independence of colonial peoples only after a period of tutelage by the 'parent' states."[10] Roosevelt was by no means revolutionary in his approach to the British Empire, but he advocated a new political order that was far less conventional or moderate than Louis suggests above. In his State of the Union Address of 1941, Roosevelt declared that American freedoms hinged on "the supremacy of human rights everywhere." Building on a Jeffersonian liberal tradition, Roosevelt identified human rights with his famous "Four Freedoms"— that is, the rights to freedom of speech, freedom of religion, freedom from want, and freedom from fear.[11] Just days after the Japanese attack on Pearl Harbor, the U.S. Secretary of State, Cordell Hull, established an interdepartmental Committee on Problems of Peace and Reconstruction, which would subsequently flesh out the administration's human rights policy on the basis of Roosevelt's "Four Freedoms" speech.[12]

Roosevelt and Churchill's disagreements over human rights surfaced initially at the Atlantic Conference in 1941, and British officials would subsequently find themselves assailed by U.S. critics who advocated the rights of colonial nations. In response, British officials attempted to establish common ground on the basis of trusteeship, which, according to Louis, "had increasingly gained recognition as a principle of administration, in the United States no less than in the European colonies."[13] Behind the wartime rhetoric, however, British and U.S. officials took different views on trusteeship, the postwar settlement, and especially the construction of the United Nations on the shattered remains of the League of Nations. Churchill, for one, believed that the U.S. government supported the principle of trusteeship as a thin veil for its own imperial ambitions after the war.[14] These differences surfaced in negotiations over the creation of the United Nations at the San Francisco Conference in 1945, during which Churchill handed control over British imperial policy to Clement Attlee and the first majority Labour government.

By this time, most British officials across the political spectrum felt compelled to endorse political rights for Britain's imperial subjects in Africa and elsewhere. As Stephen Howe suggests, this view was probably produced by a prevailing rejection of the language of racial superiority, attributable to revulsion at the Nazis; the crucial participation of imperial forces in the war; and the demands of colonial nationalists.[15] "Any politician or party which wished to retain legitimacy had to employ the discourse of universal political rights," according to Howe, "whether they did so opportunistically or…with real conviction."[16] The politics of rights subsequently overcame the politics of trusteeship, which finally gave way to the concept of "partnership" in a Commonwealth of Nations.[17]

Although the discourses of rights and trusteeship became commonplace in both British and U.S. politics by the end of the war, Britain's commitment to the Empire could not be easily reconciled with the U.S. government's postwar policies. In addressing the proposal for a new international trusteeship system, U.S. officials wanted to make international peace and security the priorities of the system, with political oversight by a supervisory body under the U.N. General Assembly.[18] By contrast, British officials argued that the trusteeship system should prioritize welfare, and they opposed political oversight by any U.N. authority.[19] In the end, given the postwar balance of power, the United Nations International Trusteeship System was established as the United States desired.

The League of Nations Covenant of 1919 had not endorsed human rights, but the United Nations Charter of 1945 would explicitly combine the League's "sacred trust" with human rights in the new International Trusteeship System.[20] Subsequently, the United Nations incorporated human rights into the international law against slavery in its Supplementary Slavery Convention of 1956. While the U.N. Charter enjoined trustees to uphold human rights, there was still no workable mechanism for international intervention. According to the Charter, human rights could be enforced by international intervention only if a state's violation of human rights threatened international peace and security.[21] Nonetheless, the United Nations exercised its authority to send representatives to evaluate the administrations of trust territories, and the territories were subject to criticism in U.N. committees and debates in the General Assembly. The capacity for international oversight, if not effective intervention, thus distinguished the United Nations from the League of Nations. As Louis asserts, "The trusteeship system had teeth and often bit."[22]

The language of trusteeship and rights that appears in the United Nations Charter reflects an ideological compromise at the political turning point between the era of European great powers and empires and the advent of U.S. and Soviet superpowers and decolonization. Scholars have commonly overlooked this ideological development, which deserves further scrutiny. One might argue, of course, that the principle of trusteeship had always entailed temporary authority, and that it had always ensured—or at least never precluded—political representation. Indeed, the U.N. Trusteeship Council chose of its own accord to suspend its operation in 1994, after the independence of Palau, the last U.N. trust territory. Nonetheless, just as scholars have productively questioned whether nationalist thought is a derivative discourse of empire, we should ask similar questions of the principles of international government.[23] More specifically, historians should assess the ways in which the privileges and rights of international government have continued to derive from an imperialist vision of civilized hierarchy, capitalist development, and the sovereignty of the state.

Appendix to Chapter 4

The statistics below, regarding purchases of cocoa by *Cadbury Brothers, Ltd.*, are drawn from the Cadbury Papers, "Statistics on Cocoa Production and Consumption, 1908–11," Ms. 307.

Note the amounts of cocoa that *Cadbury Brothers* purchased from São Tomé in 1908 and British West Africa in 1910. It appears that by 1910 the supplies of cocoa from the Gold Coast enabled Cadbury to compensate substantially for its boycott of cocoa from São Tomé.

The Gold Coast cocoa harvest increased as shown below (figures in metric tons [1000 kg]):

1903	2,315
1904	5,193
1905	5,166
1906	9,004
1907	9,503
1908	12,946
1909	20,534
1910	23,112
1911	40,357 (Gold Coast becomes the world's leading producer of cocoa)
1912	39,260

In 1908, *Cadbury* purchased 13,818,143 pounds of cocoa from the following sources:

South America	6,407,408
São Tomé	4,434,304
West Indies	1,731,968
BritishWest Africa	918,176
East Indies (Ceylon, etc.)	268,240
Sundry	58,047

In 1909, *Cadbury* purchased 12,426,570 pounds of cocoa from the following sources:

South America	7,179,312
West Indies	2,105,376
British West Africa	1,694,896
Sundry	813,738
São Tomé	537,152
E. Indies (Ceylon, etc.)	96,096

In 1910, *Cadbury* purchased 13,629,220 pounds of cocoa from the following sources:

South America	7,263,984
British West Africa	4,062,128
West Indies	1,604,624
Sundry	583,236
E. Indies (Ceylon, etc.)	115,248
São Tomé	0

Notes

Introduction

1. Henry W. Nevinson, *A Modern Slavery* (London: Harper & Brothers., 1906), 113.
2. Ibid., 104.
3. Ibid., 37.
4. Ibid., 209.
5. Seymour Drescher demonstrates that many influential Britons looked skeptically on the economic superiority of free labor and the economic success of emancipation well into the middle of the nineteenth century. As Drescher is careful to acknowledge, however, the driving forces behind popular abolitionist campaigns were moral rather than economic. With regard to the later nineteenth century, Drescher observes, "The moral dimension of the end of slavery took increasing precedence over its economic results. As decades became generations, the disappointed forecasts of dynamic revival actually enhanced the retrospective image of the material sacrifice made by Britons in the name of humanity." See Seymour Drescher, *The Mighty Experiment* (Oxford: Oxford University Press, 2002), 225. Also see ibid., 107–108, 138.
6. Ibid., 3, 85–87; James Walvin, "Freedom and Slavery and the Shaping of Victorian Britain," in *Unfree Labour in the Development of the Atlantic World*, ed. Paul E. Lovejoy and Nicholas Rogers (London: Frank Cass, 1994), 246–259.
7. Frederick Cooper, "Conditions Analogous to Slavery: Imperialism and Free Labor Ideology in Africa," in Frederick Cooper, Thomas C. Holt, and Rebecca J. Scott, *Beyond Slavery* (Chapel Hill: University of North Carolina Press, 2000), 111–112.
8. John Harris, "Back to Slavery?," *The Contemporary Review* (August 1921): 197.
9. For an introduction to the scholarship on British anti-slavery, see Drescher, *Mighty Experiment*; Seymour Drescher, *From Slavery to Freedom* (New York: New York University Press, 1999); Thomas Bender, ed., *The Antislavery Debate* (Berkeley: University of California Press, 1992); Clare Midgley, *Women against Slavery: The British Campaigns, 1780–1870* (London: Routledge, 1992); Barbara L. Solow and Stanley L. Engerman, eds., *British Capitalism and Caribbean Slavery: The Legacy of Eric Williams* (Cambridge: Cambridge University Press, 1987); Seymour Drescher, *Capitalism and Antislavery: British Mobilization in Comparative Perspective* (New York: Oxford University Press, 1987); Christine Bolt and Seymour Drescher, eds., *Anti-Slavery, Religion and Reform* (Folkestone, U.K.: William Dawson, 1980); Roger Anstey, *The Atlantic Slave Trade and British Abolition, 1760–1810* (Atlantic Highlands, N.J.: Humanities Press, 1975); David Brion Davis, *The Problem of Slavery in the Age of Revolution, 1770–1823* (Ithaca, N.Y.: Cornell University Press, 1975).
10. My views on this subject have been strongly influenced by the work of Frederick Cooper. See the following works: Cooper, Holt, and Scott, *Beyond Slavery*; Cooper, *From Slaves to Squatters: Plantation Labor and Agriculture in Zanzibar and Coastal Kenya, 1890–1925*

(New Haven, Conn.: Yale University Press, 1980); Cooper, "From Free Labor to Family Allowances: Labor and African Society in Colonial Discourse," *American Ethnologist* 16 (November 1989): 745–765. Also see Michael Salman, *The Embarrassment of Slavery* (Berkeley: University of California Press, 2001); Howard Temperley, ed., *After Slavery: Emancipation and Its Discontents* (London: Frank Cass, 2000); Suzanne Miers and Martin A. Klein, eds., *Slavery and Colonial Rule in Africa* (London: Frank Cass, 1999); Indrani Chatterjee, *Gender, Slavery and Law in Colonial India* (New Delhi: Oxford University Press, 1999); Martin A. Klein, ed., *Breaking the Chains: Slavery, Bondage, and Emancipation in Modern Africa and Asia* (Madison: University of Wisconsin Press, 1993); Michael Twaddle, ed., *The Wages of Slavery* (London: Frank Cass, 1993); Thomas C. Holt, *The Problem of Freedom* (Baltimore: Johns Hopkins University Press, 1992); Paul Lovejoy, *Transformations in Slavery* (Cambridge: Cambridge University Press, 1983); Hugh A. Tinker, *A New System of Slavery* (London: Oxford University Press, 1974).

11. Lovejoy, *Transformations*; Chatterjee, *Gender, Slavery and Law*.

12. Howard Temperley, *British Antislavery, 1833–1870* (Columbia: University of South Carolina Press, 1972).

13. Suzanne Miers, *Britain and the Ending of the Slave Trade* (New York: Africana, 1975).

14. Suzanne Miers, *Slavery in the Twentieth Century* (Walnut Creek, Calif.: AltaMira Press, 2003), xiii.

15. The following chapters also respond to a limited number of historical case studies of particular controversies over the new slaveries in Africa. The two most important of these case studies are James Duffy, *A Question of Slavery* (Cambridge, Mass.: Harvard University Press, 1967), and Adam Hochschild, *King Leopold's Ghost* (Boston: Houghton Mifflin, 1998). It is noteworthy that British abolitionists have also written histories that move beyond the Victorian campaigns against the American plantation complex. See, for example, John H. Harris, *A Century of Emancipation* (London: J.M. Dent, 1933); C.W.W. Greenidge, *Slavery* (London: Allen & Unwin, 1958).

16. Harold Spender, "The Great Congo Iniquity," *The Contemporary Review*, (July 1906): 45.

17. Cooper, "Conditions Analogous to Slavery."

18. Paul Lovejoy and Jan S. Hogendorn, *Slow Death for Slavery: The Course of Abolition in Northern Nigeria, 1897–1936* (Cambridge: Cambridge University Press, 1993); Martin A. Klein, *Slavery and Colonial Rule in French West Africa* (Cambridge: Cambridge University Press, 1998); Gervase Clarence-Smith, *Slaves, Peasants and Capitalists in Southern Angola, 1840–1926* (Cambridge: Cambridge University Press, 1979); Patrick Harries, *Work, Culture, and Identity: Migrant Laborers in Mozambique and South Africa, c. 1860–1910* (Portsmouth, N.H.: Heinemann, 1994). Also see the works cited in note 10.

19. Jacques Willequet, *Le Congo Belge et la Weltpolitik, 1894–1914* (Brussels: Presses Universitaires de Bruxelles, 1962); Heinrich Loth, *Kolonialismus und Humanitätintervention: Kritische Untersuchung der Politik Deutschlands gegenüber dem Kongostaat (1884–1908)* (Berlin: Akademie-Verlag, 1966); Jean Stengers, "Morel and Belgium," in *E.D. Morel's History of the Congo Reform Movement*, ed. William Roger Louis and Jean Stengers (Oxford: Clarendon Press, 1968); Klaus Kaiser, "'Kongogreuel'—Zur Kongoreformbewegung in England und Deutschland vor dem Ersten Weltkrieg," in *Geschichte und Humanität*, ed. Horst Gründer (Münster: LIT Verlag, 1994).

20. Edmund Burke, *The Works of the Right Honorable Edmund Burke*, rev. ed., vol. 9 (Boston: Little, Brown, 1867), 335.

21. Quoted in John H. Harris, *Africa: Slave or Free?* (London: Student Christian Movement, 1919), 239.

22. Jomo Kenyatta, *Facing Mount Kenya* (New York: Vintage Books, 1965), xviii.

23. By contrast, historians of British abolition and the British Empire have paid extensive attention to the roles of missionaries in anti-slavery protest in the first half of the nineteenth century. See, for example, Catherine Hall, *Civilising Subjects* (Chicago: University of Chicago Press, 2002).

24. Charles Swaisland, "The Aborigines' Protection Society, 1837–1909," in *After Slavery: Emancipation and Its Discontents*, ed. Howard Temperley (London: Frank Cass, 2000), 265–280.

25. Suzanne Miers, "Humanitarianism at Berlin: Myth or Reality?," in *Bismarck, Europe and Africa: The Berlin Africa Conference 1884–1885 and the Onset of Partition*, ed. Stig Förster, Wolfgang Mommsen, and Ronald Robinson (Oxford: Oxford University Press, 1988), 333–345.

26. The contingencies and revisions of humanitarian ideology are also evident in the amendments to the Universal Declaration of Human Rights since its ratification by the United Nations in 1948. See Walter Laqueur and Barry Rubin, eds., *The Human Rights Reader* (Philadelphia: Temple University Press, 1979), 195–263.

Chapter 1

1. Joseph Conrad, *Heart of Darkness*, ed. Robert Kimbrough, 3rd ed. (New York: W.W. Norton, 1988), 10. Conrad initially published this story in 1899 as a serial in *Blackwood's Magazine* of Edinburgh, Scotland.
2. Ibid., 15.
3. For a summary and critique of the conventional long view on the development of human rights theory, see Richard P. Claude, "The Classical Model of Human Rights Development," in *Comparative Human Rights*, ed. Richard P. Claude (Baltimore: Johns Hopkins University Press, 1976), 6–50.
4. William Roger Louis, "Great Britain and International Trusteeship: The Mandate System," in *The Historiography of the British Empire–Commonwealth*, ed. Robin W. Winks (Durham, N.C.: Duke University Press, 1966), 310. For the best study of trusteeship, focusing on the middle decades of the twentieth century, see William Roger Louis, *Imperialism at Bay 1941–1945: The United States and the Decolonization of the British Empire* (Oxford: Oxford University Press, 1977).
5. The principle of trusteeship has not been examined in the recent scholarship on ideologies of empire in the early modern era. See, for example, David Armitage, *The Ideological Origins of the British Empire* (Cambridge: Cambridge University Press, 2000); and Anthony Pagden, *Lords of All the World: Ideologies of Empire in Spain, Britain and France, c.1500–c.1800* (New Haven, Conn.: Yale University Press, 1995). For studies that address trusteeship, but do not examine its origins and its changing significance in the nineteenth and twentieth centuries, see Andrew Porter, "Trusteeship, Anti-Slavery, and Humanitarianism," in *The Oxford History of the British Empire*, vol. 3, *The Nineteenth Century*, ed. Andrew Porter (Oxford: Oxford University Press, 1999), 198–221; and G.R. Mellor, *British Imperial Trusteeship, 1783–1850* (London: Faber & Faber, 1951).
6. I disagree with speculation that British imperial trusteeship ultimately derived from the Roman law of trust governing property. See, for example, Louis, *Imperialism at Bay*, 88. Alternatively, J.W. Gough suggests that the concept of political trusteeship can be divided into two forms: the idea of trust as a moral responsibility or duty, and the idea of trust as "a metaphor for the private law of trusts" governing property. "It seems...possible," Gough observes, "that the idea [of political trusteeship] arose, independently at first of the legal trust, as an extension of the general meaning of trust or confidence." See J.W. Gough, *John Locke's Political Philosophy*, 2nd ed. (Oxford: Clarendon Press, 1973), 154–156, 165. Note that I choose to interpret trust in the sense which Gough privileges, rather than in terms of the private law of trust governing property. Regarding the latter, see F.W. Maitland, *Equity*, ed. A.H. Chaytor and W.J. Whittaker (Cambridge: Cambridge University Press, 1936); David Johnston, *The Roman Law of Trusts* (Oxford: Clarendon Press, 1988). Regarding the general influence of the Reformation on English and European political thought, see Quentin Skinner, *The Foundations of Modern Political Thought*, vol. 2, *The Age of Reformation* (Cambridge: Cambridge University Press, 1978).
7. The theological origins of trusteeship were, in these respects, tied to the long-term process of undermining the supreme power of the Pope. They were also tied to revisions of medieval doctrines of resistance to unjust rulers and of limited constitutional government. For the former, see J.N. Figgis, *Political Thought from Gerson to Grotius, 1414–1625* (Cambridge: Cambridge University Press, 1907); and for the latter, see Brian Tierney, *Religion, Law, and the Growth of Constitutional Thought, 1150–1650* (Cambridge: Cambridge University Press, 1982).
8. William Tyndale, *The New Testament Translated by William Tyndale, 1534* (Cambridge: Cambridge University Press, 1938), 301. Also see David Daniell, *William Tyndale: A Biography* (New Haven, Conn.: Yale University Press, 1994), 149.
9. Skinner, *Foundations*, 18.

10. Ibid., 68.
11. Ibid., 16–19.
12. I make these generalizations in order to bring us quickly to the argument at hand, which concerns modern political trusteeship. Following Henry VIII's break with Rome and his seizure of control over the Church in England in the 1530s, the principle of justification by faith was incorporated into the Protestant reform of the Church of England under Henry's son, Edward VI, during his reign between 1547 and 1553. This reform was then reversed by Queen Mary, a Catholic, during her reign between 1553 and 1558. Although Elizabeth I subsequently reinstated the Protestant reform of the Church by law, the reform of the beliefs and practices of the common people was a slower, uneven process that did not reach fruition until at least the 1580s. See Eamon Duffy, *The Stripping of the Altars* (New Haven, Conn.: Yale University Press, 1992); A.G. Dickens, *The English Reformation, 2nd ed.* (University Park: Pennsylvania State University Press, 1989).
13. Skinner, *Foundations*, 236–238.
14. Ibid., 229–230.
15. Ibid., 221–224, 235.
16. Paul Kléber Monod has demonstrated that this tumultuous era in English history can be seen as part of a general European movement "to appeal to an authority that was vested by God in the mystical body of the people rather than that of the monarch." Paul Kléber Monod, *The Power of Kings: Monarchy and Religion in Europe, 1589–1715* (New Haven, Conn.: Yale University Press, 1999), 151.
17. Gough, *Locke's Political Philosophy*, 161.
18. See Alexandra Walsham, *Providence in Early Modern England* (Oxford: Oxford University Press, 1999), esp. ch. 5.
19. John Locke, *Two Treatises of Government*, ed. Peter Laslett (Cambridge: Cambridge University Press, 1996), 113.
20. Ibid., 114.
21. Ibid., 121.
22. Ibid., 381.
23. Gough, *Locke's Political Philosophy*, 164.
24. Locke, *Two Treatises*, 381.
25. Ibid.
26. Ibid.
27. Uday Mehta, "Liberal Strategies of Exclusion," in *Tensions of Empire*, ed. Frederick Cooper and Ann Laura Stoler (Berkeley: University of California Press, 1997), 61. Mehta's further discussion regarding the political implications of Locke's views on the education of children is highly relevant to the discussion at hand. See especially 67–70.
28. Locke, *Two Treatises*, 381.
29. Ibid., 287–288.
30. This point was brought to my attention by Armitage, *Ideological Origins*, 97–98. See John Locke, *A Letter Concerning Toleration*, ed. James Tully (Indianapolis, Ind.: Hackett, 1983), 43.
31. Locke, *Two Treatises*, 109.
32. Ibid., 407–408.
33. Ibid., 407.
34. Linda Colley, *Britons: Forging the Nation, 1707–1832* (New Haven, Conn.: Yale University Press, 1992), 55.
35. H. Duncan Hall, *Mandates, Dependencies and Trusteeship* (Washington, D.C.: Carnegie Endowment for International Peace, 1948), 97–98. Members of Parliament subsequently invoked the principle of trust in debates over American colonial policy that preceded the American Revolution. See, for example, Edmund Burke's speech on conciliation with America on March 22, 1775, in George Bennett, ed., *The Concept of Empire: Burke to Attlee, 1774–1947* (London: Adam and Charles Black, 1953), 43.
36. P.J. Marshall, *Problems of Empire: Britain and India 1757–1813* (London: Allen and Unwin, 1968), 174–175.
37. Burke makes this point in explicit terms in *Reflections on the Revolution in France*, ed. J.G.A. Pocock (Indianapolis, Ind.: Hackett, 1987), 80–81. Regarding the case of India, see Frederick Whelan, *Edmund Burke and India* (Pittsburgh, Pa.: University of Pittsburgh Press, 1996), 23.

38. Edmund Burke, *The Works of the Right Honorable Edmund Burke*, rev. ed., vol. 9 (Boston: Little, Brown, 1867), 399.
39. Whelan, *Burke and India*, 8.
40. Burke, *Works*, 340.
41. Ibid., 379.
42. Ibid., 335.
43. C.B. Macpherson, *Burke* (New York: Oxford University Press, 1980), 59.
44. Ibid., 63.
45. This is a central theme in Catherine Hall, *Civilising Subjects: The Colony and Metropole in the English Imagination* (Chicago: University of Chicago Press, 2002). See, for example, 105.
46. Porter, "Trusteeship"; Mellor, *British Imperial Trusteeship*.
47. David Brion Davis, *The Problem of Slavery in the Age of Revolution, 1770–1823* (Ithaca, N.Y.: Cornell University Press, 1975), 377.
48. Ibid., 467.
49. Davis insists, "There is no consistent or inevitable connection between antislavery doctrine and the laissez-faire ideal of a competitive labour market." See ibid., 358.
50. Ibid.
51. See Brian Stanley, "'Commerce and Christianity': Providence Theory, the Missionary Movement, and the Imperialism of Free Trade, 1842–1860," *The Historical Journal*, 26, no. 1 (1983): 71–94; G.R. Searle, *Morality and the Market in Victorian Britain* (Oxford: Clarendon Press, 1998), 13.
52. Brian Harrison, "A Genealogy of Reform in Modern Britain," in *Anti-Slavery, Religion, and Reform*, ed. Christine Bolt and Seymour Drescher (Folkestone, U.K.: William Dawson, 1980), 119–148.
53. Davis, *The Problem of Slavery*, 385.
54. Regarding "Christian economics," see Searle, *Morality and the Market*; Boyd Hilton, *The Age of Atonement* (Oxford: Clarendon Press, 1988).
55. Bernard Semmel, *The Rise of Free Trade Imperialism* (Cambridge: Cambridge University Press, 1970); Anthony Howe, *Free Trade and Liberal England, 1846–1946* (Oxford: Clarendon Press, 1997).
56. Searle, *Morality and the Market*, 21.
57. Ronald Hyam, "Bureaucracy and 'Trusteeship' in the Colonial Empire," in *The Oxford History of the British Empire, vol. 4, The Twentieth Century*, ed. Judith M. Brown and William Roger Louis (Oxford: Oxford University Press, 1999), 265; J.A. Hobson, *Imperialism: A Study* (Ann Arbor: University of Michigan Press, 1965), 239.
58. Quoted by Lord Emmott in the House of Lords, May 13, 1920, *Parliamentary Debates*, fifth series, vol. 40, House of Lords (London, 1920), 317.
59. L.I. Izuakor, "Colonial Challenges and Administrative Response: Sir Charles Eliot and 'Native' Trusteeship in Kenya, 1901–1904," *Transafrican Journal of History* 17 (1988): 34–49.
60. Seymour Drescher, *The Mighty Experiment* (Oxford: Oxford University Press, 2002), 108.
61. Thomas Holt, *The Problem of Freedom* (Baltimore: Johns Hopkins University Press, 1992).
62. Suzanne Miers, *Slavery in the Twentieth Century* (Walnut Creek, Calif.: AltaMira Press, 2003), 30.
63. Drescher, *Mighty Experiment*, 176.
64. Miers, *Slavery in the Twentieth Century*, 30.
65. Ibid., 31.
66. See, for example, Martin A. Klein, *Slavery and Colonial Rule in French West Africa* (Cambridge: Cambridge University Press, 1998); Suzanne Miers and Richard Roberts, eds., *The End of Slavery in Africa* (Madison: University of Wisconsin Press, 1988).
67. Richard Drayton, *Nature's Government: Science, Imperial Britain, and the "Improvement" of the World* (New Haven, Conn.: Yale University Press, 2000); Armitage, *Ideological Origins*, 96–97; Anthony Pagden, "The Struggle for Legitimacy and the Image of Empire in the Atlantic to c.1700," in *The Oxford History of the British Empire, vol. 1, The Origins of Empire*, ed. Nicholas Canny (Oxford: Oxford University Press, 1998), especially 47–48.
68. Jörg Fisch, "Africa as *terra nullius*: The Berlin Conference and International Law," in *Bismarck, Europe and Africa: The Berlin Africa Conference 1884–1885 and the Onset of Partition*, ed. Stig Förster, Wolfgang J. Mommsen, and Ronald Robinson (Oxford: Oxford University Press, 1988), 347–375.

69. David Northrup, *Indentured Labor in the Age of Imperialism, 1834–1922* (Cambridge: Cambridge University Press, 1995); Marina Carter, *Servants, Sirdars, and Settlers: Indians in Mauritius, 1834–1874* (Delhi: Oxford University Press, 1995); Hugh Tinker, *A New System of Slavery: The Export of Indian Labour Overseas, 1830–1920* (London: Oxford University Press, 1974).

70. Quoted in Tinker, *New System of Slavery*, vi.

71. Lord Frederick Lugard, *The Dual Mandate in British Tropical Africa* (London: Frank Cass, 1965), 365.

72. H.R. Fox Bourne, *Civilisation in Congoland* (London: P.S. King, (903), 299.

73. Howard Temperley, *British Antislavery, 1833–1870* (Columbia: University of South Carolina Press, 1972); Charles Swaisland, "The Aborigines' Protection Society, 1837–1909," in *After Slavery: Emancipation and Its Discontents*, ed. Howard Temperley (London: Frank Cass, 2000), 265–280.

74. Drescher, *Mighty Experiment*, 174.

75. Seymour Drescher, "Cart Whip and Billy Roller: Antislavery and Reform Symbolism in Industrializing Britain," *Journal of Social History* 15, no. 1 (Fall 1981): 3–24.

76. Philippa Levine, *Prostitution, Race, and Politics* (New York: Routledge, 2003); Laura E. Nym Mayhall, "The Rhetorics of Slavery and Citizenship: Suffragist Discourse and Canonical Texts in Britain, 1880–1914," *Gender & History* 13, no. 3 (November 2001): 481–497; Antoinette Burton, "States of Injury: Josephine Butler on Slavery, Citizenship, and the Boer War," *Social Politics* (Fall 1998): 338–361; Searle, *Morality and the Market*, 64–76.

77. Dorothy O. Helly, *Livingstone's Legacy* (Athens: Ohio University Press, 1987), 55.

78. Patrick Brantlinger, *Rule of Darkness* (Ithaca, N.Y.: Cornell University Press, 1988), 173–197.

79. Suzanne Miers, "Humanitarianism at Berlin: Myth or Reality?" in *Bismarck, Europe and Africa: The Berlin Africa Conference 1884–1885 and the Onset of Partition*, ed. Stig Förster, Wolfgang Mommsen, and Ronald Robinson (Oxford : Oxford University Press, 1988), 334.

80. Mrs. H. Grattan Guinness, *The First Christian Mission on the Congo* (London: Hodder & Stoughton, 1880), 35.

81. Pamela Scully, *Liberating the Family?* (Portsmouth, N.H.: Heinemann, 1997).

82. Andrew Porter, "Commerce and Christianity: The Rise and Fall of a Nineteenth-Century Missionary Slogan," *The Historical Journal* 28, no. 3 (1985): 597–621.

83. Paul Lovejoy, *Transformations in Slavery* (Cambridge: Cambridge University Press, 1983), 253–254.

84. John Hargreaves, *Prelude to the Partition of West Africa* (London: Macmillan, 1963), 37–41, 64–78, 196–197. The expense and other complications of colonial administration and emancipation were exhibited following Britain's defeat of Asante and its annexation of the Gold Coast in 1874. The government's labor policies prompted slaves to reject the authority of their masters, resulting in social and economic turmoil. See Lovejoy, *Transformations*, 252–253, 279.

85. German merchants and the German government had recently been frustrated by conflicts with Britain over Angra Pequena and the aborted Anglo–Portuguese Treaty of 1884. See Wolfgang Mommsen, "Bismarck, the Concert of Europe, and the Future of West Africa, 1883–1885," in *Bismarck, Europe and Africa: The Berlin Africa Conference 1884–1885 and the Onset of Partition*, ed. Stig Förster, Wolfgang Mommsen, and Ronald Robinson (Oxford: Oxford University Press, 1988), 151–170.

86. Miers, "Humanitarianism at Berlin," 336.

87. Text of the General Act of the Conference of Berlin, February 26, 1885, in Sir Edward Hertslet, ed., *The Map of Africa by Treaty*, 3rd ed., repr., vol. 2 (London: Frank Cass, 1967), 473.

88. Frederick Cooper, "Conditions Analogous to Slavery," in Frederick Cooper, Thomas C. Holt, and Rebecca J. Scott, *Beyond Slavery* (Chapel Hill: University of North Carolina Press, 2000), 107–149.

89. Lovejoy, *Transformations*, 260; Cooper, "From Free Labor to Family Allowances: Labor and African Society in Colonial Discourse," *American Ethnologist* 16 (November 1989): 750.

90. Lovejoy, *Transformations*, 222.

91. Suzanne Miers, *Britain and the Ending of the Slave Trade* (New York: Africana, 1975). In 1889, following the death of an energetic Secretary named Frederick William Chesson, the APS proposed to amalgamate with the Anti-Slavery Society. This proposal fell through due to resistance within the Anti-Slavery Society's executive committee. The next Secretary of the APS, H.R. Fox Bourne, jealously guarded his organization's autonomy until his death in 1909.

92. See, for example, Nicholas Owen, "Critics of Empire in Britain," in *The Oxford History of the British Empire*, vol. 4, *The Twentieth Century*, ed. Judith M. Brown and William Roger Louis (Oxford: Oxford University Press, 1999), 188–211; Miles Taylor, "Patriotism, History and the Left in Twentieth-Century Britain," *The Historical Journal* 33, no. 4 (1990): 971–987.

93. James Ramsay MacDonald, *What I Saw in South Africa* (London: "The Echo," 1902), 118.

94. F.K. Prochaska states, "Of all the long-standing charitable campaigns, the foreign missionary and Bible societies were probably the most adept at getting the co-operation of the poor." See F.K. Prochaska, "Philanthropy," in *The Cambridge Social History of Britain, 1750–1950*, vol. 3, ed. F.M.L. Thompson (Cambridge: Cambridge University Press, 1993), 367.

95. Andrew Porter, "Religion and Empire: British Expansion in the Long Nineteenth Century, 1780–1914," *Journal of Imperial and Commonwealth History* 20, no. 3 (September 1992): 370–390.

96. Regarding nonconformity and politics, see David Bebbington, *The Nonconformist Conscience: Chapel and Politics, 1870–1914* (London: Allen & Unwin, 1982). Also see Greg Cuthbertson, "Pricking the 'Nonconformist Conscience': Religion against the South African War," in *The South African War Reappraised*, ed. Donal Lowry (Manchester: Manchester University Press, 2000), 169–187.

97. James Ryan, *Picturing Empire: Photography and the Visualization of the British Empire* (Chicago: University of Chicago Press, 1997); Annie E. Coombes, *Reinventing Africa* (New Haven, Conn.: Yale University Press, 1994); David Killingray and Andrew Roberts, "An Outline History of Photography in Africa to ca. 1940," *History in Africa* 16 (1989): 197–208; Elizabeth Edwards, ed., *Anthropology & Photography, 1860–1920* (New Haven, Conn.: Yale University Press, 1992).

98. John MacKenzie, *Propaganda and Empire* (Manchester: Manchester University Press, 1984), 32. Also see John A. Hodges, *The Lantern-Slide Manual* (London: Hazell, Watson, and Viney, 1892).

99. John Holt to E.D. Morel, January 11, 1901, Morel Collection, London School of Economics, F8, file 83.

100. H.R. Fox Bourne, *English Merchants: Memoirs in Illustration of the Progress of British Commerce*, vol. 2 (London: Richard Bentley, 1866), 365.

101. Regarding Fox Bourne's books, see, besides the work cited in note 100, *Famous London Merchants* (London: J. Hogg,1869); and *The Romance of Trade* (London: Cassell, Petter & Galpin, 1871).

102. Mary Kingsley, *Travels in West Africa, 4th ed.* (London: Virago Press, 1982), 7. Also see Katherine Frank, *A Voyager Out: The Life of Mary Kingsley* (Boston: Houghton Mifflin, 1986).

103. Paul Rich, *Race and Empire in British Politics* (Cambridge: Cambridge University Press, 1986), 30–31.

104. Kingsley, *Travels*, 434.

105. See, for example, H.H. Johnston, "British Missions and Missionaries in Africa," *The Nineteenth Century* (November 1887): 708–724.

106. Kingsley, *Travels*, 214.

107. Ibid., 3.

108. Ibid., 403.

109. Ibid., 659.

110. Ibid., 403, 439–440.

111. Quoted in Thomas Prasch, "Which God for Africa: The Islamic–Christian Missionary Debate in Late-Victorian England," *Victorian Studies* (Autumn 1989): 51.

112. MacDonald, *What I Saw in South Africa*, 119.

113. E.D. Morel, "The Late Miss Mary Kingsley," *The British Empire Review* (July 1900).

114. There is not an excellent biography of Morel. The best work to date remains Robert Wuliger, "The Idea of Economic Imperialism, with Special Reference to the Life and Work of E.D. Morel" (Ph.D. dissertation, University of London, 1953). Also see Catherine Cline, *E.D. Morel, 1873–1924: The Strategies of Protest* (Belfast: Blackstaff Press, 1980). The most recent treatment of Morel, found in Adam Hochschild, *King Leopold's Ghost* (Boston: Houghton Mifflin, 1998), is a reprise of previous scholarship.

115. Kingsley Nworah, "Humanitarian Pressure-Groups and British Attitudes to West Africa, 1895–1915" (Ph.D. dissertation, University of London, 1966), 81.

116. Cooper, "Conditions," 130.

117. *West African Mail*, April 3, 1903, 2.
118. Hochschild, *King Leopold's Ghost*; Angus Mitchell, "New Light on the 'Heart of Darkness,'" *History Today* 49, no. 12 (1999): 20–27.

Chapter 2

1. This sequence of events is conveyed in the following correspondence: Alice Harris to Mons. Van Calcken, May 15, 1904, Mss. Brit. Emp. S19, D5/10; John Harris to Dr. Harry Guinness, May 19, 1904, Mss. Brit. Emp. S19, D5/9, Papers of the British and Foreign Anti-Slavery and Aborigines' Protection Society, Rhodes House, Oxford University (hereafter Anti-Slavery Papers); Edgar Stannard to Dr. Harry Guinness, May 21, 1904, reproduced in the appendix of E.D. Morel, *King Leopold's Rule in Africa* (London: Heinemann, 1904), 442–447. It is noteworthy that Alice Harris had only a basic knowledge of the local Mongo language, so she probably relied upon an African translator, perhaps drawn from her students at the mission's school.
2. John Harris to Dr. Harry Guinness, May 19, 1904, Anti-Slavery Papers, Mss. Brit. Emp. S19, D5/9.
3. E.D. Morel, *The Congo Slave State: A Protest against the New African Slavery* (Liverpool: John Richardson, 1903), 5.
4. See, for example, Nicholas Owen, "Critics of Empire in Britain," in *The Oxford History of the British Empire*, vol. 4, *The Twentieth Century*, ed. Judith M. Brown and William Roger Louis (Oxford: Oxford University Press, 1999), 188–211; Miles Taylor, "Patriotism, History and the Left in Twentieth-Century Britain," *The Historical Journal* 33, no. 4 (1990): 971–987.
5. Adam Hochschild, *King Leopold's Ghost* (Boston: Houghton Mifflin, 1998).
6. The following studies treat E.D. Morel as the driving force behind the Congo reform campaign in Britain. These same studies overlook or significantly underestimate the importance of missionaries in mobilizing support in Britain: Robert Wuliger, "The Idea of Economic Imperialism, with Special Reference to the Life and Work of E.D. Morel" (Ph.D. dissertation, University of London, 1953); A.J.P. Taylor, *The Trouble Makers* (London: Hamish Hamilton, 1957); Ruth Slade, *English-Speaking Missions in the Congo Independent State (1878–1908)* (Brussels: Académie Royale des Sciences Coloniales, 1959); William Roger Louis, "The Triumph of the Congo Reform Movement, 1905–1908," in *Boston University Papers on Africa*, vol. 2, ed. Jeffrey Butler (Boston: Boston University Press, 1966); Kingsley Nworah, "Humanitarian Pressure-Groups and British Attitudes to West Africa, 1895–1915" (Ph.D. dissertation, University of London, 1966); William Roger Louis and Jean Stengers, eds., *E.D. Morel's History of the Congo Reform Movement* (Oxford: Clarendon Press, 1968); S.J.S. Cookey, *Britain and the Congo Question, 1885–1913* (London: Longmans Green, 1968); Bernard Porter, *Critics of Empire* (New York: St. Martin's Press, 1968); Catherine Anne Cline, *E.D. Morel, 1873–1924: The Strategies of Protest* (Belfast: Blackstaff Press, 1980); Jules Marchal, *E.D. Morel contre Léopold II: L'Histoire du Congo, 1900–1910*, 2 vols. (Paris: L'Harmattan, 1996); Adam Hochschild, *King Leopold's Ghost* (Boston: Houghton Mifflin, 1998).
7. Richard Koebner and Helmut Dan Schmidt, *Imperialism: The Story and Significance of a Political Word* (Cambridge: Cambridge University Press, 1964); Bernard Semmel, *The Liberal Ideal and the Demons of Empire* (Baltimore: Johns Hopkins University Press, 1993).
8. Regarding free-trade politics, see Bernard Semmel, *The Rise of Free Trade Imperialism* (Cambridge: Cambridge University Press, 1970); Anthony Howe, *Free Trade and Liberal England, 1846–1946* (Oxford: Clarendon Press, 1997); Frank Trentmann, "The Strange Death of Free Trade: The Erosion of the 'Liberal Consensus' in Britain, c.1903–32," in *Citizenship and Community*, ed. Eugenio Biagini (Cambridge: Cambridge University Press, 1996), 219–250.
9. John MacKenzie, *Propaganda and Empire* (Manchester: Manchester University Press, 1984), 32. Also see James Ryan, *Picturing Empire: Photography and the Visualization of the British Empire* (Chicago: University of Chicago Press, 1997); Annie E. Coombes, *Reinventing Africa* (New Haven, Conn.: Yale University Press, 1994).
10. Ryan, *Picturing Empire*, 17.
11. I borrow the term "evidential force" from Roland Barthes, *Camera Lucida: Reflections on Photography* (New York: Hill and Wang, 1981), 88–89.
12. Samuel Clemens, *King Leopold's Soliloquy* (Boston: P.R. Warren, 1905), 65–66.

13. James Ryan provides a useful general discussion of the photograph's relation to particular imperial ideologies and political contexts. He briefly addresses the work of the Reverend John and Alice Harris, acknowledging the need for further treatment of photography and humanitarian protest. See Ryan, *Picturing Empire*, 11–20, 222–224.

14. Cameron traveled from Bagamoya on the east coast of Africa to Luanda, Angola, on the west coast between March 1873 and November 1875.

15. Verney Lovett Cameron, *Across Africa*, 2 vols. (London: Daldy, Isbister, 1877).

16. Regarding Leopold's search for imperial territory, see Neal Ascherson, *The King Incorporated* (New York: Doubleday, 1964), especially chs. 4, 9, and 10.

17. David Lagergren, *Mission and State in the Congo* (Lund: Gleerup, 1970); Roger Anstey, *Britain and the Congo in the Nineteenth Century* (Oxford: Clarendon Press, 1962).

18. Suzanne Miers, "Humanitarianism at Berlin: Myth or Reality?," in *Bismarck, Europe and Africa: The Berlin Africa Conference 1884–1885 and the Onset of Partition*, ed. Stig Förster, Wolfgang Mommsen, and Ronald Robinson (Oxford: Oxford University Press, 1988), 333–345. Also see S.E. Crowe, *The Berlin West Africa Conference, 1884–1885* (London: Longmans Green, 1942).

19. Suzanne Miers, *Britain and the Ending of the Slave Trade* (New York: Africana, 1975).

20. Captain Guy Burrows, *The Curse of Central Africa* (London: R.A. Everett, 1903), 205.

21. Grenfell to Baynes, January 30, 1886, Baptist Missionary Society Archive, Angus Library, Regent's Park College, Oxford (hereafter BMS Papers), Grenfell to Baynes Correspondence, box A/19.

22. The stations of the Livingstone Inland Mission (LIM) had been turned over to the American Baptist Missionary Union in 1884. The Congo Balolo Mission had then been established in 1888 by the same group of British missionaries and patrons who had organized the LIM. See John Brown Myers, *The Congo for Christ: The Story of the Congo Mission* (London: S.W. Partridge, 1895).

23. Grenfell to Baynes, June 23, 1890, BMS Papers, Grenfell and Baynes Correspondence, box A/19.

24. Grenfell to Baynes, August 31, 1903, BMS Papers, Grenfell and Baynes Correspondence, box A/20.

25. John Weeks to Commissaire-General at Bangala, November 16, 1897, BMS Papers, Grenfell and Baynes Correspondence, box A/20.

26. Jules Marchal, *L'État Libre du Congo: Paradis Perdu: L'Histoire du Congo, 1876–1900*, 2 vols. (Borgloon: Bellings, 1996), 141–349; Samuel Nelson, *Colonialism in the Congo Basin, 1880–1940* (Athens: Ohio University Center for International Studies, 1994), 79–102.

27. Brian Stanley, "'The Miser of Headingley': Robert Arthington and the Baptist Missionary Society, 1877–1900," in *The Church and Wealth*, ed. W.J. Shiels and Diana Wood (Oxford: Basil Blackwell, 1987), 378.

28. Grenfell to Baynes, March 6, 1901, BMS Papers, Grenfell and Baynes Correspondence, box A/20.

29. Van Eetvelde to Baynes, August 22, 1898, BMS Papers, Baynes H26/1.

30. Grenfell to Baynes, March 6, 1901, BMS Papers, Grenfell and Baynes Correspondence, box A/20.

31. Grenfell to Baynes, August 31, 1903, BMS Papers, Grenfell to Baynes Correspondence, box A/20.

32. Translation of Van Eetvelde to Baynes, July 4, 1895, BMS Papers, Baynes H26/1.

33. Lagergren, *Mission and State*, 144–145.

34. BMS Papers, box H28.

35. Lagergren, *Mission and State*, provides the most thorough discussion of the experiences and policies of the British missions, as well as the best overview of the various denominations and nationalities of Protestant missions on the Congo. For further discussion of American missions on the Congo, see Robert Benedetto, ed., *Presbyterian Reformers in Central Africa* (Leiden: E.J. Brill, 1996).

36. Cookey, *Britain and the Congo Question*, 25.

37. Lagergren, *Mission and State*, 139.

38. William Roger Louis, "Roger Casement on the Congo," *Journal of African History* 5, no. 1 (1964): 99.

39. Cookey, *Britain and the Congo Question*, 22–55; John Hope Franklin, *George Washington Williams: A Biography* (Chicago: University of Chicago Press, 1985), 180–279; Felix Driver, "Henry Morton Stanley and His Critics: Geography, Exploration and Empire," *Past and Present* no. 133 (November 1991): 134–166.

40. Prior to Murphy's report, *The Times* published an interview with two anonymous British men, recently returned from the Congo, on October 14, 1895. Monsignor Argouard, the Bishop of the French Congo since 1890, had published accusations regarding atrocities in the Congo State in 1894 in *L'Univers* in Paris.

41. H.R. Fox Bourne, *Civilisation in Congoland* (London: P.S. King, 1903), 213.

42. William Roger Louis, "The Stokes Affair and the Beginning of the Anti-Congo Campaign," *Revue Belge de Philologie et d'Histoire* 53 (1965): 572–584; R.W. Beachey, "The Arms Trade in East Africa in the Late Nineteenth Century," *Journal of African History* 3, no. 3 (1962): 451–467.

43. Jean Stengers, "The Congo State and the Belgian Congo before 1914," in *Colonialism in Africa, 1870–1960*, vol. 1, ed. L.H. Gann and Peter Duignan (Cambridge: Cambridge University Press, 1969), 280.

44. Lagergren, *Mission and State*, 146.

45. Ibid., 153–154.

46. See article 23, "Receiving Children, Adoption, Ransoming," in "Regulations for the Congo Mission," issued by the BMS General Committee on September 30, 1897. BMS Papers, H28/10.

47. Grenfell to Baynes, April 27, 1902, BMS Papers, Grenfell to Baynes Correspondence, box A/20; John Harris to Standing Committee, April 25, 1903, Anti-Slavery Papers, Mss. Brit. Emp., S19, D5/7.

48. Lagergren, *Mission and State*, 153, ftn. 5.

49. *Liverpool Daily Post*, April 4, 1902.

50. Grenfell to Baynes, June 4, 1904, BMS Papers, Grenfell and Baynes Correspondence, box A/20.

51. For a summary of Morel's politics, see Paul Rich, *Race and Empire in British Politics* (Cambridge: Cambridge University Press, 1986), 27–49.

52. *Manchester Guardian*, September 13, 1901.

53. Guinness marked his new alliance with Morel by publishing "The Congo Evil: How to Deal with It," in Morel's *West African Mail*, April 17, 1903.

54. *Parliamentary Debates*, fourth series, vol. 122, House of Commons (London, 1903), 1297–1298.

55. Ibid., 1311.

56. Ibid., 1304.

57. Translation of *Bulletin Officiel de L'Etat Indépendant du congo* (June 1903): 144.

58. Ibid., 145.

59. Ibid., 152–155.

60. Ibid., 156.

61. Ibid., 165–167.

62. Ibid., 163.

63. Ibid., 168.

64. Ibid., 167.

65. Ibid., 145.

66. BMS Papers, BMS General Committee Minutes, January 20, 1904, 10.

67. Roger Casement to Harry Farnall, private, May 28, 1903, Public Records Office, Kew (hereafter PRO), FO10/804.

68. *Accounts and Papers of the British Parliament* (hereafter *Accounts and Papers*), 1904, vol. 62, Cd. 1933, "Correspondence and Report from His Majesty's Consul at Boma Respecting the Administraton of the Independent State of the Congo" (hereafter Casement Report), 52.

69. Louis, "Roger Casement on the Congo," 104.

70. Casement to Grenfell, June 5, 1901, BMS Papers, Grenfell and Baynes Correspondence, box A/20.

71. Casement to Lansdowne, June 29, 1903, PRO, FO10/804.

72. J. Harris to the CBM Standing Committee, June 23, 1903, Anti-Slavery Papers, D5/7. Danielson had recently been dismissed by the local Standing Committee of the CBM for acts of misconduct, including conflicts with traders, quarrels with his fellow missionaries, and abuse of the mission's African workmen.

73. J. Harris to the CBM Standing Committee, August 5, 1903, Anti-Slavery Papers, D5/7.

74. Casement Report, 47.

75. Casement Diary, 1903, PRO, HO161/2. On the same day, Casement wrote a letter to the Foreign Office, indicating that he had heard sixteen BMS ministers denounce the deputation. See Casement to Lansdowne, July 18, 1903, PRO, FO10/805.

76. Casement Diary, 1903, PRO, HO161/2.
77. Casement Report, 61.
78. Ibid., 57.
79. *Accounts and Papers*, 1904, vol. 62, Cd. 2097, "Further Correspondence Respecting the Administration of the Independent State of the Congo," 26.
80. Casement Report, 60–61.
81. Ibid., 31.
82. *Accounts and Papers*, 1904, vol. 62, Cd. 2097, "Further Correspondence," 16, 34. Armstrong took his photograph of Epondo at Bonginda on September 8, 1903.
83. Casement to Lansdowne, September 15–16, 1903, PRO, FO10/805.
84. Casement Report, 77.
85. Robert Harms, "The World ABIR Made: The Maringa–Lopori Basin, 1885–1903," *African Economic History* 22 (1983): 125.
86. John Harris to Dr. Harry Guinness, March 20, 1904, Morel Collection, London School of Economics (hereafter Morel Papers), F8, file 74.
87. John Harris to Judge Bosco, July 2, 1904, Anti-Slavery Papers, Mss. Brit. Emp. S19, D5/10.
88. John Harris to F.B. Meyer, August 20, 1904, Anti-Slavery Papers, Mss. Brit. Emp. S19, D5/10.
89. Translation of Alice Harris to Msgr. Van Calcken, May 15, 1904, Anti-Slavery Papers, Mss. Brit. Emp. S19, D5/10.
90. Jean Stengers, "Le Rôle de la Commission d'Enquête de 1904–1905 au Congo," *Annuaire de l'Institut de Philologie et d'Histoire Orientales et Slaves*, 10 (1950): 701–726.
91. John Harris to the Council of the CBM, December 18, 1904, Anti-Slavery Papers, Mss. Brit. Emp., S19, D5/11.
92. E.D. Morel to Alfred Emmott, January 28, 1904, Morel Papers, F4, CRA, 1903–1908.
93. Guinness to Morel, February 2, 1904, Morel Papers, F4, CRA, 1903–1908.
94. Morel to Guinness, February 5, 1904, cited in Slade, *English-Speaking Missions*, 280.
95. I thank Professor Andrew Walls for informing me about Guinness's earlier work in the photography studio.
96. I have not found a list of the specific images that Guinness used in this lecture series, but it is probable that he displayed the photos by the Reverend W.D. Armstrong.
97. Guinness to Morel, February 2, 1904, Morel Papers, F4, CRA, 1903–1908.
98. Guinness to Morel, February 8, 1904, Morel Papers, F4, CRA, 1903–1908.
99. Lady J.A. Chalmers to Morel, March 8, 1904, Morel Papers, file 9; Morel to Lady J.A. Chalmers, March 10, 1904, Morel Papers, Copybook, January–May 1904.
100. E.D. Morel to John Holt, January 19, 1904, cited in Slade, *English-Speaking Missions*, 300, ftn. 2.
101. Ruth Slade, "King Leopold II and the Attitude of English and American Catholics towards the Anti-Congolese Campaign," *Zaire* 11 (June 1957): 593–612; Jean Stengers, "Morel and Belgium," in Louis and Stengers, ed. *E.D. Morel's History*, 221–251.
102. H.R. Fox Bourne to E.D. Morel, December 29, 1903, Morel Papers, F8, file 67.
103. Casement to Morel, January 25, 1904, Morel Papers, F8, file 16.
104. E.D. Morel to Alfred Emmott, January 26, 1904, Morel Papers, F4, CRA, 1903–1908.
105. Morel to Lady J.A. Chalmers, March 10, 1904, Morel Papers, Copybook, January–May 1904.
106. Casement to Dilke, February 1, 1904, Anti-Slavery Papers, Mss. Brit. Emp. S22, 261, vol. 2, APS.
107. In June 1904 the APS Committee chose three of its members, Fox Bourne, Charles Dilke, and Francis W. Fox, to serve as representatives on the Preliminary Committee of the CRA. Fox Bourne to Morel, January 29, 1904, Morel Papers, F4(a), CRA, 1903–1908; Fox Bourne to Morel, June 3, 1904, Morel Papers, F8, file 67.
108. Morel to Alfred Emmott, May 31, 1904, Morel Papers, Copybook, May 1904–March 1905; Morel to Edward Russell, March 9, 1904, Morel Papers, Copybook, January–May 1904.
109. Regarding the Brussels Conference on the slave trade and liquor traffic, see Miers, *Britain and the Ending of the Slave Trade*.
110. "Programme of the C.R.A.," supplement published in *West African Mail*, May 1904.
111. Morel, *King Leopold's Rule*. Alice Harris's photographs are attributed to John Harris in Morel's text.
112. The CRA established a Finance Committee in March 1907 to raise funds to meet the overwhelming number of requests for lantern lectures and pamphlet literature. It was not until

November 1908, however, that the CRA centralized its collection of funds in London by requiring auxiliaries to forward their gifts. Until that time, treasury duties were divided between London and Liverpool. To make matters more obscure, Morel did not publish registered lists of CRA subscribers until 1907 because he did not want to reveal the meager basis of the organization's funding. The CRA began keeping certified accounts in 1907 only to refute charges that it was a lobby funded entirely by merchant interests. By this time, missionaries had shifted the focus of CRA funding away from merchants, as will be demonstrated below.

113. E.D. Morel to William Cadbury, no date (but references within the letter indicate that it was written in the first week of April 1905), Morel Papers, Copybook, March 1905–November 1905.

114. CRA supporters included six Liberal MPs, six Conservative MPs, and one independent MP.

115. The past presidents were the Reverends John Clifford, R.F. Horton, J. Munro Gibson, and F.B. Meyer.

116. Although Morel would join the Labour Party in 1918, he did not have connections to the British labor movement in 1904. See E.D. Morel, *The Black Man's Burden* (London: National Labour Press, 1920), 153.

117. Roger Casement to E.D. Morel, December 14, 1904, Morel Papers, F8, file 17.

118. E.D. Morel to Alice Stopford Green, December 28, 1904, Morel Papers, Copybook, February 1904–January 1905.

119. Lansdowne minute, March 11, 1905, FO 10/815, cited in William Roger Louis, "Triumph of the Congo Reform Movement," 282.

120. Britain had joined several other European powers in signing the Belgian Neutrality Treaty in 1837, obligating Britain to come to Belgium's aid in the event of invasion.

121. E.W. Brooks to Morel, June 12, 1905, Morel Papers, F9.

122. E.D. Morel to William Cadbury, June 26, 1905, Morel Papers, F8, file 11.

123. Roger Casement to Morel, August 28, 1905, Morel Papers, F8, file 20.

124. John Harris to Morel, August 19, 1905, Morel Papers, F8, file 75.

125. *The Friend* (October 13, 1905): 670–672.

126. "C.R.A. Official Organ" (October 1905): 402.

127. "The Congo Atrocities. A Lecture to Accompany a Series of 60 Photographic Slides for the Optical Lantern." Morel Papers, sec. A (hereafter Congo Atrocities Lecture).

128. Quoted in William Roger Louis, "Morel and the Congo Reform Association, 1904–13," in Louis and Stengers, eds., *E.D. Morel's History*, 210.

129. Congo Atrocities Lecture, 24.

130. Ibid., 29.

131. Ibid., 17, 30.

132. Ibid., 31.

133. *La Vérité sur le Congo* (November 15, 1905): 455. This photograph was reprinted from *Petit Bleu* (October 17, 1905).

134. Alfred Emmott to Morel, December 9, 1905, cited in Wuliger, "The Idea of Economic Imperialism," 110. Also see Morel to Herbert Samuel, September 5, 1905, Morel Papers, Copybook, March–November 1905.

135. Morel to J. Harris, August 22, 1905, Morel Papers, Copybook, March–November 1905.

136. Grenfell to Baynes, August 12, 1905, BMS Papers, Grenfell and Baynes Correspondence, box A/20.

137. Morel to F.B. Meyer, February 1, 1906, Morel Papers, Copybook, November 1905–May 1906.

138. Morel to Reverend W.H. Haden, October 17, 1906, Morel Papers, file 1, box "Morel Cuttings."

139. *Regions Beyond* (May 1906): 113–114.

140. Marchal, *E.D. Morel contre Léopold II*, vol. 2., 362–363.

141. The following is a list of other missionaries, returned from the Congo, who lectured on behalf of the Congo reform campaign. This list is drawn from notices of lantern lectures in the "C.R.A. Official Organ." Brethren of the Congo Balolo Mission: Rev. Arthur Bowen, Rev. C.E. Franck, Rev. Herbert Frost, Rev. Somerville Gilchrist, Rev. B.J. Lower, Rev. Charles Padfield, Rev. William Wilkes, Rev. John Whitehead, Rev. Peter Whytock; brethren of the Baptist Missionary Society: Rev. John Howell, Rev. Kenred Smith, Rev. J.R.M. Stephens; brethren of the American Baptist Missionary Union: Emily Banks, Joseph Clark.

142. See note 127, above.

143. Regarding the organization and role of Town Meetings, see Morel to F.B. Meyer, November 27, 1905, Morel Papers, Copybook, November 1905–May 1906; Morel to Mrs. Emmott, October 1, 1906, and Morel to John Harris, December 17, 1906, Morel Papers, file 1, box

"Morel Cuttings," volume of out correspondence; Morel to Robert Emmett, November 5, 1909, Morel Papers, F9.

144. In fiscal 1907–1908, the London auxiliary turned a profit on eighty-six lectures, collecting numerous small donations for a total of £346.19.3.

145. Arnold Rowntree gave £10 and Barrow Cadbury gave £50. By this time, William Cadbury had begun to finance Morel personally rather than through gifts to the CRA.

146. E.D. Morel, "The Congo Reform Association and Mr. Belloc," *The New Age* (December 21, 1907); press clipping in Morel Papers, file 1, vol. 1907–1908.

147. For evidence of women's significant contributions to British overseas missions at the turn of the century, see F.K. Prochaska, *Women and Philanthropy in Nineteenth-Century England* (Oxford: Oxford University Press, 1980), 231–235. Also see Rhonda Anne Semple, *Missionary Women: Gender, Professionalism and the Victorian Idea of Christian Mission* (Woodbridge, U.K.: Boydell Press, 2003).

148. Morel to John Harris, April 26, 1906, Morel Papers, Copybook, November 1905–May 1906.

149. Morel to John Harris, February 28, 1907, Morel Papers, Copybook, January–October 1907.

150. The CRA attempted to systematize and then centralize its accounts in 1907–1908, but the extant records of CRA finances are haphazard and incomplete. I present below a rough profile of CRA funding between 1904 and 1913, with irregularities in chronology determined by the archival records: January 25, 1904, to January 6, 1905: £895.19.7; January 7, 1905, to April 19, 1906: more than £1,200, but precise figures unavailable; April 20, 1906, to March 31, 1907: £815.0.3; April 1, 1907, to March 31, 1908: £1,720.7.0; April 1908 to November 1908: unavailable; November 3, 1908, to December 31, 1908: £461.15.5; January 1, 1909, to October 31, 1909: £1,955.1.6; November 1, 1909, to October 31, 1910: £1,899.4.8; November 1, 1910, to October 31, 1911: £879.19.10; November 1, 1911, to September, 30, 1912: £683.14.5; October 1, 1912, to June 13, 1913: unavailable.

151. Morel to Reverend William Wilkes, August 25, 1909, Emmott Papers, II, Mss. Emmott 4.

152. Morel to John Harris, May 23, 1911, Morel Papers, F8, file 77.

153. Regarding conflicts over authority within the CRA between Morel and John Harris, see Marchal, *E.D. Morel contre Léopold II*, vol. 2, 359–363, 437.

154. See Louis and Stengers, eds., *E.D. Morel's History.*

155. John Harris to Miss C.W. Mackintosh, December 6, 1915, Anti-Slavery Papers, D3/13.

156. Louis and Stengers, eds., *E.D. Morel's History.*

157. Hochschild, *King Leopold's Ghost*, 305–306.

Chapter 3

1. For a discussion of the negotiations that shaped this convention, see Peter Richardson, *Chinese Mine Labour in the Transvaal* (London: Macmillan, 1982), 32–46.

2. *Accounts and Papers of the British Parliament* (hereafter *Accounts and Papers*), 1904, vol. 62, Cd. 2183, "Further Correspondence Relating to Labour in the Transvaal Mines," 26–27. For a description of the compound, see the correspondence of W.M. Squire in *The Friend* 44, no. 32 (1904), 525.

3. Samuel Ian Gordon, "The Chinese Labor Controversy in British Politics and Policy-Making" (Ph.D. dissertation, University of Ulster, Jordanstown, 1987); Richardson, *Chinese Mine Labour*; Donald Denoon, *A Grand Illusion: The Failure of Imperial Policy in the Transvaal Colony during the Period of Reconstruction, 1900–1905* (London: Longman, 1973); Ronald Hyam, *Elgin and Churchill at the Colonial Office, 1905–1908* (London: Macmillan, 1968).

4. There were 10,240 British-born whites in the mine industry in March 1904. Selborne to Lyttelton, May 29, 1905, *Accounts and Papers*, 1905, vol. 55, Cd. 2563, "Further Correspondence Relating to Affairs in the Transvaal and Orange River Colony," 29–30.

5. Gordon, "Chinese Labor Controversy," 140.

6. Surendra Bhana and Joy B. Brain, *Setting Down Roots: Indian Migrants in South Africa, 1860–1911* (Johannesburg: Witwatersrand University Press, 1990).

7. A.G. Shiell, "Chinese Slavery" (pamphlet), Bodleian Library, Oxford, Milner Papers (hereafter Milner Papers), IV, K/341.

8. For a relevant, general discussion of Conservative discourses on empire and South Africa, see Andrew S. Thompson, "The Language of Imperialism and the Meanings of Empire: Imperial Discourse in British Politics, 1895–1914," *Journal of British Studies* 36 (April 1997): 147–177.

9. Jonathan Hyslop, "The Imperial Working Class Makes Itself 'White': White Labourism in Britain, Australia, and South Africa before the First World War," *Journal of Historical Sociology* 12, no. 4 (December 1999): 414.

10. Morel to Samuel, September 5, 1905, London School of Economics, E.D. Morel Papers, Copy Book, March–November 1905.

11. *The Times,* February 23, 1906.

12. Melanie Yap and Dianne Leong Man, *Colour, Confusion and Concessions: The History of the Chinese in South Africa* (Hong Kong: Hong Kong University Press, 1996).

13. *Accounts and Papers,* 1906, vol. 80, Cd. 3251, "The Asiatic Law Amendment Ordinance, No. 29 of 1906." In a related vein, see Nayan Shah, *Contagious Divides: Epidemics and Race in San Francisco's Chinatown* (Berkeley: University of California Press, 2001).

14. Alan H. Jeeves, *Migrant Labour in South Africa's Mining Economy: The Struggle for the Gold Mines' Labour Supply, 1890–1920* (Kingston, Ont.: McGill–Queen's University Press, 1985), 13. For a concise summary of the factors which necessitated an increase in the African labor force on the Rand before the war, see Richardson, *Chinese Mine Labour,* 8–12.

15. Richardson, *Chinese Mine Labour,* 13.

16. For a general discussion of the postwar crisis in the mine industry, see ibid., 12–26. On the specific subject of postwar African labor in the Transvaal, see Donald Denoon, "The Transvaal Labour Crisis, 1901–6," *Journal of African History* 7, no. 3 (1967): 481–494.

17. Richardson, *Chinese Mine Labour,* 20. Also see Robert Davies, "Mining Capital, the State and Unskilled White Workers in South Africa, 1901–1913," *Journal of Southern African Studies* 3, no. 1 (October 1976): 41–69.

18. "Minutes of the Proceedings of the South African Inter-Colonial Conference on Customs and Other Matters, held at Bloemfontein, 10–23 March 1903," Milner Papers, IV, H/281, 77.

19. Gordon, "Chinese Labor Controversy," 11.

20. For discussion of the role of Chinese labor in the mines' broader strategy for recovery, see Richardson, *Chinese Mine Labour,* 18, 24.

21. Ibid., 29.

22. *The Times,* January 15, 1903, and the response by Lionel Phillips, *The Times,* January 19, 1903.

23. For a copy of Farrar's speech printed in the *Rand Daily Mail* on April 1, 1903, see *Accounts and Papers,* 1904, vol. 61, Cd. 1895, "Further Correspondence Relating to the Affairs of the Transvaal and Orange River Colony," 8–15.

24. Davies, "Mining Capital," 45, 58.

25. *Accounts and Papers,* 1904, vol. 61, Cd. 1895, "Further Correspondence," 55.

26. See Botha interview in *De Volksstem,* January 6, 1904, *Accounts and Papers,* 1904, vol. 61, Cd. 1899, "Further Correspondence Regarding the Transvaal Labor Question," 7–8.

27. Creswell to Seely, April 18, 1904, Nuffield College Library, Oxford, Mss Mottistone, 8.

28. On June 13, 1903, a deputation of mine owners, led by Farrar, had asked Milner to establish this commission. See Lionel Phillips, *Transvaal Problems: Some Notes on Current Politics* (London: John Murray, 1905), 49.

29. Transvaal Chamber of Mines, *Annual Report, 1903,* cvii, cxxxi, 155–169.

30. Sir George Farrar, "'Transvaal Labour Importation Ordinance,' Speech Given on the Introduction of the Ordinance in the Legislative Council of the Transvaal Colony, 28 December 1903" (Johannesburg: Transvaal Leader Office, 1904).

31. Davies, "Mining Capital," 45, 58.

32. Memorandum on Asiatic labour, November 6, 1903, Milner Papers, IV, C/237.

33. Gordon, "Chinese Labor Controversy," 82–85.

34. See, for example, P. Leys, "South Africa, II: Chinese Labour for the Rand," *The Nineteenth Century* (February 1902): 181–186.

35. See, for example, Campbell-Bannerman to James Bryce, December 31, 1903, Campbell-Bannerman Papers, British Library, Add. 41211.

36. *The Liberal Magazine* (February 1904): 10–11.

37. Herbert Samuel's diary of 1904, House of Lords Record Office, Samuel Papers, A/22.

38. Gordon, "Chinese Labor Controversy," 117.

39. James Ramsay MacDonald, *What I Saw in South Africa* (London: "The Echo," 1902), 75, 110, 119.

40. The LRC was a federation of trade unions, trades councils, the Independent Labour Party, and the Fabian Society.
41. LRC leaflet no. 11, "Slavery in the Transvaal" (London, 1904). A large collection of pamphlets and leaflets on Chinese labor in the Transvaal can be obtained from the Center for Research Libraries, Africana, MF7016, reels 8 and 9. Another good collection is located in the Commonwealth Collections at Cambridge University Library. There are also scattered pamphlets in the British Library.
42. LRC leaflet no. 14, "Voter Registration" (London, 1904).
43. Greg Cuthbertson, "Pricking the 'Nonconformist Conscience': Religion against the South African War," in *The South African War Reappraised*, ed. Donal Lowry (Manchester: Manchester University Press, 2000), 169–187.
44. Gordon, "Chinese Labor Controversy," 153–154.
45. Ibid., 139–141.
46. H.R. Fox Bourne, *Forced Labour in British South Africa* (London: P.S. King, 1903), 43.
47. *The Aborigines' Friend* (October 1905): 415–416.
48. *The Aborigines' Friend* (February 1904): 1–16. Also see Ross Forman, "Randy on the Rand: Portuguese African Labor and the Discourse of 'Unnatural vice' in the Transvaal in the Early Twentieth Century," *Journal of the History of Sexuality* (October 2002): 570–609, and relevant sections of Philippa Levine, *Prostitution, Race, and Politics: Policing Venereal Disease in the British Empire* (New York: Routledge, 2003).
49. APS to Chamberlain, with minute, January 16, 1902, CO 291/50, cited in Denoon, *A Grand Illusion*, 103.
50. E.D. Morel, *The Black Man's Burden* (London: National Labour Press, 1920), 153.
51. Persia Campbell Crawford, *Chinese Coolie Emigration to Countries within the British Empire* (London: P.S. King, 1923), 170.
52. Regarding Coates, see Gordon, "Chinese Labor Controversy," 139; Lyttelton to Milner, April 14, 1904, Milner Ms. dep. 171, ff. 373–376, cited in Gordon, 158.
53. ISAA leaflet no. 60, "Chinese Labour. Five Reasons for Supporting the Government on Chinese Labour" (London, 1904); Sir Gilbert Parker, "'Our Imperial Responsibilities in the Transvaal,' an Address to the Junior Constitutional Club, Piccadilly, 23 March 1904" (London, 1904).
54. Ibid., p. 24.
55. ISAA leaflet no. 73, "Chinese Labour. Dignified Rebuke from Nonconformist Ministers in the Transvaal to Their Brethren in England" (London, 1904); Conservative Publication Department leaflet, N.U. no. 468, "Chinese Labour. A Protest from Transvaal Nonconformist Ministers" (London, 1904).
56. Conservative Publication Department, leaflet C.C.O. no. 464, "Chinese Labour for the Transvaal Mines: Nonconformists Condemn Agitation Against It" (London, 1904). Indeed, at least three missionary organizations would engage in evangelical work in the compounds. These groups were the South African Compounds and Interior Mission, the Salvation Army, and the South African Baptist Missionary Society. See "Foreign Labour Department Annual Report, 1904–5," in *Accounts and Papers*, 1906, vol. 80, Cd. 3025, "Further Correspondence Relating to Labour in the Transvaal Mines," 159.
57. A.K. Russell, *Liberal Landslide: The General Election of 1906* (Newton Abbot, U.K.: David & Charles, 1973), 187.
58. John Burns, MP, "BONDAGE for Black. SLAVERY for Yellow Labour" (pamphlet) (London: Kent & Matthews, 1904). Reprinted from the *Independent Review* (May 1904).
59. Peter Richardson, "Coolies, Peasants, and Proletarians: The Origins of Chinese Indentured Labour in South Africa, 1904–1907," in *International Labour Migration: Historical Perspectives*, ed. Shula Marks and Peter Richardson (London: University of London Press, 1984), 168.
60. Transvaal Chamber of Mines, *Annual Report, 1904*, xxvii.
61. Transvaal Chamber of Mines, *Annual Report, 1909*, xlii. The Chamber provides the following figures for indentured Chinese in the Transvaal for years ending December 31: 1905: 47,217; 1906: 52,889; 1907: 35,676; 1908: 12,283; 1909: 1,910—shipped out in February 1910.
62. Crawford, *Chinese Coolie Emigration*, 209; "Foreign Labour Department Annual Report, 1904–5," 168.
63. Regarding importers' obligations to families, see Government Notice no. 777 of 1904, in "Handbook of Ordinances, Proclamations, Regulations and Instructions, Connected with the Importation of Foreign Labour into the Transvaal" (Pretoria, 1906).
64. Davies, "Mining Capital," 47.

65. William Evans, "General Report on Chinese Labour," in *Accounts and Papers*, 1905, vol. 55, Cd. 2401, "Further Correspondence Relating to Labour in the Transvaal Mines," 81.

66. Of 1,741 laborers imported from southern China by June 1905, 137 died on the Rand and 537 were sent home after being incapacitated by disease or injury. "Foreign Labour Department Annual Report, 1904–5," 151.

67. Peter Richardson, "Coolies and Randlords: The North Randfontein Chinese Miners' 'Strike' of 1905," *Journal of Southern African Studies* 2, no. 2 (April 1976): 167–168.

68. Government Notice no. 78 of 1906, in "Handbook of Ordinances, Proclamations, Regulations and Instructions, Connected with the Importation of Foreign Labour into the Transvaal" (Pretoria, 1906).

69. "Foreign Labour Department Annual Report, 1904–5," 161.

70. Selborne to Lyttelton, August 7, 1905, Public Records Office (hereafter PRO), CO291/84.

71. Phillips, *Transvaal Problems*, 116.

72. Denoon, *Grand Illusion*, 155–158.

73. See statistics in *Accounts and Papers*, appendix IV, 165.

74. Transvaal Chamber of Mines, *Annual Report, 1906*, xxix.

75. Lawley to Lyttelton, dispatch 369, May 8, 1905, CO291/82, 425, cited in Gordon, "Chinese Labor Controversy," 203.

76. *Accounts and Papers*, 1905, vol. 55, Cd. 2401, "Further Correspondence Relating to Labour in the Transvaal Mines," 52.

77. For an in-depth study of this case, see Richardson, "Coolies and Randlords," 151–177.

78. Denoon, *Grand Illusion*, 154.

79. Selborne to Lyttelton, August 7, 1905, PRO, CO291/84.

80. Reported in the *Daily News*, February 22, 1905; cited in Gordon, "Chinese Labor Controversy," 219.

81. Campbell-Bannerman to H. Gladstone, November 23, 1904, Campbell-Bannerman Papers, British Library, Add. 41217.

82. Richard Price, *An Imperial War and the British Working Class* (London: Routledge & Kegan Paul, 1972), 235–241. For a dissenting view on Price's argument, see Paul Readman, "The Conservative Party, Patriotism, and British Politics: The Case of the General Election of 1900," *Journal of British Studies* 40 (January 2001): 107–145.

83. *Evening Standard*, April 17, 1905.

84. Lyttelton to Selborne, May 31, 1905, *Accounts and Papers*, 1906, vol. 80, Cd. 2786, "Further Correspondence Relating to Labour in the Transvaal Mines," 2.

85. Gordon, "Chinese Labor Controversy," 235.

86. Lawley to Witwatersrand Mine Owners, June 13, 1905, PRO, CO291/84.

87. Selborne to Lyttelton, August 7, 1905, PRO, CO291/84.

88. Afrikaner delegation to the Lieutenant Governor, September 6, 1905, *Accounts and Papers*, Cd. 2786, "Further Correspondence Relating to Labour in the Transvaal Mines," 11–19.

89. Selborne to Lyttelton, September 18, 1905, Cd. 2786, 9–10.

90. Conservative Publication Department, "Chinese Labour Brings More Employment for Whites in the Transvaal" (flyer) (London, 1905).

91. Russell, *Liberal Landslide*, 196.

92. Ibid., 66.

93. Ibid., 69.

94. Hyam, *Elgin and Churchill*, 66.

95. *The Times*, December 22, 1905.

96. Russell, *Liberal Landslide*, 106–107.

97. Hyam, *Elgin and Churchill*, 69.

98. Gordon, "Chinese Labor Controversy," 266.

99. Hyam, *Elgin and Churchill*, 50

100. Ibid., 74–75.

101. Ibid., 78.

102. Gordon, "Chinese Labor Controversy," 358.

103. Elgin to Governor, November 28, 1907, *Accounts and Papers*, 1908, vol. 73, Cd. 3994, "Correspondence Relating to the Transvaal Indentured Labour Laws Temporary Continuance Act, 1907," 9.

104. MacDonald, *What I Saw in South Africa*, 118.

105. Hyslop, "Imperial Working Class," 404.

106. Ibid., 398–399.
107. Jonathan Crush, Alan Jeeves,and David Yudelman, *South Africa's Labor Empire: A History of Black Migrancy to the Gold Mines* (Boulder, Colo.: Westview Press, 1991), 2.

Chapter 4

1. Bernard Porter, "The Pro-Boers in Britain," in *The South African War: The Anglo–Boer War, 1899–1902*, ed. Peter Warwick (Harlow, U.K.: Longman, 1980), 250.
2. *Daily Mail*, July 26, 1906.
3. Defense "Particulars," April 13, 1909, Cadbury Papers, University of Birmingham (hereafter Cadbury Papers), Ms. 1/2.
4. Charles Dellheim, "The Creation of a Company Culture: Cadburys, 1861–1931," *American Historical Review* 92, no. 1 (1987): 14, 16, 36; Geoffrey I. Nwaka, "Cadbury and the Dilemma of Colonial Trade in Africa, 1901–1910," *Bulletin de l'I.F.A.N.* 42, ser. B, no. 4 (1980): 782; James Duffy, *A Question of Slavery* (Cambridge, Mass.: Harvard University Press, 1967), 183, 193–194. Historians of Angola have assumed that Cadbury aggressively questioned the system of exploitation in Portuguese West Africa. See, for example, F. Clement C. Egerton, *Angola in Perspective* (London: Routledge, 1957), 95–96; Lawrence Henderson, *Angola: Five Centuries of Conflict* (Ithaca, N.Y.: Cornell University Press, 1979), 115–116.
5. Dellheim, "Creation of a Company Culture," 21–22.
6. In Britain, for example, cocoa consumption increased from 4,713 tons in 1880 to 16,888 tons in 1900. See Arthur W. Knapp, *The Cocoa and Chocolate Industry* (New York: Isaac Pitman, 1930), 27. For international statistics, see the trade journal *The Gordian*.
7. Gervase Clarence-Smith, *The Third Portuguese Empire, 1825–1975: A Study in Economic Imperialism* (Manchester: Manchester University Press, 1985), 87.
8. Ibid., 11, 81, 85.
9. Duffy, *A Question of Slavery*, 63.
10. Gervase Clarence-Smith, *Slaves, Peasants and Capitalists in Southern Angola, 1840–1926* (Cambridge: Cambridge University Press, 1979), 31.
11. Ibid.
12. Ibid., 38.
13. Ibid., 31.
14. Charles Swan, *The Slavery of To-day* (Glasgow: Pickering & Inglis, 1909), 184–186; Henry Nevinson, *A Modern Slavery* (London: Harper and Bros., 1906), 50; Reverend Cunningham, letter published in *Echoes of Service* no. 446, part 1 (January 1900), 26; F.S. Arnot to Fox Bourne, September 19, 1905, Papers of the British and Foreign Anti-Slavery and Aborigines' Protection Society, Rhodes House, Oxford University (hereafter Anti-Slavery Papers), Mss. Brit. Emp. S22, G268/B.
15. Nevinson, *A Modern Slavery*, 104–107, 149.
16. John Harris, *Portuguese Slavery: Britain's Dilemma* (London: Methuen, 1913), 60.
17. Nevinson, *A Modern Slavery*, 173. For a description of the registration process and sea voyage, see especially pp. 168–186.
18. W.G. Clarence-Smith, "Labour Conditions in the Plantations of São Tomé and Príncipe, 1875–1914," in *The Wages of Slavery*, ed. Michael Twaddle (London: Frank Cass, 1993), 149.
19. Ibid., 155.
20. António de Almada Negreiros, *Colonies Portugaises: Ile de San-Thomé* (Paris: A. Challamel, 1901), 9–10.
21. Clarence-Smith, "Labour Conditions," 158–159.
22. Ibid., 149.
23. Ibid., 159.
24. Ibid., 151–152.
25. Ibid., 153–155.
26. Ibid., 156–157.
27. Ibid., 158–160.
28. Ibid., 161.
29. For general discussion of British protests against slavery in the Portuguese empire between 1850 and 1882, see Duffy, *A Question of Slavery*, 75–76, 102–116.

30. Verney Lovett Cameron, *Across Africa*, vol. 2 (London: Daldy, Isbister, 1877), 137.

31. Duffy, 77–82.

32. Joseph A. Pease to Sir Edward Grey, MP, June 5, 1894, Public Records Office, Kew (hereafter, PRO), FO63/1447.

33. Duffy, *A Question of Slavery*, 101.

34. Bentley to Baynes, April 21, 1884, Baptist Missionary Society Archive, Angus Library, Regent's Park College, Oxford University (hereafter BMS Papers), Bentley to Baynes Correspondence, A/31.

35. The Anti-Slavery Society's annual report for 1903, for instance, observes that missionaries were the main sources of humanitarian information from Portuguese West Africa. British and Foreign Anti-Slavery Society, Annual Report, 1903, Rhodes House Library, Oxford, 100.221 r.78, p. 15.

36. For a summary of the Plymouth Brethren's expansion in Africa between 1884 and 1914, see W.T. Stunt et al., *Turning the World Upside Down* (Eastbourne, U.K.: Upperton Press, 1972), 363–417. According to Robert Rotberg, the Plymouth Brethren's files of missionary correspondence from Africa in this early period were incinerated during a "spring cleaning" at the Brethren's headquarters in Bath in 1939. Consequently, the discussion below depends on letters and diaries reprinted in the Brethren's journal, *Echoes of Service*. See Robert Rotberg, *Christian Missionaries and the Creation of Northern Rhodesia, 1880–1924* (Princeton, N.J.: Princeton University Press, 1965), 198.

37. Rotberg characterizes the missionaries as "Msiri's captives and errand boys." Robert Rotberg, "Plymouth Brethren and the Occupation of Katanga, 1886–1907," *Journal of African History*, 5, no. 2 (1964): 290.

38. F.S. Arnot, *Missionary Travels in Central Africa* (Bath: Office of Echoes of Service, 1914), 94–97.

39. Rotberg, "Plymouth Brethren," 293.

40. F.S. Arnot, *Echoes of Service* (October 1889): 318.

41. Dugald Campbell, *Echoes of Service* (December 1893, part II).

42. William Lewis, *Echoes of Service* (December 1899, part II): 375; Lizzie Brayshaw, *Echoes of Service* (January 1899, part II): 29.

43. Harris, *Portuguese Slavery*, 38–39.

44. William Cadbury to H.H. Johnston, July 9, 1904, Cadbury Papers, Ms. 4/88.

45. William Cadbury to Sales Committee, October 31, 1906, Cadbury Papers, Ms. 2041.

46. William Cadbury, "A Private Inside History of the Connection of *Cadbury Bros., Ltd.*, with African Slavery" (November 1949), Cadbury Papers, Ms. 183.

47. William Cadbury to Joseph Sturge, May 1, 1901, Cadbury Papers, Ms. 4/4.

48. Michael Anthony Samuels, *Education in Angola, 1878–1914* (New York: Teachers College Press, 1970), 87–88.

49. Duffy, *A Question of Slavery*, 171.

50. William Cadbury to Travers Buxton, June 10, 1902, Cadbury Papers, Ms. 4/10.

51. APS minutes, June 5, 1902, Anti-Slavery Papers, Mss. Brit. Emp. S20, E5/10.

52. Fox Bourne to Secretary of State, Foreign Office, June 11, 1902, PRO, FO63/1447.

53. Casement to Secretary of State, September 17, 1902, PRO, FO63/1447.

54. Duffy, *A Question of Slavery*, 160, 182.

55. Ibid., 175–176.

56. Ibid., 147.

57. Ibid., 182–183.

58. William Cadbury to Fox Bourne, May 20, 1903, Cadbury Papers, Ms. 4/41; Holt to Morel, July 4, 1903, E.D. Morel Collection, London School of Economics (hereafter Morel Papers), file 85.

59. Henry Nevinson to William Cadbury, October 10, 1904, Cadbury Papers, Ms. 180/845; Cadbury to Buxton, October 21, 1904, Cadbury Papers, Ms. 4/117.

60. William Cadbury to H.R. Fox Bourne, February 9, 1905, Cadbury Papers, Ms. 4/151.

61. E.D. Morel to William Cadbury, no date, Morel Papers, Letter Book, March 1905–November 1905.

62. E.D. Morel to William Cadbury, June 26, 1905, Morel Papers, F8, file 11.

63. William Cadbury to Morel, July 5, 1905, Morel Papers, F8, file 11. Cadbury later extended his payments under this arrangement for another six months in 1907. William Cadbury to Morel, Morel Papers, March 11, 1907, F8, file 12.

64. Morel to William Cadbury, July 31, 1908, Cadbury Papers, Ms. 180/807.

65. William Roger Louis, "Critical Notes," in *E.D. Morel's History of the Congo Reform Movement*, ed. William Roger Louis and Jean Stengers (Oxford: Clarendon Press, 1968), 258–260.
66. H.R. Fox Bourne to William Cadbury, August 14, 1905, Cadbury Papers, Ms. 4/177.
67. E.D. Morel to William Cadbury, August 4, 1905, Morel Papers, F8, file 11.
68. E.D. Morel to William Cadbury, November 7, 1908, Cadbury Papers, Ms. 180/822.
69. Nevinson, *A Modern Slavery*, 37.
70. Ibid., 57.
71. Ibid., 167.
72. George Cadbury to Sir Edward Grey, October 27, 1906, Cadbury Papers, Ms. 5/39.
73. Duffy, *A Question of Slavery*, 194–199.
74. Report of Joseph Burtt and Dr. Horton, 1907, Appendix A in William Cadbury, *Labour in Portuguese West Africa* (London: Routledge, 1910; repr. New York: Negro Universities Press, 1969), 130–131.
75. Duffy, *A Question of Slavery*, 198–199.
76. Fox Bourne to William Cadbury, June 26, 1907, Cadbury Papers, Ms. 5/139.
77. Cadbury Bros., Ltd., to Rowntree Bros., Ltd., July 26, 1907, Cadbury Papers, Ms. 5/174; J.S. Fry and Sons, Ltd., to Cadbury Bros., Ltd., August 1, 1907, Cadbury Papers, Ms. 5/180.
78. John Holt was certainly in contact with William Cadbury regarding cocoa production in West Africa. As a firm ally and friend of Morel, Holt was also no doubt aware of Cadbury's dilemma over slavery. In addition, Holt was a well-known adversary of Sir Alfred Jones, and had advised Morel of Jones's machinations in support of the Congo Free State.
79. William Cadbury to E.D. Morel, September 14, 1907, Cadbury Papers, Ms. 180/749.
80. Cadbury Bros., Ltd., to Rowntree & Co., Ltd., October 7, 1907, Cadbury Papers, Ms. 6/16; William Cadbury to E.D. Morel, October 22, 1907, Cadbury Papers, Ms. 180/753.
81. E.D. Morel to William Cadbury, October 23, 1907, Cadbury Papers, Ms. 180/754.
82. William Cadbury, private memo to Messrs. Cadbury, Fry, and Rowntree, undated, Cadbury Papers, Ms. 305.
83. William Cadbury's statement to cocoa proprietors, November 28, 1907, Lisbon, Friends House Library, London.
84. William Cadbury to E.D. Morel, February 3, 1908, Cadbury Papers, Ms. 180/774.
85. William Cadbury to E.D. Morel, March 26, 1908, Cadbury Papers, Ms. 180/776.
86. Cadbury sent a copy to Morel, who said, "The article you send me is atrocious, but just the sort of thing one might expect from that quarter. I long to have a wack [*sic*] at these stupid attacks against you, and I think my time will come before very long." E.D. Morel to William Cadbury, September 29, 1908, Morel Papers, Letter Book, October 1907–December 1908.
87. List of philanthropic subscriptions submitted to the defense in *Cadbury v. Standard*, Cadbury Papers, Ms. 143.
88. *Birmingham Daily Post*, December 7, 1909.
89. *Birmingham Daily Post*, November 30, 1909.
90. *Birmingham Daily Post*, December 2, 1909.
91. Duffy, *A Question of Slavery*, 209.
92. William Cadbury to E.D. Morel, March 17, 1909, Cadbury Papers, Ms. 180/839.
93. John Harris, *Dawn in Darkest Africa* (London: Smith, Elder, 1912).
94. Duffy, *A Question of Slavery*, 212.
95. For a summary of the controversy after 1910, see ibid., 211–229.
96. A.G. Gardiner, *Life of George Cadbury* (London: Cassell, 1923); Iolo Williams, *The Firm of Cadbury, 1831–1931* (London: Constable, 1931).
97. "A Private Inside History of the Connection of Cadbury Bros., Ltd. with African Slavery."
98. Ibid.

Chapter 5

1. J. Harris to Basil Matthews of the Laymens' Missionary Society, August 27, 1914, Papers of the British and Foreign Anti-Slavery and Aborigines' Protection Society, Rhodes House, Oxford University (hereafter Anti-Slavery Papers), Mss. Brit. Emp. S19, D3/11.
2. J. Harris to Booker T. Washington, September 30, 1914, Anti-Slavery Papers, Mss. Brit. Emp. S19, D3/11.

3. James Ramsay MacDonald, *Labour and the Empire* (London: George Allen, 1907; repr. London: Routledge/Thoemmes Press, 1999), 98.

4. William Roger Louis, "African Origins of the Mandates Idea," *International Organization* (Winter 1965): 20–36.

5. Historians of the British Empire have been apt to gloss over the changes in trusteeship. For example, Ronald Robinson comments, "For as long as anybody cares to remember trusteeship was the code of the British colonial empire." Ronald Robinson, "The Moral Disarmament of African Empire, 1919–1947," *Journal of Imperial and Commonwealth History* 8, no. 1 (1979): 87.

6. Précis for lecture titled "Germany's Lost Colonial Empire," Anti-Slavery Papers, Mss. Brit. Emp. S22, G485, 1916–1918.

7. E.D. Morel, "The African Problem and the Peace Settlement," UDC pamphlet no. 22a (July 1917), 5.

8. MacDonald, *Labour and the Empire*, 100.

9. Minutes of the War Cabinet, January 3, 1918, Public Records Office, Kew (hereafter PRO), CAB 23/5.

10. Jan Smuts, "The League of Nations: A Practical Suggestion" (London: Hodder and Stoughton, 1918). Also see George Curry, "Woodrow Wilson, Jan Smuts, and the Versailles Settlement," *American Historical Review* 66, no. 4 (July 1961): 968–986; Lloyd E. Ambrosius, *Woodrow Wilson and the American Diplomatic Tradition* (Cambridge: Cambridge University Press, 1987), especially chs. 2, 3, and 5.

11. David Hunter Miller, *The Drafting of the Covenant*, vol. 1 (New York: Putnam's, 1928), 101, 105, 109.

12. Smuts, "The League of Nations," 15.

13. There is a large body of scholarship on the organization of the mandates system. For a solid introduction to the mandates system in Africa, see Michael D. Callahan, *Mandates and Empire: The League of Nations and Africa, 1914–1931* (Brighton, U.K.: Sussex Academic Press, 1999).

14. Smuts, "The League of Nations," 9.

15. Minutes of the War Cabinet, January 3, 1918, PRO, CAB 23/5.

16. Kevin Grant, "'A Civilised Savagery': British Humanitarian Politics and European Imperialism in Africa, 1884–1926" (Ph.D. dissertation, University of California, Berkeley, 1997), ch. 6.

17. E.D. Morel, *The Black Man's Burden* (London: National Labour Press, 1920), 228.

18. *Anti-Slavery Reporter* (October 1914): 113–114.

19. *Anti-Slavery Reporter* (April 1915): 1–9.

20. See, for example, Sir Harry Johnston's lecture, "Africa after the War," to the Royal Geographic Society on February 24, 1915, reprinted in the *Anti-Slavery Reporter* (March 1915): 2–3.

21. *Anti-Slavery Reporter* (July 1915): 32–34.

22. Nicoletta F. Gullace, "Sexual Violence and Family Honor: British Propaganda and International Law during the First World War," *American Historical Review* 102, no. 3 (June 1997): 714–747.

23. Jean Stengers, "British and German Imperial Rivalry: A Conclusion," in *Britain and Germany in Africa*, ed. Prosser Gifford and William Roger Louis (New Haven, Conn.: Yale University Press, 1967), 345.

24. John Harris to N. Garbah, May 21, 1915, Anti-Slavery Papers, Mss. Brit. Emp. S19, D3/12.

25. Anti-Slavery Society to Andrew Bonar Law, July 6, 1915, Anti-Slavery Papers, Mss. Brit. Emp. S19, D6/1; J. Harris to W. Cadbury, August 9, 1915, Anti-Slavery Papers, Mss. Brit. Emp. S19, D3/12.

26. File on the Cameroons, titled "German Atrocities and Lies," PRO, CO649/6, file 26770.

27. See, for example, Alice Harris's lecture schedule for February 1916, in A. Harris to Yeaxlee, January 26, 1916, Anti-Slavery Papers, Mss. Brit. Emp. S19, D3/13.

28. *Anti-Slavery Reporter* (July 1916): 24.

29. Marvin Swartz, *The Union of Democratic Control in British Politics during the First World War* (Oxford: Clarendon Press, 1971), 47, 49, 58, 85. Swartz explains that the UDC began with three general objectives: "(1) Parliamentary control over foreign policy and prevention of secret diplomacy; (2) negotiations after the war with Continental democracy to form an international understanding depending on popular parties rather than on governments;

(3) peace terms that neither humiliated the defeated nation nor artificially rearranged frontiers so as to provide cause for future wars." Ibid., 25.

30. The first attack came in the spring of 1915, from Cecil Chesterton in the *New Witness*. The attack was carried forward by the *Globe*, the *Morning Post*, and other publications. J. Harris to C.P. Scott, August 10, 1915, Anti-Slavery Papers, Mss. Brit. Emp. S19, D3/12.

31. Anti-Slavery Society Committee meeting, July 6, 1916, Minute Book, December 1915–July 1920, Anti-Slavery Papers, E2/14.

32. Regarding Dickinson, see A.J.P. Taylor, *The Trouble Makers* (London: Pimlico, 1993), 141. Later pressure groups included the League of Free Nations Association, established in September 1918, and the League of Nations Union, established in November 1918.

33. J.A. Hobson, *Towards International Government* (London: George Allen and Unwin, 1915).

34. Henry Winkler, "The Development of the League of Nations Idea in Great Britain, 1914–1919," *Journal of Modern History* 20, no. 2 (June 1948): 108–109.

35. Henry Winkler, "British Labor and the Origins of the Idea of Colonial Trusteeship, 1914–1919," *The Historian* 13, no. 2 (Spring 1951): 156.

36. For a summary of the British conquest of Germany's African empire, see William Roger Louis, *Great Britain and Germany's Lost Colonies, 1914–1919* (Oxford: Clarendon Press, 1967).

37. Anti-Slavery Society to Arthur Balfour, Foreign Secretary, January 22, 1917, Anti-Slavery Papers, Mss. Brit. Emp. S19, D6/2.

38. John Harris, *Germany's Lost Colonial Empire and the Essentials of Reconstruction* (London: Simpkin, Marshall, Hamilton, Kent, 1917), 12–13.

39. Ibid., 23–30.

40. Ibid., 16.

41. Ibid., 18–19.

42. Department of Information, "Reports on Various Branches of Propaganda Work and Recommendations," December 7, 1917, PRO, INF4/4B.

43. Morel, *The African Problem and the Peace Settlement*, 15.

44. Ibid., 18.

45. Ibid., 26–29.

46. Louis, *Great Britain and Germany's Lost Colonies*, 56.

47. For a detailed account of the determination of British war aims in Africa, see Peter J. Yearwood, "Great Britain and the Repartition of Africa, 1914–19," *Journal of Imperial and Commonwealth History* 18 (1990): 316–341.

48. John Gallagher, "The Decline, Revival and Fall of the British Empire," in John Gallagher, *The Decline, Revival and Fall of the British Empire: The Ford Lectures and Other Essays*, ed. Anil Seal (Cambridge: Cambridge University Press, 1982), 86–87.

49. Arthur Henderson, *The Aims of Labour* (London: Headley Bros., 1918), 85.

50. Ibid., 87.

51. Minutes of the War Cabinet, December 31, 1917, PRO, CAB 23/4.

52. *The Times*, January 7, 1918.

53. Louis, *Great Britain and Germany's Lost Colonies*, 100.

54. Ibid., 103.

55. Ibid., 124.

56. Miller, *The Drafting of the Convenant*, vol. 1, especially ch.1.

57. With regard to the particular issue of self-determination, see Kevin Grant, "Trust and Self-Determination: Anglo–American Ethics of Empire and International Government," in *Critiques of Capitalism in Modern Britain and America*, ed. Mark Bevir and Frank Trentmann (New York: Palgrave Macmillan, 2002).

58. Miller, *The Drafting of the Convenant*, vol. 1, 101, 105, 109; see also vol. 2, 28, 103, 152.

59. William Roger Louis, "Great Britain and International Trusteeship: The Mandate System," in *The Historiography of the British Empire–Commonwealth*, ed. Robin Winks (Durham, N.C.: Duke University Press, 1966).

60. House of Lords Debate, May 13, 1920, *The Parliamentary Debates*, fifth Series, vol. 40, House of Lords (London, 1920), 319.

61. On the contrary, Ronald Robinson observes with reference to imperial officials of this era: "If the men of the empire made a habit of moralizing their mundane purposes, it is reasonable to suppose that this was because theology was as vital to the imperial process as surplus capital or high velocity guns." See Ronald Robinson, "Andrew Cohen and the Transfer of

Power in Tropical Africa, 1940–1951," in *Decolonisation and After: The British and French Experience,* ed. W.H. Morris-Jones and Georges Fischer (London: Frank Cass, 1980), 57.

62. Jan Smuts, "The Basis of Trusteeship in African Native Policy," a speech delivered in Cape Town on January 21, 1942 (Cape Town: South African Institute of Race Relations, 1942), 7.

63. Ibid., 12.

64. Nicholas Owen has made a similar observation. See Nicholas Owen, "Critics of Empire in Britain," in *The Oxford History of the British Empire,* vol. 4, *The Twentieth Century,* ed. Judith M. Brown and William Roger Louis (Oxford: Oxford University Press, 1999), 194–195.

65. Ibid., 193.

66. Robert Ferrell, *Woodrow Wilson and World War I, 1917–1921* (New York: Harper & Row, 1985), 152.

67. John Harris, *Africa: Slave or Free?* (London: Student Christian Movement, 1919), 230.

68. Ibid., 231.

69. Ibid., 192.

70. Lord Frederick Lugard, *The Dual Mandate in British Tropical Africa,* 5th ed. (London: Archon Books, 1965), 391.

71. Morel, *The Black Man's Burden,* vii.

72. Ibid., 224–225.

73. Ibid., 56–57, 107, 166.

74. Ibid., 228.

75. Ibid., 167.

76. Ibid.

77. Ibid., 170.

78. Ibid., 235, 240.

79. See Perham's introduction to Lugard, *The Dual Mandate,* 5th ed., xxix.

80. Ibid., p. 228

81. Morel published a glowing review of Shaw's book, *A Tropical Dependency,* in the *Daily Chronicle* on December 20, 1905.

82. Lugard, *The Dual Mandate,* 5th ed., 354.

83. Ibid., 355.

84. Ibid., 365.

85. Ibid., 367.

86. Ibid., 368.

87. Ibid., 374–375.

88. Ibid., 375, 396.

89. Ibid., 411.

90. See Chapter 1.

91. See, for example, J.H. Oldham, *Christianity and the Race Problem* (London: Student Christian Movement, 1926).

92. Lugard, *The Dual Mandate,* 5th ed., 617.

93. Confidential Harris to Lugard, April 4, 1922; J. Harris to Sir Arthur, October 9, 1922; J. Harris to Lord Buxton, October 10, 1922; J. Harris to Charles Roberts, December 18, 1922, Anti-Slavery Papers, Mss. Brit. Emp. S22, G444.

94. Verbatim record of the third Assembly of the League of Nations, 5th plenary session, September 6, 1922, PRO, FO371/8334 (W7898/7715/98).

95. Steel-Maitland's resolution had been sent to the Sixth Committee, revised by the Subcommittee on Mandates and Slavery, then resubmitted to the Assembly, which adopted it on September 21. The Council then agreed to act upon the resolution on September 26. See verbatim record of the third Assembly of the League of Nations, 5th plenary session, PRO, FO371/8334 (W7898/7715/98); Council of the League, record of meeting, September 26, 1922, PRO, FO371/8331 (W8464/5594/98).
   In July 1923, the Council extended this request for information to the following nonmembers of the League: Abyssinia, Afghanistan, Ecuador, Hedjaz, Mexico, Turkey, and the United States.

96. The Foreign Office considered reporting its evidence of slavery in Portuguese West Africa, but ruled this out due to fears of compromising migrant labor from Portuguese East Africa to the Union of South Africa. See minutes exchanged between Foreign Office officials between October and December 1922, PRO, FO371/8335 (W8530/8041/98). Predictably, the Undersecretary of State for the Colonies informed the Secretary of the Cabinet

that there was no cause for concern about slavery in Britain's colonies, protectorates, or mandated territories. See Undersecretary to Secretary of the Cabinet, October 31, 1922, PRO, FO371/8335 (W9655/8041/98).

97. The Foreign Office's brief reply included references to the British naval patrol intercepting slave traffic from East Africa to Persia, and the "Involuntary Servitude [Abolition] Ordinance" passed in Tanganyika on June 9, 1922. Charles Tufton, for the Secretary of Foreign Affairs, to the Secretary-General of the League of Nations, December 11, 1922, PRO, FO371/8335 (W8530/8041/98).

98. J. Harris to E.D. Morel, May 7, 1923, E.D Morel Collection, London School of Economics (hereafter Morel Papers), F8, file 78.

99. Minute by R. Sperling, December 4, 1922, PRO, FO371/8335 (W8530/8041/98).

100. Eric Drummond informed Harris of this change in policy in a letter of July 21, 1923. See Harris to Gilbert Murray, August 8, 1923, Anti-Slavery Papers, Mss. Brit. Emp. S22, G445.

101. R. Sperling to J. Harris, September 4, 1923, Anti-Slavery Papers, Mss. Brit. Emp. S22, G445.

102. League of Nations, "The Question of Slavery," August 10, 1923, A.18.1923.VI (Geneva, 1923).

103. E.M.B. Ingram to Lord Cecil, undated, PRO, FO371/8448 (A6594/5476/52); Foreign Office confidential to Lord Robert Cecil, December 5, 1923, PRO, FO371/8448 (A6594/5476/52). Harris's resolution had been facilitated by the Rt. Hon. Edward Wood, who sat on the Sixth Committee of the Assembly. Subsequently, the Foreign Office asserted that Wood had acted "in direct contravention" of government policy. Confidential memorandum for Lord Robert Cecil, December 5, 1923, PRO, FO371/8448 (A6594/5476/52).

104. Minute by A. Cadogan, January 9, 1924, upon Eric Drummond to Curzon, December 22, 1923, PRO, FO371/8448 (A7575/5476/52).

105. Minutes of deputation, February 22, 1924, PRO, FO371/9531 (A1292/366/52); A. Cadogan to Lord Parmoor, March 7, 1924, PRO, FO371/9531 (A1502/366/52). Note that Belgium, France, Poland, and Switzerland all recommended private organizations and individuals as consultants on slavery. See Secretary-General, memorandum on "Question of Slavery," June 10, 1924, PRO, FO371/9531 (A3785/366/52).

106. Eric Drummond to Sir Eyre Crowe, April 18, 1924, PRO, FO371/9531 (A2607/366/52).

107. H. Duncan Hall, *Mandates, Dependencies and Trusteeship* (Washington, D.C.: Carnegie Endowment for International Peace, 1948), 33.

108. The following eight men composed the Temporary Slavery Commission: M. Gohr (Belgium), Director-General in the Ministry of the Colonies; M. Freire d'Andrade (Portugal), former Minister of Foreign Affairs and a current member of the Permanent Mandates Commission; M. Louis Dantes Bellegarde (Haiti), former Minister of Haiti to France and the first delegate of Haiti to the third Assembly of the League of Nations; M. Delafosse (France), former colonial Governor-General and a member of the French Colonial Academy; Mr. H.A. Grimshaw, representing the International Labour Organisation; Sir Frederick Lugard, former Governor of Nigeria and a current member of the Permanent Mandates Commission; M. Roncagli (Italy), Secretary-General of the Italian Geographical Society; M. Van Rees (Netherlands), former Vice President of the Council of the Dutch East Indies and current Vice President of the Permanent Mandates Commission.

109. League of Nations, "Temporary Slavery Commission: Minutes of the First Session, 9–12 July 1924," A.18.1924.VI (Geneva, 1924), 6. Regarding humanitarian controversies over Mui-Tsai, see Susan Pedersen, "The Maternalist Moment in British Colonial Policy: The Controversy over 'Child Slavery' in Hong Kong 1917–1941," *Past and Present* no. 171 (2001): 161–202.

110. League of Nations, "Temporary Slavery Commission: Minutes of the First Session, 9–12 July 1924," 6.

111. Ibid.

112. Robert Cecil to Austin Chamberlain, June 19, 1925, with enclosure of excerpt of letter from Lugard to Cecil, undated, PRO, FO371/10617 (A3180/531/52).

113. League of Nations, "Temporary Slavery Commission: Minutes of the First Session, 9–12 July 1924," 6.

114. Robert Vansittart to various departments, July 2, 1925, PRO, FO371/10617 (A3225/531/52).

115. Minutes of the Inter-Departmental Committee on Slavery and the Slave Trade, July 7, 1925, PRO, FO371/10617 (A3541/531/52); for many memorandums and minutes upon the draft of the Convention, see FO371/11133 and FO371/11134.

116. League of Nations, "The Question of Slavery," September 26, 1925, A.130.1925.VI (Geneva, 1925), 2.
117. Ibid.
118. Ibid.
119. Lugard, *The Dual Mandate*, 5th ed.,194.
120. John Harris, "Freeing the Slaves," *Contemporary Review* (December 1925): 743–750.
121. Anti-Slavery Society resolution, July 1, 1926, PRO, FO371/11134 (A3548/110/52).
122. Frederick Cooper, "Conditions Analogous to Slavery," in Frederick Cooper, Thomas C. Holt, and Rebecca J. Scott, *Beyond Slavery* (Chapel Hill: University of North Carolina Press, 2000), 108.
123. Morel, *The Black Man's Burden*, 170.

Epilogue

1. John Harris, *Africa: Slave or Free?* (London: Student Christian Movement, 1919), 239; Jan Smuts, "The Basis of Trusteeship in African Native Policy," a speech delivered in Cape Town on January 21, 1942 (Cape Town: South African Institute of Race Relations, 1942), 7.
2. E.D. Morel, *The Black Man's Burden* (London: National Labour Press, 1920), 197.
3. Stephen Howe, *Anticolonialism in British Politics: The Left and the End of Empire, 1918–1964* (Oxford: Clarendon Press, 1993), 28.
4. See, for example, Leonard Woolf, *Imperialism and Civilization* (New York: Harcourt, Brace, 1928), 116, 175–182; Howe, *Anticolonialism in British Politics*.
5. Woolf, *Imperialism and Civilization*, 60.
6. William Roger Louis, *Imperialism at Bay: The United States and the Decolonization of the British Empire, 1941–1945* (Oxford: Oxford University Press, 1978), 100; Ronald Hyam, "Bureaucracy and 'Trusteeship' in the Colonial Empire," in *The Oxford History of the British Empire, vol. 4, The Twentieth Century*, ed. Judith M. Brown and William Roger Louis. (Oxford: Oxford University Press, 1999).
7. Smuts, "The Basis of Trusteeship," 10.
8. See, for example, Ronald Robinson, "Andrew Cohen and the Transfer of Power in Tropical Africa, 1940–1951," in *Decolonisation and After: The British and French Experience*, ed. W.H. Morris-Jones and Georges Fischer (London: Frank Cass, 1980).
9. Arthur Creech Jones, as the Undersecretary of State at the Colonial Office, recognized that colonial nationalism changed ideas about trusteeship. See A. Creech Jones, MP, "International Trusteeship of Colonies," an address to the annual meeting of the British and Foreign Anti-Slavery and Aborigines' Protection Society, June 7, 1945 (London: British and Foreign Anti-Slavery and Aborigines' Protection Society, 1945), 3. As indicated in chapter 5, I do not intend to suggest that Britain had lost its will to rule.
10. Louis, *Imperialism at Bay*, 4.
11. M. Glenn Johnson, "The Contributions of Eleanor and Franklin Roosevelt to the Development of International Protection for Human Rights," *Human Rights Quarterly* 9, no. 1 (February 1987): 19–48.
12. Cordell Hull, *The Memoirs of Cordell Hull* (New York: Macmillan, 1948), 1635.
13. Louis, *Imperialism at Bay*, 12.
14. Ibid., 8.
15. Howe, *Anticolonialism in British Politics*, 325–326. In a related vein, Ronald Hyam observes that the politics of trusteeship shifted into "multiracialism" and "non-racialism." See Hyam, "Bureaucracy and Trusteeship," 265.
16. Howe, *Anticolonialism in British Politics*, 325.
17. Hyam, "Bureaucracy and Trusteeship," 274.
18. The U.S. policy on trusteeship was largely determined by the State Department's Committee on Dependent Areas. For a definitive account of Anglo–American policy making and negotiations, see Louis, *Imperialism at Bay*.
19. Charmian Edwards Toussaint, *The Trusteeship System of the United Nations* (New York: Praeger, 1956), 20–29.
20. See the Charter of the United Nations (1945), chapter XII, articles 73 and 76.
21. Charter of the United Nations (1945), chapter VII.
22. Louis, *Imperialism at Bay*, 117.
23. See, for example, Frantz Fanon, *The Wretched of the Earth* (New York: Grove Press, 1963); Partha Chatterjee, *Nationalist Thought and the Colonial World: A Derivative Discourse?* (London: Zed, 1986; Minneapolis: University of Minnesota Press, 1993).

Bibliography

Archives

Private Organizations

Aborigines' Protection Society, Rhodes House, Oxford.
Baptist Missionary Society, Angus Library, Regents Park College, Oxford.
British and Foreign Anti-Slavery Society, Rhodes House, Oxford.
Cadbury Papers, University of Birmingham.
Society of Friends, Friends House Library, London.

Personal Papers

Henry Campbell-Bannerman, British Library, London.
Roger Casement, National Library of Ireland, Dublin.
Charles Dilke, British Library, London.
Alfred Emmott, Nuffield College Library, Oxford.
Herbert Gladstone, British Library, London.
Lord Alfred Milner, Bodleian Library, Oxford.
E.D. Morel, British Library of Political and Economic Science,
      London School of Economics.
Herbert Samuel, House of Lords Record Office.
J.E.B. Seely, Mottistone Papers, Nuffield College Library, Oxford.
John St. Loe Strachey, House of Lords Record Office.

British Governmental Collections

British Public Record Office Kew
CAB 23/4–5
CO291/84
CO649/6
FO10/804–805
FO63/1447
FO371/8331
FO371/8334–8335
FO371/8448
FO371/9443

FO371/9531–9532
FO371/10617
FO371/11133–11134
HO161/2
INF4/4B

Governmental Publications

Great Britain

Parliamentary Debates, fourth and fifth series
Accounts and Papers of the British Parliament
"Correspondence Relating to the Transvaal Indentured Labour Laws Temporary Continuance Act, 1907," 1908, vol. 73, Cd. 3994.
"The Asiatic Law Amendment Ordinance, no. 29 of 1906," 1906, vol. 80, Cd. 3251.
"Further Correspondence Relating to Labour in the Transvaal Mines," 1906, vol. 80, Cd. 3025.
"Further Correspondence Relating to Labour in the Transvaal Mines," 1906, vol. 80, Cd. 2786.
"Further Correspondence Relating to Affairs in the Transvaal and Orange River Colony," 1905, vol. 55, Cd. 2563.
"Further Correspondence Relating to Labour in the Transvaal Mines," 1905, vol. 55, Cd. 2401.
"Further Correspondence Relating to Labour in the Transvaal Mines," 1904, vol. 62, Cd. 2183.
"Further Correspondence Respecting the Administration of the Independent State of the Congo," 1904, vol. 62, Cd. 2097.
"Correspondence and Report from his Majesty's Consul at Boma Respecting the Administration of the Independent State of the Congo," 1904, vol. 62, Cd. 1933.
"Further Correspondence Regarding the Transvaal Labour Question," 1904, vol. 61, Cd. 1899.
"Further Correspondence Relating to the Affairs of the Transvaal and Orange River Colony," 1904, vol. 61, Cd. 1895.

L'État Indépendant du Congo

Bulletin Officiel de l'État Indépendant du Congo.

Transvaal Colony

"Handbook of Ordinances, Proclamations, Regulations and Instructions, Connected with the Importation of Foreign Labour into the Transvaal" (Pretoria, 1906).

Newspapers and Periodicals Consulted

Aborigines' Friend
Anti-Slavery Reporter
Birmingham Daily Post
British Empire Review
Contemporary Review
Daily Chronicle
Daily Mail
Echoes of Service
Evening Standard
La Vérité sur le Congo
Liberal Magazine
Liverpool Daily Post
L'Univers
Manchester Guardian
Nineteenth Century and After
Regions Beyond

The Friend
The Gordian
The Times
West African Mail

Primary Sources: Published Books

Arnot, F.S. *Missionary Travels in Central Africa.* Bath: Office of Echoes of Service, 1914.

Bennett, George, ed. *The Concept of Empire: Burke to Attlee, 1774–1947.* London: Adam and Charles Black, 1953.

Bentley, Rev. W. Holman. *Pioneering on the Congo,* 2 vols. London: Religious Tract Society, 1900.

Bourne, H. R. Fox. *The Aborigines' Protection Society: Chapters in Its History.* London: P.S. King, 1899.

Bourne, H. R. Fox. *Blacks and Whites in South Africa.* London: P.S. King, 1900.

Bourne, H. R. Fox. *Civilisation in Congoland.* London: P.S. King, 1903.

Bourne, H. R. Fox. *English Merchants: Memoirs in Illustration of the Progress of British Commerce,* vol. 2. London: Richard Bentley, 1886.

Bourne, H. R. Fox. *Famous London Merchants: A Book for Boys.* London: J. Hogg, 1869.

Bourne, H. R. Fox. *Forced Labour in British South Africa.* London: P.S. King, 1903.

Bourne, H. R. Fox. *The Romance of Trade.* London: Cassell, Petter & Galpin, 1871.

Burke, Edmund. *Reflections on the Revolution in France,* edited by J.G.A. Pocock. Indianapolis, Ind.: Hackett, 1987.

Burke, Edmund. *The Works of the Right Honorable Edmund Burke,* rev. ed., vol. 14. Boston: Little, Brown, 1867.

Burrows, Captain Guy. *The Curse of Central Africa.* London: R.A. Everett, 1903.

Cadbury, William. *Labour in Portuguese West Africa,* 2nd ed. London: Routledge, 1910. Reprinted New York: Negro Universities Press, 1969.

Cell, John W., ed. *By Kenya Possessed: The Correspondence of Norman Leys and J.H. Oldham, 1918–1926.* Chicago: University of Chicago Press, 1976.

Clemens, Samuel. *King Leopold's Soliloquy: A Defense of His Congo Rule.* Boston: P.R. Warren, 1905.

Conrad, Joseph. *Congo Diary and Other Uncollected Pieces,* edited by Zdislaw Najder. Garden City, N.Y.: Doubleday, 1978.

Conrad, Joseph. *Heart of Darkness,* edited by Robert Kimbrough, 3rd ed. New York: W.W. Norton, 1988.

Creswell, F.H.P. *The Chinese Labour Question from Within.* London: P.S. King, 1905.

Doyle, Sir Arthur Conan. *The Crime of the Congo.* New York: Doubleday, Page, 1909.

Glave, E.J. *Six Years of Adventure in Congo-land.* London: S. Low, Marston, 1893.

Harris, John. *A Century of Emancipation.* London: J.M. Dent, 1933.

Harris, John. *Africa: Slave or Free?* London: Student Christian Movement, 1919.

Harris, John. *Dawn in Darkest Africa.* London: Smith, Elder, 1912.

Harris, John. *Germany's Lost Colonial Empire and the Essentials of Reconstruction.* London: Simpkin, Marshall, Hamilton, Kent, 1917.

Harris, John. *Portuguese Slavery: Britain's Dilemma.* London: Methuen, 1913.

Henderson, Arthur. *The Aims of Labour.* London: Headley Bros., 1918.

Hertslet, Sir Edward. *The Map of Africa by Treaty,* 3rd ed., repr., vol. 2. London: Frank Cass, 1967.

Hinde, Sidney. *The Fall of the Congo Arabs.* London: Methuen, 1897.

Hobson, J.A. *Imperialism: A Study.* London, 1902. Reprinted Ann Arbor: University of Michigan Press, 1965.

Hobson, J.A. *Towards International Government.* London: George Allen and Unwin, 1915.

Hull, Cordell. *The Memoirs of Cordell Hull.* New York: Macmillan, 1948.

Kenyatta, Jomo. *Facing Mount Kenya.* New York: Vintage Books, 1965.

Kingsley, Mary. *Travels in West Africa, Congo Français, Corisco and Cameroons.* London: Macmillan, 1897. Reprinted London: Virago Press, 1982.

Kingsley, Mary. *West African Studies.* London: Macmillan, 1899.

Locke, John. *A Letter Concerning Toleration,* edited by James Tully. Indianapolis, Ind.: Hackett, 1983.

Locke, John. *Two Treatises of Government,* edited by Peter Laslett. Cambridge: Cambridge University Press, 1996.

Lugard, Lord Frederick. *The Dual Mandate in British Tropical Africa.* London, 1922. Reprinted London: Frank Cass, 1965.

MacDonald, James Ramsay. *Labour and the Empire.* London: George Allen, 1907.
MacDonald, James Ramsay. *What I Saw in South Africa.* London: "The Echo," 1902.
Mackintosh, C.W. *Dr. Harry Guinness.* London: Regions Beyond Missionary Union, 1916.
Miller, David Hunter. *The Drafting of the Covenant,* 2 vols. New York: Putnam's, 1928.
Morel, E.D. *The Black Man's Burden.* London: National Labour Press, 1920.
Morel, E.D. *The Congo Slave State: A Protest against the New African Slavery.* Liverpool: John Richardson, 1903.
Morel, E.D. *History of the Congo Reform Movement,* edited by William Roger Louis and Jean Stengers. Oxford: Clarendon Press, 1968.
Morel, E.D. *King Leopold's Rule in Africa.* London: Heinemann, 1904.
Myers, John Brown. *The Congo for Christ: The Story of the Congo Mission.* London: S. W. Partridge, 1895.
Negreiros, António de Almada. *Colonies Portugaises: Ile de San-Thomé.* Paris: A. Challamel, 1901.
Nevinson, Henry W. *A Modern Slavery.* London: Harper and Brothers., 1906.
Phillips, Lionel. *Transvaal Problems: Some Notes on Current Politics.* London: John Murray, 1905.
Stanley, Henry M. *The Congo and the Founding of Its Free State: A Story of Work and Exploration,* 2 vols. New York: Harper and Brothers, 1885.
Swan, Charles. *The Slavery of To-day.* Glasgow: Pickering & Inglis, 1909.
Transvaal Chamber of Mines. *Annual Report.* 1903, 1904, 1909.
Ward, Herbert. *Five Years with the Congo Cannibals.* London: Chatto & Windus, 1890.
Weeks, John. *Among Congo Cannibals.* London: Seeley, Service, 1913.
Woolf, Leonard, *Imperialism and Civilization.* New York: Harcourt, Brace, 1928.

Primary Sources: Articles, Pamphlets, and Leaflets

Anon. "The Question of Slavery." September 26, 1925. League of Nations Publication A.130.1925.VI.
Anon. "Temporary Slavery Commission: Minutes of the First Session, 9–12 July 1924." League of Nations Publication A.18.1924.VI.
Anon. "The Question of Slavery." August 10, 1923. League of Nations Publication A.18.1923.VI.
Anon. "Chinese Labour Brings More Employment for Whites in the Transvaal." London: Conservative Publication Department, 1905.
Anon. "Chinese Labour. A Protest from Transvaal Nonconformist Ministers." London: Conservative Publication Department, 1904.
Anon. "Chinese Labour. Dignified Rebuke from Nonconformist Ministers in the Transvaal to Their Brethren in England." London: Imperial South African Association, 1904.
Anon. "Chinese Labour. Five Reasons for Supporting the Government on Chinese Labour." London: Imperial South African Association, 1904.
Anon. "Chinese Labour for the Transvaal Mines: Nonconformists Condemn Agitation Against It." London: Conservative Publication Department, 1904.
Anon. "Slavery in the Transvaal." London: Labour Representation Committee, 1904.
Anon. "Voter Registration." London: Labour Representation Committee, 1904.
Baptist Missionary Society. "The Congo Question and the Baptist Missionary Society." London: Baptist Mission House, 1909.
Bourne, H.R. Fox. "Slave Traffic in Portuguese Africa." London: P.S. King, 1908.
Burns, John. "BONDAGE for Black, SLAVERY for Yellow Labour." Reprinted from the *Independent Review.* London: Kent & Matthews, 1904.
Cadbury, William A. "Statement Made by William A. Cadbury on Behalf of the English Cocoa Makers, to a Committee of the Proprietors of the Cocoa Estates of S. Thomé and Principé, Lisbon, Nov. 28th 1907." Press release. 1907.
Farrar, Sir George. "'Transvaal Labour Importation Ordinance,' Speech Given on the Introduction of the Ordinance in the Legislative Council of the Transvaal Colony, 28 December 1903." Johannesburg: Transvaal Leader Office, 1904.
Federation for the Defence of Belgian Interests Abroad. "The Truth on the Congo Free State." Brussels, May 1905.
Guinness, Mrs. H. Grattan. "The First Christian Mission on the Congo." London: Hodder & Stoughton, 1880.
Harris, Alice Seeley. "Enslaved Womanhood of the Congo." London: Congo Reform Association, 1908 or 1909.
Harris, John. "Back to Slavery?" *The Contemporary Review* (August 1921): 190–197.

Johnston, H.H. "British Missions and Missionaries in Africa." *The Nineteenth Century* (July–December 1887): 708–724.

Jones, Arthur Creech. "International Trusteeship of Colonies." An address to the annual meeting of the British and Foreign Anti-Slavery and Aborigines' Protection Society, June 7, 1945. London: British and Foreign Anti-Slavery and Aborigines' Protection Society, 1945.

Leys, P. "South Africa, II: Chinese Labour for the Rand." *The Nineteenth Century* (February 1902): 181–186.

Morel, E.D. "Evidence Laid before the Congo Commission of Inquiry." Liverpool: Congo Reform Association, July 1905.

Morel, E.D. "The African Problem and the Peace Settlement." UDC pamphlet no. 22a. London, July 1917.

Morel, E.D. "The Economic Aspect of the Congo Problem." Liverpool: Congo Reform Association, 1908.

Parker, Sir Gilbert. "'Our Imperial Responsibilities in the Transvaal,' an Address to the Junior Constitutional Club, Piccadilly, 23 March 1904." London: Junior Constitutional Club, 1904.

Shiell, A.G. "Chinese Slavery." London, 1904.

Smuts, Jan. "The Basis of Trusteeship in African Native Policy." A speech delivered in Cape Town on January 21, 1942. Cape Town: South African Institute of Race Relations, 1942.

Smuts, Jan. "The League of Nations: A Practical Suggestion." London: Hodder & Stoughton, 1918.

Spender, Harold. "The Great Congo Iniquity." *The Contemporary Review* (July 1906): 43–55.

Secondary Sources: Published Books

Ambrosius, Lloyd E. *Woodrow Wilson and the American Diplomatic Tradition.* Cambridge: Cambridge University Press, 1987.

Anstey, Roger. *The Atlantic Slave Trade and British Abolition, 1760–1810.* Atlantic Highlands, N.J.: Humanities Press, 1975.

Anstey, Roger. *Britain and the Congo in the Nineteenth Century.* Oxford: Clarendon Press, 1962.

Armitage, David. *The Ideological Origins of the British Empire.* Cambridge: Cambridge University Press, 2000.

Ascherson, Neal. *The King Incorporated: Leopold II in the Age of Trusts.* New York: Doubleday, 1964.

Barthes, Roland. *Camera Lucida: Reflections on Photography.* New York: Hill and Wang, 1981.

Bebbington, David. *The Nonconformist Conscience: Chapel and Politics, 1870–1914.* London: Allen and Unwin, 1982.

Bender, Thomas, ed. *The Antislavery Debate: Capitalism and Abolitionism as a Problem in Historical Interpretation.* Berkeley: University of California Press, 1992.

Benedetto, Robert, ed. *Presbyterian Reformers in Central Africa.* Leiden: E.J. Brill, 1996.

Bhana, Surendra, and Joy B. Brian. *Setting Down Roots: Indian Migrants in South Africa, 1860–1911.* Johannesburg: Witwatersrand University Press, 1990.

Bolt, Christine, and Seymour Drescher, eds. *Anti-Slavery, Religion and Reform.* Folkestone, U.K.: William Dawson, 1980.

Brantlinger, Patrick. *Rule of Darkness.* Ithaca, N.Y.: Cornell University Press, 1988.

Callahan, Michael D. *Mandates and Empire: The League of Nations and Africa, 1914–1931.* Brighton, U.K.: Sussex Academic Press, 1999.

Carter, Marina. *Servants, Sirdars, and Settlers: Indians in Mauritius, 1834–1874.* Delhi: Oxford University Press, 1995.

Chatterjee, Indrani. *Gender, Slavery and Law in Colonial India.* New Delhi: Oxford University Press, 1999.

Chatterjee, Partha. *Nationalist Thought and the Colonial World: A Derivative Discourse?* London: Zed, 1986; Minneapolis: University of Minnesota Press, 1993.

Clarence-Smith, Gervase. *Slaves, Peasants and Capitalists in Southern Angola, 1840–1926.* Cambridge: Cambridge University Press, 1979.

Clarence-Smith, Gervase. *The Third Portuguese Empire, 1825–1975: A Study in Economic Imperialism.* Manchester: Manchester University Press, 1985.

Cline, Catherine. *E.D. Morel, 1873–1924: The Strategies of Protest.* Belfast: Blackstaff Press, 1980.

Colley, Linda. *Britons: Forging the Nation, 1707–1832.* New Haven, Conn.: Yale University Press, 1992.

Cookey, S.J.S. *Britain and the Congo Question, 1885–1913.* London: Longmans, Green, 1968.

Coombes, Annie E. *Reinventing Africa: Museums, Material Culture, and Popular Imagination in Late Victorian and Edwardian England.* New Haven, Conn.: Yale University Press, 1994.

Cooper, Frederick. *From Slaves to Squatters: Plantation Labor and Agriculture in Zanzibar and Coastal Kenya, 1890–1925.* New Haven, Conn.: Yale University Press, 1980.

Cooper, Frederick, Thomas C. Holt, and Rebecca J. Scott. *Beyond Slavery: Explorations of Race, Labor, and Citizenship in Postemancipation Societies.* Chapel Hill: University of North Carolina Press, 2000.

Coupland, Sir Reginald. *The British Anti-Slavery Movement.* London: Butterworth, 1933.

Crawford, Persia Campbell. *Chinese Coolie Emigration to Countries within the British Empire.* London: P.S. King, 1923.

Crowe, S.E. *The Berlin West African Conference, 1884–1885.* London: Longmans Green, 1942.

Crush, Jonathon, Alan Jeeves, and David Yudelman. *South Africa's Labor Empire: A History of Black Migrancy to the Gold Mines.* Boulder, Colo.: Westview Press, 1991.

Daniell, David. *William Tyndale: A Biography.* New Haven, Conn.: Yale University Press, 1994.

Darwin, John. *Britain and Decolonisation: The Retreat from Empire in the Post-War World.* New York: St. Martin's Press, 1988.

Davis, David Brion. *The Problem of Slavery in the Age of Revolution, 1770–1823.* Ithaca, N.Y.: Cornell University Press, 1975.

Davis, David Brion. *The Problem of Slavery in Western Culture.* Ithaca, N.Y.: Cornell University Press, 1966.

Denoon, Donald. *A Grand Illusion: The Failure of Imperial Policy in the Transvaal Colony during the Period of Reconstruction, 1900–1905.* London: Longman, 1973.

Dickens, A.G. *The English Reformation,* 2nd ed. University Park: Pennsylvania State University Press, 1991.

Drescher, Seymour. *Capitalism and Antislavery: British Mobilization in Comparative Perspective.* New York: Oxford University Press, 1987.

Drescher, Seymour. *From Slavery to Freedom: Comparative Studies in the Rise and Fall of Atlantic Slavery.* New York: New York University Press, 1999.

Drescher, Seymour. *The Mighty Experiment: Free Labor vs. Slavery in British Emancipation.* New York: Oxford University Press, 2002.

Duffy, Eamon. *The Stripping of the Altars: Traditional Religion in England, c. 1400–c. 1580.* New Haven, Conn.: Yale University Press, 1992.

Duffy, James. *A Question of Slavery.* Cambridge, Mass.: Harvard University Press, 1967.

Edwards, Elizabeth, ed. *Anthropology & Photography, 1860–1920.* New Haven, Conn.: Yale University Press, 1992.

Egerton, F. Clement C. *Angola in Perspective: Endeavour and Achievement in West Africa.* London: Routledge and Kegan Paul, 1957.

Egerton, George W. *Great Britain and the Creation of the League of Nations.* Chapel Hill: University of North Carolina Press, 1978.

Fanon, Frantz. *The Wretched of the Earth.* New York: Grove Press, 1963.

Ferrell, Robert. *Woodrow Wilson and World War I, 1917–1921.* New York: Harper & Row, 1985.

Figgis, J.N. *Political Thought from Gerson to Grotius, 1414–1625.* Cambridge: Cambridge University Press, 1907.

Frank, Katherine. *A Voyager Out: The Life of Mary Kingsley.* Boston: Houghton Mifflin, 1986.

Franklin, John Hope. *George Washington Williams: A Biography.* Chicago: University of Chicago Press, 1985.

Gann, L.H., and Peter Duignan. *The Rulers of Belgian Africa, 1884–1914.* Princeton, N.J.: Princeton University Press, 1979.

Gardiner, A.G. *Life of George Cadbury.* London: Cassell, 1923.

Gough, J.W. *John Locke's Political Philosophy,* 2nd ed. Oxford: Clarendon Press, 1973.

Greenidge, C.W.W. *Slavery.* London: Allen and Unwin, 1958.

Hall, Catherine. *Civilising Subjects: The Colony and Metropole in the English Imagination.* Chicago: University of Chicago Press, 2002.

Hall, H. Duncan. *Mandates, Dependencies and Trusteeship.* Washington, D.C.: Carnegie Endowment for International Peace, 1948.

Hargreaves, John. *Prelude to the Partition of West Africa.* London: Macmillan, 1963.

Harries, Patrick. *Work, Culture and Identity: Migrant Laborers in Mozambique and South Africa, c.1860–1910.* Portsmouth: N.H.: Heinemann, 1994.

Helly, Dorothy O. *Livingstone's Legacy.* Athens: Ohio University Press, 1987.

Henderson, Lawrence. *Angola: Five Centuries of Conflict.* Ithaca, N.Y.: Cornell University Press, 1979.

Hilton, Boyd. *The Age of Atonement: The Influence of Evangelicalism on Social and Economic Thought, 1795–1865.* Oxford: Clarendon Press, 1988.

Hochschild, Adam. *King Leopold's Ghost: A Story of Greed, Terror, and Heroism in Colonial Africa.* Boston: Houghton Mifflin, 1998.

Hodges, John A. *The Lantern-Slide Manual.* London: Hazell, Watson and Viney, 1892.

Holt, Thomas C. *The Problem of Freedom: Race, Labor and Politics in Jamaica and Britain, 1832–1938.* Baltimore: Johns Hopkins University Press, 1992.

Howe, Anthony. *Free Trade and Liberal England, 1846–1946.* Oxford: Clarendon Press, 1997.

Howe, Stephen. *Anticolonialism in British Politics: The Left and the End of Empire, 1918–1964.* Oxford: Clarendon Press, 1993.

Hyam, Ronald. *Elgin and Churchill at the Colonial Office, 1905–1908: The Watershed of the Empire–Commonwealth.* London: Macmillan, 1968.

Inglis, Brian. *Roger Casement.* Belfast: Blackstaff Press, 1993.

Jeeves, Alan H. *Migrant Labour in South Africa's Mining Economy: The Struggle for the Gold Mines' Labour Supply, 1890–1920.* Kingston, Ont.: McGill–Queen's University Press, 1985.

Klein, Martin A. *Slavery and Colonial Rule in French West Africa.* Cambridge: Cambridge University Press, 1998.

Klein, Martin A., ed., *Breaking the Chains: Slavery, Bondage, and Emancipation in Modern Africa.* Madison: University of Wisconsin Press, 1993.

Knapp, Arthur W. *The Cocoa and Chocolate Industry: The Tree, the Bean, the Beverage.* New York: Isaac Pitman, 1930.

Koebner, Richard, and Helmut Dan Schmidt. *Imperialism: The Story and Significance of a Political Word.* Cambridge: Cambridge University Press, 1964.

Lagergren, David. *Mission and State in the Congo, 1885–1903.* Lund: Gleerup, 1970.

Laqueur, Walter, and Barry Rubin, eds. *The Human Rights Reader.* Philadelphia: Temple University Press, 1979.

Levine, Philippa. *Prostitution, Race, & Politics: Policing Venereal Disease in the British Empire.* New York: Routledge, 2003.

Loth, Heinrich. *Kolonialismus und "Humanitätintervention": Kritische Untersuchung der Politik Deutschlands gegenüber dem Kongostaat (1884–1908).* Berlin: Akademie-Verlag, 1966.

Louis, William Roger. *Great Britain and Germany's Lost Colonies, 1914–1919.* Oxford: Clarendon Press, 1967.

Louis, William Roger. *Imperialism at Bay, 1941–1945: The United States and the Decolonization of the British Empire.* Oxford: Oxford University Press, 1977.

Lovejoy, Paul. *Transformations in Slavery: A History of Slavery in Africa.* Cambridge: Cambridge University Press, 1983.

Lovejoy, Paul, ed., *The Ideology of Slavery in Africa.* Beverly Hills, Calif.: Sage, 1981.

Lovejoy, Paul E., and Jan S. Hogendorn. *Slow Death for Slavery: The Course of Abolition in Northern Nigeria, 1897–1936.* Cambridge: Cambridge University Press, 1993.

MacKenzie, John. *Propaganda and Empire: The Manipulation of British Opinion, 1880–1960.* Manchester: Manchester University Press, 1984.

Macpherson, C.B. *Burke.* New York: Oxford University Press, 1980.

Maitland, F.W. *Equity,* edited by A.H. Chaytor and W.J. Whittaker. Cambridge: Cambridge University Press, 1936.

Marchal, Jules. *E.D. Morel contre Léopold II: L'Histoire du Congo, 1900–1910,* 2 vols. Paris: L'Harmattan, 1996.

Marchal, Jules. *L'État Libre du Congo: Paradis Perdu. L'histoire du Congo, 1876–1900,* vol. 2. Borgloon: Bellings, 1996.

Marshall, P.J. *Problems of Empire: Britain and India 1757–1813.* London: Allen and Unwin, 1968.

Mellor, G.R. *British Imperial Trusteeship, 1783–1850.* London: Faber & Faber, 1951.

Midgley, Clare. *Women against Slavery: The British Campaigns, 1780–1870.* London: Routledge, 1992.

Miers, Suzanne. *Britain and the Ending of the Slave Trade.* New York: Africana, 1975.

Miers, Suzanne. *Slavery in the Twentieth Century: The Evolution of a Global Problem.* Walnut Creek, CA: AltaMira Press, 2003.

Miers, Suzanne, and Martin A. Klein, eds. *Slavery and Colonial Rule in Africa.* Portland, Ore.: Frank Cass, 1999.

Miers, Suzanne, and Igor Kopytoff, eds. *Slavery in Africa: Historical and Anthropological Perspectives*. Madison: University of Wisconsin Press, 1977.

Miers, Suzanne, and Richard Roberts, eds. *The End of Slavery in Africa*. Madison: University of Wisconsin Press, 1988.

Monod, Paul Kléber. *The Power of Kings: Monarchy and Religion in Europe, 1589–1715*. New Haven, Conn.: Yale University Press, 1999.

Nelson, Samuel. *Colonialism in the Congo Basin, 1880–1940*. Athens: Ohio University Center for International Studies, 1994.

Northrup, David. *Indentured Labor in the Age of Imperialism, 1834–1922*. Cambridge: Cambridge University Press, 1995.

Pagden, Anthony. *Lords of All the World: Ideologies of Empire in Spain, Britain and France, c.1500–c.1800*. New Haven, Conn.: Yale University Press, 1995.

Porter, Bernard. *Critics of Empire: British Radical Attitudes to Colonialism in Africa, 1895–1914*. New York: St. Martin's Press, 1968.

Price, Richard. *An Imperial War and the British Working Class: Working-Class Attitudes and Reactions to the Boer War, 1899–1902*. London: Routledge & Kegan Paul, 1972.

Prochaska, F.K. *Women and Philanthropy in Nineteenth-Century England*. Oxford: Clarendon Press, 1980.

Reid, B.L. *The Lives of Roger Casement*. New Haven, CT: Yale University Press, 1976.

Rich, Paul. *Race and Empire in British Politics*. Cambridge: Cambridge University Press, 1986.

Richardson, Peter. *Chinese Mine Labour in the Transvaal*. London: Macmillan, 1982.

Rotberg, Robert. *Christian Missionaries and the Creation of Northern Rhodesia, 1880–1924*. Princeton, N.J.: Princeton University Press, 1965.

Russell, A.K. *Liberal Landslide: The General Election of 1906*. Newton Abbot, U.K.: David & Charles, 1973.

Ryan, James. *Picturing Empire: Photography and the Visualization of the British Empire*. Chicago: University of Chicago Press, 1997.

Salman, Michael. *The Embarrassment of Slavery: Controversies over Bondage and Nationalism in the American Colonial Philippines*. Berkeley: University of California Press, 2001.

Samuels, Michael Anthony. *Education in Angola, 1878–1914: A History of Culture Transfer and Administration*. New York: Teachers College Press, 1970.

Scully, Pamela. *Liberating the Family?: Gender and British Slave Emancipation in the Rural Western Cape, South Africa, 1823–1853*. Portsmouth, N.H.: Heinemann, 1997.

Searle, G.R. *Morality and the Market in Victorian Britain*. Oxford: Clarendon Press, 1998.

Semmel, Bernard. *Imperialism and Social Reform: English Social–Imperial Thought, 1895–1914*. New York: Anchor Books, 1968.

Semmel, Bernard. *The Liberal Ideal and the Demons of Empire: Theories of Empire from Adam Smith to Lenin*. Baltimore: Johns Hopkins University Press, 1993.

Semmel, Bernard. *The Rise of Free Trade Imperialism*. Cambridge: Cambridge University Press, 1970.

Semple, Rhonda Anne. *Missionary Women: Gender, Professionalism and the Victorian Idea of Christian Mission*. Woodbridge, U.K.: Boydell Press, 2003.

Shah, Nayan. *Contagious Divides: Epidemics and Race in San Francisco's Chinatown*. Berkeley: University of California Press, 2001.

Skinner, Quentin. *The Foundations of Modern Political Thought*, vol. 2, *The Age of Reformation*. Cambridge: Cambridge University Press, 1978.

Slade, Ruth. *English-Speaking Missions in the Congo Independent State (1878–1908)*. Brussels: Académie Royale des Sciences Coloniales, 1959.

Slade, Ruth. *King Leopold's Congo*. Oxford: Oxford University Press, 1962.

Solow, Barbara L., and Stanley L. Engerman, eds. *British Capitalism and Caribbean Slavery: The Legacy of Eric Williams*. Cambridge: Cambridge University Press, 1987.

Stanley, Brian. *The Bible and the Flag*. Leicester, U.K.: Apollos, 1990.

Stanley, Brian. *The History of the Baptist Missionary Society, 1792–1992*. Edinburgh: T. & T. Clark, 1992.

Stunt, W.T. *Turning the World Upside Down*. Eastbourne, U.K.: Upperton Press, 1972.

Swartz, Marvin. *The Union of Democratic Control in British Politics during the First World War*. Oxford: Clarendon Press, 1971.

Taylor, A.J.P. *The Trouble Makers: Dissent over Foreign Policy, 1792–1938*. London: Hamish Hamilton, 1957.

Temperley, Howard. *British Antislavery, 1833–1870*. Columbia: University of South Carolina Press, 1972.

Temperley, Howard. *White Dreams, Black Africa: The Antislavery Expedition to the River Niger, 1841–1842*. New Haven: Yale University Press, 1991.

Temperley, Howard, ed. *After Slavery: Emancipation and Its Discontents*. London: Frank Cass, 2000.

Thorne, Susan. *Congregational Missions and the Making of an Imperial Culture in Nineteenth-Century England*. Stanford: Stanford University Press, 1999.

Tierney, Brian. *Religion, Law, and the Growth of Constitutional Thought, 1150–1650*. Cambridge: Cambridge University Press, 1982.

Tinker, Hugh. *A New System of Slavery: The Export of Indian Labour Overseas, 1830–1920*. London: Hansib, 1974.

Toussaint, Charmian Edwards. *The Trusteeship System of the United Nations*. New York: Praeger, 1956.

Twaddle, Michael, ed. *The Wages of Slavery: From Chattel Slavery to Wage Labour in Africa, the Caribbean, and England*. London: Frank Cass, 1993.

Tyndale, William. *The New Testament Translated by William Tyndale, 1534*. Cambridge: Cambridge University Press, 1938.

Van Onselen, Charles. *Chibaro: African Mine Labour in Southern Rhodesia, 1900–1933*. Johannesburg: Ravan Press, 1976.

Walsham, Alexandra. *Providence in Early Modern England*. Oxford: Oxford University Press, 1999.

Walvin, James. *Slavery and British Society, 1776–1846*. Baton Rouge: Louisiana State University Press, 1982.

Whelan, Frederick. *Edmund Burke and India: Political Morality and Empire*. Pittsburgh, Pa.: University of Pittsburgh Press, 1996.

Willequet, Jacques. *Le Congo Belge et la Weltpolitik, 1894–1914*. Brussels: Presses Universitaires de Bruxelles, 1962.

Williams, Iolo. *The Firm of Cadbury, 1831–1931*. London: Constable, 1931.

Winkler, Henry. *The League of Nations Movement in Great Britain, 1914–1919*. Metuchen, N.J.: Scarecrow, 1967.

Yap, Melanie, and Dianne Leong Man. *Colour, Confusion and Concessions: The History of the Chinese in South Africa*. Hong Kong: Hong Kong University Press, 1996.

Secondary Sources: Published Articles, Essays, and Reviews

Beachey, R.W. "The Arms Trade in East Africa in the Late Nineteenth Century." *Journal of African History* 3, no. 3 (1962): 451–467.

Burton, Antoinette. "States of Injury: Josephine Butler on Slavery, Citizenship, and the Boer War." *Social Politics* (Fall 1998): 338–361.

Clarence-Smith, W.G. "Labour Conditions in the Plantations of São Tomé and Príncipe, 1875–1914." In *The Wages of Slavery*, edited by Michael Twaddle. London: Frank Cass, 1993.

Claude, Richard P. "The Classical Model of Human Rights Development." In *Comparative Human Rights*, edited by Richard P. Claude. Baltimore: Johns Hopkins University Press, 1976.

Cline, Catherine Ann. "The Church and the Movement for Congo Reform." *Church History* 32, no. 1 (March 1963): 46–56.

Cooper, Frederick, "Conditions Analogous to Slavery: Imperialism and Free Labor Ideology in Africa." In Frederick Cooper, Thomas C. Holt, and Rebecca J. Scott, *Beyond Slavery: Explorations of Race, Labor, and Citizenship in Postemancipation Societies*. Chapel Hill: University of North Carolina Press, 2000.

Cooper, Frederick. "From Free Labor to Family Allowances: Labor and African Society in Colonial Discourse." *American Ethnologist* 16 (November 1989): 745–765.

Curry, George. "Woodrow Wilson, Jan Smuts, and the Versailles Settlement." *American Historical Review* 66, no. 4 (July 1961): 968–986.

Cuthbertson, Greg. "Pricking the 'Nonconformist Conscience': Religion against the South African War." In *The South African War Reappraised*, edited by Donal Lowry. Manchester: Manchester University Press, 2000.

Davies, Robert. "Mining Capital, the State and Unskilled White Workers in South Africa, 1901–1913." *Journal of Southern African Studies* 3, no. 1 (October 1976): 41–69.

Dellheim, Charles. "The Creation of a Company Culture: Cadburys, 1861–1931." *American Historical Review* 92, no. 1 (1987): 13–44.

Denoon, Donald. "The Transvaal Labour Crisis, 1901–6." *Journal of African History* 7, no. 3 (1967): 481–494.

Drescher, Seymour. "Cart Whip and Billy Roller: Antislavery and Reform Symbolism in Industrializing Britain." *Journal of Social History* 15, no. 1 (Fall 1981): 3–24.

Driver, Felix. "Henry Morton Stanley and His Critics: Geography, Exploration and Empire." *Past and Present* no.133 (November 1991): 134–166.

Engerman, Stanley. "Slavery and Emancipation in Comparative Perspective: A Look at Some Recent Debates." *Journal of Economic History* 46, no. 2 (June 1986): 317–339.

Fisch, Jörg. "Africa as *terra nullius*: The Berlin Conference and International Law." In *Bismarck, Europe and Africa: The Berlin Conference 1884–1885 and the Onset of Partition*, edited by Stig Förster, Wolfgang J. Mommsen, and Ronald Robinson. Oxford: Oxford University Press, 1988.

Flint, John. "Mary Kingsley—A Reassessment." *Journal of African History* 4, no. 1 (1963): 95–104.

Forman, Ross. "Randy on the Rand: Portuguese African Labor and the Discourse of 'Unnatural Vice' in the Transvaal in the Early Twentieth Century." *Journal of the History of Sexuality* 11, no. 4 (October 2002): 570–609.

Gallagher, John. "The Decline, Revival and Fall of the British Empire." In John Gallagher, *The Decline, Revival and Fall of the British Empire: The Ford Lectures and Other Essays*, edited by Anil Seal. Cambridge: Cambridge University Press, 1982.

Grant, Kevin. "Christian Critics of Empire: Missionaries, Lantern Lectures, and the Congo Reform Campaign in Britain." *Journal of Imperial and Commonwealth History* 29, no. 2 (May 2001): 27–58.

Grant, Kevin. "Trust and Self-Determination: Anglo–American Ethics of Empire and International Government." In *Critiques of Capital in Modern Britain and America*, edited by Mark Bevir and Frank Trentmann. New York: Palgrave Macmillan, 2002.

Gullace, Nicoletta F. "Sexual Violence and Family Honor: British Propaganda and International Law during the First World War." *American Historical Review* 102, no. 3 (June 1997): 714–747.

Harms, Robert. "The World ABIR Made: The Maringa–Lopori Basin, 1885–1903."*African Economic History* 22 (1983): 125–139.

Harrison, Brian. "A Genealogy of Reform in Modern Britain." In *Anti-Slavery, Religion, and Reform*, edited by Christine Bolt and Seymour Drescher. Folkestone, U.K.: William Dawson, 1980.

Hyam, Ronald. "Bureaucracy and 'Trusteeship' in the Colonial Empire." In *The Oxford History of the British Empire*, vol. 4, *The Twentieth Century*, edited by Judith M.Brown and William Roger Louis. Oxford: Oxford University Press, 1999.

Hyslop, Jonathan. "The Imperial Working Class Makes Itself 'White': White Labourism in Britain, Australia, and South Africa before the First World War." *Journal of Historical Sociology* 12, no. 4 (December 1999): 398–421.

Izuakor, L.I. "Colonial Challenges and Administrative Response: Sir Charles Eliot and 'Native' Trusteeship in Kenya, 1901–1904." *Transafrican Journal of History* 17 (1988): 34–49.

Johnson, M. Glenn. "The Contributions of Eleanor and Franklin Roosevelt to the Development of International Protection for Human Rights." *Human Rights Quarterly* 9, no. 1 (February 1987): 19–48.

Kaiser, Klaus. "'Kongogreuel'—Zur Kongoreformbewegung in England und Deutschland vor dem Ersten Weltkrieg." In *Geschichte und Humanität*, edited by Horst Gründer. Münster: LIT Verlag, 1994.

Killingray, David, and Andrew Roberts. "An Outline History of Photography in Africa to ca. 1940," *History in Africa* 16 (1989): 197–208.

Louis, William Roger. "African Origins of the Mandates Idea." *International Organization* (Winter 1965): 20–36.

Louis, William Roger. "Critical Notes." In *E.D. Morel's History of the Congo Reform Movement*, edited by William Roger Louis and Jean Stengers. Oxford: Clarendon Press, 1968.

Louis, William Roger. "Great Britain and German Expansion in Africa, 1884–1919." In *Britain and Germany in Africa*, edited by Prosser Gifford and William Roger Louis. New Haven, Conn.: Yale University Press, 1967.

Louis, William Roger. "Great Britain and International Trusteeship: The Mandate System." In *The Historiography of the British Empire–Commonwealth*, edited by Robin W. Winks. Durham, N.C.: Duke University Press, 1966.

Louis, William Roger. "Morel and the Congo Reform Association, 1904–1913." In *E.D. Morel's History of the Congo Reform Movement*, edited by William Roger Louis and Jean Stengers. Oxford: Clarendon Press, 1968.

Louis, William Roger. "Roger Casement and the Congo." *Journal of African History* 5, no. 1 (1964): 99–120.

Louis, William Roger. "The South West African Origins of the Sacred Trust." *African Affairs* 66, no. 262 (1967): 20–39.

Louis, William Roger. "The Stokes Affair and the Beginning of the Anti-Congo Campaign." *Revue Belge de Philologie et d'Histoire* 53 (1965): 572–584.

Louis, William Roger. "The Triumph of the Congo Reform Movement, 1905–1908." In *Boston University Papers on Africa*, vol. 2, edited by Jeffrey Butler. Boston: Boston University Press, 1966.

Mayhall, Laura E. Nym. "The Rhetorics of Slavery and Citizenship: Suffragist Discourse and Canonical Texts in Britain, 1880–1914." *Gender & History* 13, no. 3 (November 2001): 481–497.

Mehta, Uday. "Liberal Strategies of Exclusion." In *Tensions of Empire: Colonial Cultures in a Bourgeois World*, edited by Frederick Cooper and Ann Laura Stoler. Berkeley: University of California Press, 1997.

Miers, Suzanne, "Humanitarianism at Berlin: Myth or Reality?" In *Bismarck, Europe and Africa: The Berlin Africa Conference 1884–1885 and the Onset of Partition*, edited by Stig Förster, Wolfgang Mommsen, and Ronald Robinson. Oxford: Oxford University Press, 1988.

Mitchell, Angus. "New Light on the 'Heart of Darkness.'" *History Today* 49, no. 12 (1999): 20–27.

Mommsen, Wolfgang. "Bismarck, the Concert of Europe, and the Future of West Africa, 1883–1885." In *Bismarck, Europe and Africa: The Berlin Africa Conference 1884–1885 and the Onset of Partition*, edited by Stig Förster, Wolfgang Mommsen, and Ronald Robinson. Oxford: Oxford University Press, 1988.

Nwaka, Geoffrey I. "Cadbury and the Dilemma of Colonial Trade in Africa, 1901–1910." *Bulletin de l'I.F.A.N.* 42, ser B, no. 4 (1980): 780–793.

Owen, Nicholas. "Critics of Empire in Britain." In *The Oxford History of the British Empire*, vol. 4, *The Twentieth Century*, edited by Judith M. Brown and William Roger Louis. Oxford: Oxford University Press, 1999.

Pagden, Anthony. "The Struggle for Legitimacy and the Image of Empire in the Atlantic to c. 1700." In *The Oxford History of the British Empire*, vol. 1, *The Origins of Empire*, edited by Nicholas Canny. Oxford: Oxford University Press, 1998.

Pedersen, Susan. "The Maternalist Moment in British Colonial Policy: The Controversy over 'Child Slavery' in Hong Kong 1917–1941." *Past and Present* no. 171 (2001): 161–202.

Porter, Andrew. "Commerce and Christianity: The Rise and Fall of a Nineteenth-Century Missionary Slogan." *The Historical Journal* 28, no. 3 (1985): 597–621.

Porter, Andrew. "Religion and Empire: British Expansion in the Long Nineteenth Century, 1780–1914." *Journal of Imperial and Commonwealth History* 20, no. 3 (September 1992): 370–390.

Porter, Andrew. "Scottish Missions and Education in Nineteenth-Century India: The Changing Face of 'Trusteeship.'" *Journal of Imperial and Commonwealth History* 16, no. 3 (1988): 35–57.

Porter, Andrew. "Trusteeship, Anti-Slavery, and Humanitarianism." In *The Oxford History of the British Empire*, vol. 3, *The Nineteenth Century*, edited by Andrew Porter. Oxford: Oxford University Press, 1999.

Prasch, Thomas. "Which God for Africa: The Islamic–Christian Missionary Debate in Late-Victorian England." *Victorian Studies* (Autumn 1989): 51–73.

Prochaska, F.K. "Philanthropy." In the *Cambridge Social History of Britain, 1750–1950*, vol. 3, edited by F.M.L. Thompson. Cambridge: Cambridge University Press, 1993.

Readman, Paul. "The Conservative Party, Patriotism, and British Politics: The Case of the General Election of 1900." *Journal of British Studies* 40 (January 2001): 107–145.

Richardson, Peter. "Coolies and Randlords: The North Randfontein Chinese Miners' 'Strike' of 1905." *Journal of Southern African Studies* 2, no. 2 (April 1976): 151–177.

Richardson, Peter. "Coolies, Peasants, and Proletarians: The Origins of Chinese Indentured Labour in South Africa, 1904–1907." In *International Labour Migration: Historical Perspectives*, edited by Shula Marks and Peter Richardson. London: University of London Press, 1984.

Robinson, Ronald. "Andrew Cohen and the Transfer of Power in Tropical Africa, 1940–1951." In *Decolonisation and After: The British and French Experience*, edited by W.H. Morris-Jones and Georges Fischer. London: Frank Cass, 1980.

Robinson, Ronald. "The Moral Disarmament of African Empire, 1919–1947." *Journal of Imperial and Commonwealth History* 8, no. 1 (1979): 86–104.

Rotberg, Richard. "Plymouth Brethren and the Occupation of Katanga, 1886–1907." *Journal of African History* 5, no. 2 (1964): 285–297.

Slade, Ruth. "English Missionaries and the Beginning of the Anti-Congolese Campaign in England." *Revue Belge de Philologie et d'Histoire* 33, no. 1 (1955): 37–73.

Slade, Ruth. "King Leopold II and the Attitude of English and American Catholics Towards the Anti-Congolese Campaign." *Zaire* 11 (June 1957): 593–612.

Stanley, Brian. "'Commerce and Christianity': Providence Theory, the Missionary Movement, and the Imperialism of Free Trade, 1842–1860." *The Historical Journal* 26, no. 1 (1983): 71–94.

Stanley, Brian. "'The Miser of Headingley': Robert Arthington and the Baptist Missionary Society, 1877–1900." In *The Church and Wealth*, edited by W.J. Shiels and Diana Wood. London: Basil Blackwell, 1987.

Stengers, Jean. "British and German Imperial Rivalry: A Conclusion." In *Britain and Germany in Africa*, edited by Prosser Gifford and William Roger Louis. New Haven, Conn.: Yale University Press, 1967.

Stengers, Jean. "The Congo State and the Belgian Congo before 1914." In *Colonialism in Africa, 1870–1960*, vol. 1, edited by L.H. Gann and Peter Duignan. Cambridge: Cambridge University Press, 1969.

Stengers, Jean. "Le Rôle de la Commission d'Enquête de 1904–1905 au Congo." *Annuaire de l'Institut de Philologie et d'Histoire Orientales et Slaves* 10 (1950): 701–726.

Stengers, Jean. "Morel and Belgium." In *E.D. Morel's History of the Congo Reform Movement*, edited by William Roger Louis and Jean Stengers. Oxford: Clarendon Press, 1968.

Stengers, Jean. "Quand Léopold II s'est-il rallié à l'annexation du Congo par la Belge?" *Bulletin des Séances, Institut Royal Colonial Belge* 23, no. 3 (1952): 783–824.

Swaisland, Charles. "The Aborigines' Protection Society, 1837–1909." In *After Slavery: Emancipation and Its Discontents*, edited by Howard Temperley. London: Frank Cass, 2000.

Taylor, Miles. "Patriotism, History and the Left in Twentieth-Century Britain." *The Historical Journal* 33, no. 4 (1990): 971–987.

Thompson, Andrew S. "The Language of Imperialism and the Meanings of Empire: Imperial Discourse in British Politics, 1895–1914." *Journal of British Studies* 36 (April 1997): 147–177.

Trentmann, Frank. "The Strange Death of Free Trade: The Erosion of 'Liberal Consensus' in Great Britain, c. 1903–1932." In *Citizenship and Community: Liberals, Radicals, and Collective Identities in the British Isles, 1865–1931*, edited by Eugenio F. Biagini. Cambridge: Cambridge University Press, 1996.

Walvin, James. "Freedom and Slavery and the Shaping of Victorian Britain." In *Unfree Labour in the Development of the Atlantic World*, edited by Paul E. Lovejoy and Nicholas Rogers. London: Frank Cass, 1994.

Walvin, James. "Symbols of Moral Superiority: Slavery, Sport and the Changing World Order, 1800–1950." In *Manliness and Morality: Middle-Class Masculinity in Britain and America, 1800–1940*, edited by J.A. Mangan and James Walvin. Manchester: Manchester University Press, 1987.

Winkler, Henry. "British Labor and the Origins of the Idea of Colonial Trusteeship, 1914–1919." *The Historian* 13, no. 2 (Spring 1951): 154–172.

Winkler, Henry. "The Development of the League of Nations Idea in Great Britain, 1914–1919." *Journal of Modern History* 20, no. 2 (June 1948): 95–112.

Yearwood, Peter J. "Great Britain and the Repartition of Africa, 1914–19." *Journal of Imperial and Commonwealth History* 18 (1990): 316–341.

Dissertations

Gordon, Samuel Ian. "The Chinese Labor Controversy in British Politics and Policy-Making." D.Phil. dissertation, University of Ulster, Jordanstown, 1987.

Grant, Kevin. "A Civilised Savagery: British Humanitarian Politics and European Imperialism in Africa, 1884–1926." Ph.D. dissertation, University of California, Berkeley, 1997.

Nworah, Kingsley. "Humanitarian Pressure-Groups and British Attitudes to West Africa, 1895–1915." Ph.D. dissertation, University of London, 1966.

Southall, Roger J. "Cadbury on the Gold Coast, 1907–1938: The Dilemma of the 'Model Firm' in a Colonial Economy." Ph.D. dissertation, University of Birmingham, 1975.

Wuliger, Robert. "The Idea of Economic Imperialism, with Special Reference to the Life and Work of E.D. Morel." Ph.D. dissertation, University of London, 1953.

Index

CPSIA information can be obtained
at www.ICGtesting.com
Printed in the USA
FSOW03n1219171116
27468FS